D1270402

The Police Procedural

The Police Procedural

George N. Dove

Bowling Green University Popular Press
Bowling Green, Ohio 43403

Copyright © 1982 by the Bowling Green University Popular Press

Library of Congress Catalog Card Number: 81-84214

ISBN: 0-87972-188-X Clothbound
0-87972-189-8 Paperback

CONTENTS

Chapter I

Introduction

ITS ABILITY to freshen itself up, every couple of generations, with new kinds of detectives, new styles of detection, even new types of crimes, settings, and atmosphere, is one thing that has caused the detective story to flourish. The first real breakthrough came in the early 1840s when, against a background of tawdry Newgate Calendars and lurid Vidocq *Memoires,* Edgar Allan Poe wrote his three Dupin stories, and the ratiocinative tale of detection was born. A half century later Arthur Conan Doyle began the Sherlock Holmes series, introducing the charismatic detective and the story rich in circumstantial atmosphere, destined to become the most significant development in the history of detective fiction, because the Holmes stories provided the impetus for the eventual flowering, in the early part of the twentieth century, of the classic formal-problem story, an era we have come to call the Golden Age of detective fiction.

In the 1920s and '30s, when the Golden Age had settled into a period of mellow fruitfulness, a group of writers in the United States (most of them associated with *Black Mask* magazine) began to produce a new kind of story, in which the detective was no longer a gifted consulting detective or a brilliant amateur but a hard-bitten private investigator who was more notable for canniness and agility than for ratiocinative powers, and who tended to use his gun or his fists instead of his brain and who consequently earned the designation of hard-boiled private eye. Then, in the late 1940s and early 1950s another kind of story began to appear, one in which the mystery is solved by regular police detectives, usually working in teams and using ordinary police routines. This kind of narrative is customarily called the "police procedural" story, and it is the subject of this book.

Although we habitually speak of "schools" of detective fiction writing, we should not imply that the detective story has gone through periods of development in which one type of narrative has

1

superseded its predecessor. As a matter of fact, the classic formal-problem story is still the most popular, as exemplified in the successes of writers like Harry Kemelman and Emma Lathen, and in the continuing popularity of people no longer producing, like Agatha Christie, Rex Stout, Erle Stanley Gardner, and Ellery Queen. Nor has there been a decline in the private investigator type of story, as the work of Ross Macdonald, Robert Parker, and Bill Pronzini will testify. Indeed, several writers have successfully merged elements of two of the schools of detection, as Rex Stout did with the use of a classic ratiocinative sleuth (Nero Wolfe) and a hard-boiled type (Archie Goodwin) in the same stories, and as Thomas Chastain has done more recently in his combination of elements of the private investigator with some from the police procedural.

The easiest way to define the police procedural is to call it the *Dragnet* kind of story, in which a mystery is solved by police detectives like Joe Friday and Frank Smith. Not every story about policemen is a procedural; the first qualification is that it must be built around a mystery, as are all other kinds of detective stories. This qualification would exclude police novels like those of Joseph Wambaugh, in which the policemen are not detectives and hence do not solve mysteries. The term "procedural" refers to the methods of detection employed, the procedures followed by policemen in real life. Where the classic detective solves mysteries through the use of his powers of observation and logical analysis, and the private investigator through his energy and his tough tenacity, the detective in the procedural story does those things ordinarily expected of policemen, like using informants, tailing suspects, and availing himself of the resources of the police laboratory. This qualification almost automatically suggests another one: the policemen in the procedurals almost always work in teams, sharing the responsibilities and the dangers, and also the credit, of the investigation, with the result that the resolution of the mystery is usually the product of the work of a number of people instead of the achievement of a single protagonist as in the classic formal-problem tale and the hard-boiled private eye story. The conventions of popular fiction demand that there be a main-character detective in the procedural, but he or she does not solve the crime without the collaborative efforts of other police.

As devotees of detective fiction know, the writers of the

procedural story did not "invent" the police detective. He has been around from the beginning, often in minor roles like those of the Paris police in Poe's Dupin tales and the Scotland Yard representatives in the Sherlock Holmes stories, and like the multitudinous cops in the hard-boiled tales of Dashiell Hammett and Raymond Chandler. As a matter of fact, the detective-heroes of most of the early novels were policemen, like Emile Gaboriau's M. Lecoq, Wilkie Collins' Sergeant Cuff, and Anna Katharine Green's Ebenezer Gryce. Then, of course, there has been a body of distinguished detective fiction featuring such great names as Georges Simenon's Jules Maigret and Ngaio Marsh's Roderick Alleyn, who are policemen. Couldn't these stories be called police procedurals? The answer is no, for two reasons. The first is that, while detectives like Lecoq and Maigret operate within the police establishment and are assisted by other policemen, they always solve the mystery single-handed, whereas the success of a procedural policeman like J.J. Marric's George Gideon is customarily dependent in part on the efforts of his team-mates and subordinates. The second reason is closely related to the first: the methods employed by people like Maigret are almost inevitably dependent on powers of observation and perception and hence are more closely related to those of Sherlock Holmes and the other geniuses of the classic school than to those of the procedural cops. For these reasons, they should properly be called the Great Policemen of detective fiction, a special class of the detectives of the classic school.

Meanwhile, we need to take into account one special feature of the procedural that distinguishes it from the other traditions of detective fiction and also largely determines its direction: the police procedural is the only kind of detective story in which the detective has a recognizable counterpart in real life. Almost nobody (outside, possibly, the group who studied under Dr. Joseph Bell) has ever seen a great transcendent genius who through powers of observation and logic can solve problems in crime-detection that baffle ordinary mortals. Very few people have ever met a private detective. Consequently, those superior geniuses of the classic school and those noble private eyes of the hard-boiled tradition are not required to conform to any preconceptions carried over from the non-fictional world. Everybody, on the other hand, knows the police detective, especially in an age of electronic journalism that keeps him before our eyes. He is the serious-looking individual in the plain suit who is interviewed on the television news after a big homicide or robbery, who uses expressions like "tentative identification," who refers to dead people as "decedents" and to living ones as "subjects," and who almost always concludes with a statement that the investigation is continuing and that apprehension is expected within the next twenty-four hours.

Thus, the procedural is the only kind of detective fiction that did not originate in a purely literary tradition. We do not demand that the classic sleuth conform to any reality other than that established in the earlier stories, with the result that all of them, right down to Kemelman's Rabbi Small and Lathen's John Putnam Thatcher, are the literary descendants of Poe's Dupin through Conan Doyle's Holmes. The same is true of the private eyes of the Hammett-Chandler tradition, who are products of literary convention rather than real-life models: as George Grella has pointed out, the hard-boiled writers took the professional private investigator of real life and transformed him into the familiar figure of the popular media, quite a different personality from his original.[1] Consequently, the conventions and formulas of the classic and hard-boiled schools are almost entirely mythical, in the sense that they have no parallels outside fiction. As we will see in Chapter 8, the police procedural has also developed some mythical components, but the formula almost always has two faces, one determined by the demands of the real world and the other by narrative necessity.

The fact that the reality in the police procedural is based upon the non-fictional world naturally sets some limits on these stories and imposes some restraints upon the writers. One advantage immediately denied to the writer, as Hillary Waugh has pointed out, is the "attractive superman hero," because the nature of the police detective's job and his place in society does not conform to a super-human image.[2] There are, as we will see, some really fascinating protagonists in the procedurals, but writers almost inevitably endow their police detectives with enough human frailties to keep them at least reasonably in line with the public image of the policeman. Another condition imposed on the procedural by the readers' preconceptions affects the kinds of mysteries to be solved. The cases a police detective deals with are crimes that *must* be investigated, regardless of whether a Philo Vance might be interested because of the intriguing intricacies of the problem or whether family and friends can afford to hire a Lew Archer. It is true that detectives of both the classic and the hard-boiled traditions often undertake investigations out of sympathy for the victim and his or her friends; the procedural detective also frequently feels sympathy for a victim, but he works on the case because it is his job. Thus the writer of police procedurals must forego the temptation to endow his protagonist with the formidable intellect of a Nero Wolfe or the egocentric ethical system of a Mike Hammer, and must put his policeman in a position to work on whatever cases come his way, regardless of whether he finds them to his liking.

Having accepted these limitations on his or her detective, however, the procedural writer can still reserve the right to choose those mysteries with which the stories will deal. This is important to remember, because although policemen in real life spend most of their time working on crimes that are not spectacular and are often senseless, the procedural author is not automatically limited to those unremarkable problems. We are reminded throughout the procedural literature of the humdrum nature of a policeman's job, but the case chosen for any given story must be such as to hold the reader's interest. The degree of "realism" demanded, in other words, must always be tempered by the mystery writer's art; a story that undertakes to be a photographically accurate representation of the normal daily routine of ordinary policemen might be strongly "realistic," but nobody would want to read it.

Although the procedural story need not be a literal rendering, it must be at least a plausible representation, which means that the writer of this kind of mystery needs to know the police world, not just the procedures and routines, but the policeman's way of thinking and the sub-culture of which he is a member. Of the twenty-five writers we will be dealing with in this study, an impressive number had had experience on a police force, and one of them (Maurice Procter) retired to writing fiction after a career of considerable length as a policeman. Of the others, almost all have had intimate personal acquaintance with police departments and have read up on the field of criminology. Here is another difference between the procedural writers and those in the other schools of detective fiction. It is possible to write a mystery featuring a gifted amateur detective without having been one; Arthur Conan Doyle was successful in applying Sherlock Holmes' methods to real-life cases, but he is the remarkable exception. The same can be said for the hard-boiled story; Dashiell Hammett worked for a time as a Pinkerton agent, but his successors and imitators can turn out good private-detective fiction without such first-hand experience. The writer of the classic formal-problem story needs to know his Poe and his Conan Doyle, and the writer of hard-boiled stories his Hammett and Chandler, but anybody who writes about policemen (including those in the two traditions just mentioned) had better know his cops.

The fact that police fiction has a counterpart in the non-fiction world offers an opportunity—or perhaps, more accurately, a temptation—to the critic-historian to make comparisons. Are the policemen in procedural stories like those in real life? The answer to that question would undoubtedly tell us a great deal about ourselves as image-builders, and about the interpretative processes of popular fiction, but we will not seek it in this study. With the exception of a brief mention of the disparity between the quality of married life among fictional policemen and those in real life, we will concern ourselves here only with the world of fiction. There are two reasons for eschewing comparisons, one of which is that in this book we are undertaking an interpretation of a body of fiction that would only be confused by comparisons with reality; the other is that we are dealing with the perceptions of authors and readers, surely a broad enough study in itself.

The critical assumption in this study is that any work of art should be judged basically in terms of its purposes. If a story is written for the purpose of being popular, then the only basis for evaluation is the degree to which it achieves popularity. The task of the critic, then, is not to evaluate (the reading public does that) but to interpret. Thus there will be in the following pages no ranking of books or authors in terms of excellence, no lists of Bests and Worsts, and no Desert Island Ten. Our aim instead will be to interpret the special nature of the police procedural as a sub-class of the mystery-detection genre, with particular attention to the public image as it is developed in these stories. We will, of course, find many occasions to call attention to the degrees of narrative quality—or lack of it—in the stories, but this too is part of the interpretation.

In Chapter 2 we will undertake a brief introduction to the

twenty-five writers of police procedurals whose work is the subject of this study. Chapter 3, a review of policemen in the other traditions of detective fiction, is intended primarily as background for understanding the special nature of the policemen in the procedural stories. Chapter 4 deals with distinctive qualities and characteristics of the novels with which this book is concerned. Chapter 5 is intended to introduce a few of the "procedures" that give the procedural its name. In Chapters 6 and 7 we will be concerned with the police sub-culture as it emerges in the stories, first from the viewpoint of the fictional policeman as a member of the police system, and then in the wider context of the place of the police system in society. Chapter 8 is a summary section, dealing with the formulaic and mythic components of the procedural and with the special conception of reality in this kind of story. Because the police procedural is a worldwide kind of story, offering opportunities for comparisons between the images of policemen in different geographical areas, Chapter 9 will examine some of the more noticeable differences between those images in America and in Europe. The next four chapters, 10-13, will deal with some groups of special interest, the woman police detective and the black, Jewish, and Hispanic detective. Chapters 14-22 are discussions of other writers whose work has achieved recognition and whose main characters are not women or members of ethnic groups. In the final chapter we will examine some of the literary qualities of the police procedural stories and will have something special to say about two writers who have extended the procedural format beyond its original conception.

This study will be concerned with police procedural *novels* only, a limitation that must preclude consideration of short stories in print and also the procedural in motion pictures and television. Our writers have done a few short stories about the police featured in the novels, but the procedural formula does not adapt readily to the short tale, which does not permit much development of teams of policemen and police routines. As a usual thing, the short stories about the procedural cops almost automatically fall into the Great Policeman class, with the detective working essentially on his own. An exception to this generalization occurs in a collection of short stories like Michael Gilbert's *Petrella at Q*, which is really an episodic novel. As for the procedural in motion pictures and on

8   Police Procedural

televison, the subject is too broad for inclusion here, except for a
brief treatment of the radio and television series *Dragnet*, which had
a tremendous influence on the early direction of the procedural
novel.

Chapter 2

The First Thirty-Five Years

THE EASIEST WAY to get a reliable picture of what the police procedural novel is like, and at the same time to see how it has developed during the past thirty-five years, is to make a summary review of the work of the writers with whom this book is concerned. In this chapter our twenty-five authors are listed in the order of the beginnings of their procedural series, with a few brief comments on the special characteristics of their stories. Most of them will be treated in more detail later on.

Historians of detective fiction date the beginning of the police procedural in 1945, with the publication of *V as in Victim*, by Lawrence Treat. As we observed in Chapter 1, the policeman in detective fiction did not make his appearance with the emergence of the procedural school but had been very much in evidence from the beginnings of the detective story. Indeed, the cop as leading figure appeared on the scene before Poe began his Dupin tales, in the predecessor of the formal ratiocinative tale of detection, Vidocq's *Memoires*, in 1829. The pioneers in the book-length detective story, moreover, made policemen their protagonists, and we must not neglect to mention that long succession of policemen who played minor but memorable roles during the formative years of the mystery, like Poe's Prefect G——, Dickens' Inspector Bucket, and Conan Doyle's Gregson and Lestrade. Finally, there are the hero-detectives of the Great Policeman school, like Georges Simenon's Maigret and Ngaio Marsh's Alleyn, whose reputations were already secure before the beginnings of the procedural tale. If we want to draw up a list of "predecessors" of the procedural policemen, we should not omit the Keystone Kops of the silent movies, whose descendants may be identified in some of the bumbling characters in the stories of Ed McBain and Maj Sjowall and Per Wahloo, and most certainly not Dick Tracy, by all odds the most popular policeman in fiction.

Treat's *V as in Victim*, however, introduced a new way of dealing with the police story. The cops bore the burden of detection, but they were not "heroes," nor did they display any suggestion of awe-inspiring powers of ratiocination. For the most part they worked in teams, using the methodology normally employed by policemen in real life.

There are usually special social and cultural conditions that stimulate the emergence of any type of writing at a given time. K. Arne Blom suggests that the end of World War II produced a kind of readiness for a more realistic tale of detection, in that, after six years of conflict that had disrupted old values, readers found it hard to escape reality and wanted to read about it in order to better understand themselves and the world.[1] If this interpretation is acceptable, it would appear that the time was right in 1945 for the emergence of the police procedural, because it is the "realistic" quality of this type of story that has rather consistently caught the attention of the public and the critics. Anthony Boucher refers to Lawrence Treat as "the prime pioneer in the naturalistic novel of police procedural,"[2] and Ellery Queen speaks of "the realistic procedural approach."[3] As we will see later, the procedural tale has developed qualities beyond the immersion in reality and the naturalistic approach, but the label of "realism" remains firmly attached to this kind of tale of detection.

What Lawrence Treat did in *V as in Victim* was to give the story three directions that at least partially define the police procedural and differentiate it from other types of detective fiction. First, he showed his policemen employing those procedures and following the routines that we normally expect: questioning witnesses and suspects, using the police lab for the analysis of evidence, setting up tailings and stake-outs. Knowledge of police work is fundamental in Treat's approach to mystery-writing; in his introduction to the MWA *Mystery Writer's Handbook* he suggests an essential home reference-shelf for every mystery writer, which would include up-to-date editions of texts on criminal investigation, forensic medicine, and police science.[4] Besides his own extensive reading in these fields, Treat also prepared himself for writing police fiction by hanging around the NYPD lab and by serving an unofficial hitch on San Diego's Homicide Squad, absorbing the color of police life as well as details of procedure and technique. Second, he introduced the reader to the police mind, a constellation of attitudes and prejudices that characterize the main police detective in the story, Mitch Taylor. Mitch is a good enough cop who likes to think about everybody outside the police world as "civilians," but he is not a gung-ho policeman, and when he goes home at the end of his shift he is ready to dump his police commitments in somebody else's lap while he enjoys the company of his beloved Amy. His bias is anti-intellectual, his approach to police work casual and unsystematic. Third, Treat established in this story a tension between the old-fashioned, largely disorganized approach to police work and the emerging development of police technology. Jub Freman, the other detective in the story, is a police scientist who can identify paint-scrapings by spectroscopic analysis, identify a suspect by making a cast of tooth-marks on a cigar butt, and bring out bloodstains by employing a chemical reagent. The tension between old methods and new is dramatized in the story by a guarded wariness between Mitch and Jub, though Mitch grudgingly admits that "most cops don't use the lab enough" (I, iv).[5]

V as in Victim has one other quality that must not escape notice: it is a good mystery story, with suspense sustained right up until the conclusion, skillful handling of clues, and strict observance of the Fair Play convention. It has the structure of the formal-problem tale, with the customary seven-step sequence of the Poe-Conan Doyle tradition: the Problem, the Initial Solution, the Complication, the Period of Confusion, the Dawning Light, the Solution, and the Explanation. Treat had devised a new atmosphere for detection, but his narrative method was in the mystery tradition.

Treat wrote eight other novels in the Taylor-Freeman series, but he substantially wrote Mitch Taylor out of the story, shifting the role of protagonist to Jub Freeman and, later, to the "old screwball" Lieutenant Bill Decker. Mitch makes a few cameo appearances and has a couple of starring roles, but Treat apparently found the brilliant scientific work of Freeman and the energetic approach of Decker better story-material than the beat-cop nonchalance of Mitch Taylor.

If we should find it necessary to award the title of "Father of the Police Procedural," we might immediately recognize several viable claimants, including Lawrence Treat, Hillary Waugh and John Creasey. In terms of ability to seize the public imagination and to place a permanent stamp on the subsequent development of the procedural, however, it would be difficult to find a more likely candidate than Sergeant Joe Friday (LAPD, Badge No. 714) of the radio-television series *Dragnet*, whom Anthony Boucher called "the world's best-known policeman."[6]

Dragnet started as a radio series in the summer of 1949, earned tremendous popularity, and was moved to NBC television in 1952, with Jack Webb continuing as producer, director and star. It is difficult to make an adequate estimate of the reputation of this program, and especially the person of Sergeant Friday, because both became part of the American folklore in the 1950s. Rare indeed was the comedian, professional or amateur, who did not undertake at least one imitation of Friday's ballpoint monotone and his flat cliches, notably "just the facts, ma'am." The fast, economical movement of the episodes set the pace for other subsequent broadcast programs and for writers of the procedural stories, as did the whip-cracking dialogue that was an element of the *Dragnet* style:

> VICTIM: I've told you the whole story.
> FRIDAY: Just one thing you left out.
> VICTIM: What's that?
> FRIDAY: The truth.[7]

Dragnet continued on television for seven years and was revived later for another successful run. It is rare, as Julian Symons points out, for any form of crime fiction to take anything from the movies or television, but the surge in production of procedural stories in print during *Dragnet*'s heyday (and the popularity in Britain of programs like *Z Cars*) would seem to indicate that the public appetite had been whetted for stories about "ordinary" policemen doing the things Joe Friday and Frank Smith did.[8]

The second novelist to produce a police procedural was Maurice Procter, who set his stories in his home county of Yorkshire, where he had been a policeman since reaching adulthood. *The Chief Inspector's Statement* (U.S. title, *The Pennycross Murders*), published in 1951, is the first-person account by Chief Inspector Philip Hunter of Scotland Yard of the investigation of a series of crimes in Pennycross, a village in Yorkshire. The title should not mislead us: this is not an official report rendered in the flat police language customary in such documents, but Hunter's personal account of the case, including his own experience of falling in love with a sister of one of the victims. Although he leads the investigation, Hunter works with his fellow-officers as a member of the team, and the story gives a plausible account of police routines and police attitudes. Procter wrote one other Hunter story, *I Will Speak Daggers* (1956), but his reputation today rests on the series featuring Detective Inspector Harry Martineau, beginning with *Hell Is a City* (U.S. title, *Somewhere in This City*) in 1954. The Martineau stories are set in the fictitious "Granchester," a port city in Yorkshire, and they are notable for their representation of such plausible police methods as the use of informants, advanced laboratory work, and employment of the "good cop-bad cop" roles during the questioning of suspects.

No other police procedural has achieved the critical acclaim awarded to Hillary Waugh's *Last Seen Wearing---*) which was published in 1952. Julian Symons included it (upon the recommendation of Raymond Chandler) in his list of the hundred best crime novels, and it is the only procedural in the editions of classic mysteries re-published by the Mystery Library. Waugh achieved two successes in this novel, neither of which is easy in a procedural. He developed a compelling sense of suspense without resort to gaudy sensationalism, and he devised a clean, uncluttered single plot that is in the best tradition of the classic tale of detection.

Waugh did not develop this novel into a series, but he moved his locale from "Bristol," Massachusetts (the imaginary college town that is the setting of *Last Seen Wearing—*) to "Stockford," Connecticut, another fictitious small city, where the chief of police is Fred Fellows, one of the best-drawn policemen in the procedural craft. Fellows made his first appearance in *Sleep Long, My Love* in 1959 as a compassionate policeman with a capacity for seeing beyond the obvious. Waugh calls him "an imaginative thinker,"[9] and Fellows' second-in-command accuses him of never being satisfied with an obvious reason (xxiii). Fellows' tobacco-chewing folksiness is deceptive; he has one of the best minds to be found among fictional detectives. In 1968 Waugh initiated a second series with *"30" Manhattan East,* featuring Frank Sessions of New York Homicide. The Manhattan setting is about as different from

Stockford as could be imagined, but Sessions shares Fellows' sense of justice, his ethical commitment, and his sharp analytical mentality.

In any discussion of the early development of the police procedural the name of John Creasey is likely to emerge, largely as a result of his creation of George Gideon of Scotland Yard, probably the best known of procedural policemen. Under the pseudonym of J.J. Marric, Creasey introduced Gideon in *Gideon's Day* (1955), and the twenty-first and last novel in the series, *Gideon's Drive*, was published in 1976, three years after Creasey's death. As a policeman Gideon is courageous and resourceful, and as an administrator (he is commander of the CID, London Metropolitan Police) he earns both the apprehensive awe and the intense loyalty of his subordinates. Creasey did one thing in the development of the portrait of George Gideon that has become almost a standard of the procedural story, a reasonably full account of Gideon as husband and father, a policeman often torn between his commitment to his profession and the demands of family life.

Gideon's Day is developed along six separate story-lines that are related to one another only in respect that they represent the several cases Gideon works on during his fifteen-hour "day." Creasey continued the multiple-plot structure in the subsequent Gideon stories and was able to handle his inter-plotting in such a way as to add plausibility to the accounts. One difference between policemen and the other kinds of detectives in fiction is that cops can seldom afford to work on only one case at a time. In the hands of a skillful writer, the device is not only credible but supportive of the sense of mystery and suspense.

Creasey's other police series, which he published under his own name, actually antedates Treat's *V as in Victim* by three years and would be considered the first of the procedural type except for the fact that it began as an example of the Great Policeman school and was not transformed into a procedural series until the Gideon saga was well under way. Inspector Roger West of Scotland Yard appears in *Inspector West Takes Charge* (1942) as a loner who works most closely with a gifted amateur sleuth and who uses his police subordinates chiefly to run errands and to gather information. He continued in this Maigret-like role until the late 1950s, when Creasey transformed him into a team man of the pattern of George

Gideon. The West series went through forty-three novels, ending with the publication of *A Sharp Rise in Crime* in 1978.

Evan Hunter, author of several highly regarded "serious" novels, is better known to mystery fans under the pseudonym of Ed McBain, who with the publication of *Cop Hater* in 1956 began the 87th Precinct saga, the longest (and in the opinion of many readers the best) of the police procedural series.

Two qualities distinguish the 87th Precinct stories as procedurals. The first is McBain's success in treating the business of law enforcement as a team effort instead of the work of one or two outstanding heroes. If there is a star on the 87th Squad it is Detective Steve Carella, partly because Carella is the most capable policeman on the force and partly because readers and editors have demanded that he be given a greater share of the spotlight than the rest of the "boys" of the Eight-Seven. As a matter of fact McBain had planned to kill Carella off at the end of the third book in the series but was dissuaded by his outraged editor.[10] Aside from Carella's pre-eminence, though, the sense of teamwork is strong in the series, with the detectives working in pairs or larger groups on most cases.

McBain's other excellence in the handling of police work is his understanding of police routines, which are described in almost loving detail and which add immeasurably to the plausibility of the stories. In almost every one of the 87th Precinct stories there is at least one discourse on the several methods of tailing a suspect, or the workings of a computerized communications system, usually handled with a touch of good-humored irony.

One unique feature of the McBain narrative technique is the pervasive presence of the comic spirit in the series, represented in a dollop of humor at moments when the sense of tragedy is about to become too heavy. It is as if the author steps in occasionally to remind us not to take things too seriously, to retain our balance. Critics sometimes miss the intent of this process and take McBain to task for "wackiness" and "ghoulish humor."

Despite the length of the 87th Precinct series, McBain has refused to settle upon a formula, with the result that he is one of the most versatile writers in the field. In *Killer's Wedge* (1959), for example, he meshes two parallel stories, one a locked-room mystery in the best formal-problem tradition, the other a sensational thriller in which an aggrieved woman threatens to blow up the precinct station along with most of the detective squad, and he merges the central predicaments of the two elements into the theme stated in the title. *He Who Hesitates* (1956) is a genuine tour-de-force, with all the action of the story, including the activities of the police, seen through the eyes of a murderer.

The Scottish writer of a series of procedurals, Bill Knox, sets the scene of his stories in the tough Millside Division of Glasgow, beginning with *Deadline for a Dream* in 1957. Each of his three main characters embodies a superlative of a sort, Colin Thane being one of the most thoroughly professional of policemen, his team-mate Phil Moss the owner of what must be the most thunderous ulcer in mystery fiction, and their superior, William "Buddha" Ilford, one of the most overbearing of division commanders. A special quality of the Knox stories is their meticulous description of police routines and methods, including the use of some highly sophisticated technology.

For Love of Imabelle (1957) was the first of the bitter stories written by Chester Himes about the Harlem police team of Grave Digger Jones and Coffin Ed Johnson. Most of the novels in this series are procedurals, in that they are mysteries solved by police officers using police routines, but the sense of social injustice hangs heavy over the stories and tends to become the dominant theme. Jones and Johnson are certainly two of the roughest detectives in fiction, whose habit of controlling a potential mob by bellowing "Straighten up!" and "Count off!" has its effect in Harlem where, as we are told, people do not respect black cops (ix). Into this violent world, however, Himes can inject a caustic humor that verges on the theater of the absurd, like the story of the "Holy Dream" in *Cotton Comes to Harlem* (iii) or the bizarre adventure of the naked white policeman in the same story (x).

Michael Gilbert will probably be better remembered for his spy fiction and his lawyer-stories than for his police procedurals, but *Blood and Judgment* (1959) introduced one of the most picturesque of procedural policemen, Patrick Petrella of Q Division, London Metropolitan Police. The son of a Spanish policeman whose special assignment was to protect General Franco, and an English mother who had her own ideas about the proper upbringing of boys, Petrella's approach to police work usually shows the influence of his sedate English boarding-school rearing, but can on occasion reflect his hot Spanish heritage. Most of Petrella's appearances have been in short stories, which were collected under the title *Petrella at Q* in 1977.

Gilbert has created two other policemen who deserve mention. Chief Inspector (later Chief Superintendent) Hazlerigg was introduced in *Close Quarters* (1947) and appeared in several subsequent stories, sometimes as a representative of the Great Policeman school who solves mysteries almost without the assistance of his subordinates, and sometimes only in a cameo role in stories where the main detective work is carried on by civilians. Detective Chief Inspector William Mercer has appeared in only one book-length procedural story, *The Body of a Girl* (1972), though Gilbert did revive him for a series of three short stories in *Ellery Queen's Mystery Magazine* in 1979.

If accolades are to be awarded to any of these writers of early police procedurals, Michael Gilbert would easily receive the one for command of incisive English prose. Here, for example, is his description in *Death Has Deep Roots* of the sorrowful Sergeant Crabbe, who has come to the uncomfortable conclusion that he can do nothing to help one of the parties interested in the case: "He bestowed upon McCann the look which a St. Bernard might have given if, after a long trek through the snow, he had found the traveler already frozen to death" (vi).

Elizabeth Linington writes three series of procedurals, the one featuring Luis Mendoza under the pseudonym of Dell Shannon, the Vic Varallo series as by Lesley Egan, and the Ivor Maddox series under her own name. Mendoza appeared upon the scene in *Case Pending* (1960), Varallo in *Case for Appeal* (1961), and Maddox in *Greenmask!* (1964). Linington's novels are characterized by the remarkable number of story-lines, representing the number of cases (twenty-four in *Spring of Violence*) on which her policemen are employed, and by an often-stated conception of police work as the never-ending struggle between good and evil.

Police methods receive frequent mention in her books, but they are seldom handled with any degree of detail. More often than not she backs away from the report of procedures, treating them whimsically or even flippantly.

Nicolas Freeling created Inspector Peter Simon Joseph Van der Valk in *Love in Amsterdam* in 1962 and killed him off ten novels later in *A Long Silence* (U.S. title, *Aupres de ma Blonde*) in 1972. Van der Valk is probably the most complex and unorthodox policeman in procedural fiction. Steinbrunner and Penzler call him "a leftist intellectual," *Time* magazine "a plebeian with little formal education," a painter in one of the novels calls him "a ham actor," and to one of his superiors he is "a lunatic."[11]

Not all the Van der Valk stories are procedurals in the sense of the involvement of a police team carrying out a cooperative effort. In several of them Van der Valk works not only alone but in secret, and in one he not only solves the mystery but makes a determination regarding the appropriateness of punishment. For the reader especially interested in the procedural formula the stories are rich in commentary on police life and the police mind, usually from Van der Valk himself, who is far better read than most fictional policemen and whose thinking on police methods and the police sub-culture is often profound and almost inevitably eccentric.

Not many mystery novels have received as many honors as John Ball's *In the Heat of the Night* (1965), the first in the series featuring Virgil Tibbs of the Pasadena police force. It received the "best first" award from the Mystery Writers of America and the Gold Dagger from the Crime Writers' Association, and it continues to show up on lists of "bests" and "favorites."

The Tibbs stories have two special qualities that are important in the development of the procedural form. First, they comprise a running commentary on the nature of police work as a profession. Virgil Tibbs is a black policeman, but his consciousness of his race is not so significant a theme as his dedication to integrity and competence. Second, the author shows remarkable flexibility in his ability to stay within the procedural formula while at the same time varying his thematic approach from one novel to another. *Johnny Get Your Gun* (1969), for example, is a good instance of the mystery story as social commentary, while *Five Pieces of Jade* (1972) in both subject and treatment is an almost classic example of the traditional formal-problem story.

Ball has written one procedural novel outside the Tibbs series, *Police Chief* (1977), in which Sergeant Jack Tallon of the Pasadena police department moves to the state of Washington as chief of a small-city department.

Sweden has experienced a resurgence of mystery-story writing during the past two or three decades, but no Swedish writers have attracted world-wide attention as have the husband-wife team of Maj Sjowall and Per Wahloo, whose series of procedurals began with *Roseanna* in 1965 and ended with *The Terrorists* in 1975, the year of Wahloo's death.

Martin Beck is usually listed as the main character of the series, but the real "hero" is the National Homicide Squad and various other police who work with them, including the guilt-ridden Lennart Kollberg (who eventually quits police work), the uncivil Gunvald Larsson, the phlegmatic but phenomenally retentive Fredrik Melander, and even the "Keystone Klutzes,"[12] Kristiansson and Kvant, the inept patrolmen who can never do anything right. The stories are especially abundant in details of police off-duty, as they are in social criticism. Collectively, they create the impression that crime is not so much a social evil as it is a symptom of the much deeper discontents of civilization.

Hamilton Jobson, like Maurice Procter, writes police procedurals in which the policemen are local people, not Scotland Yard men. Detective Chief Superintendent Matt Anders, who was introduced in *Therefore I Killed Him* (1968), is a capable professional who stands by his subordinates and whose calm manner impresses those civilians with whom he comes into contact. The second novel in the series, *The Evidence You Will Hear* (1975), qualifies as a "pure" procedural, in which the detection is carried forward by straight police work and in which the spotlight is shared successively by the policemen at work on the case.

The first policewoman to be treated in depth in a procedural series was Dorothy Uhnak's Christie Opara, who appeared in *The Bait* (1968), *The Witness* (1969) and *The Ledger* (1970). Uhnak, who served for fourteen years with the New York Transit Police and has a bachelor's degree in criminal justice, has a firm knowledge of both the practical and theoretical aspects of police work, and an especially strong sensitivity to the problems of a woman police officer.

Uhnak abandoned the Opara series in 1973 to produce the best-selling *Law and Order*, a story of three generations of New York patrolmen, a police novel but not a mystery. She returned to the procedural format with *The Investigation* in 1977, another best-seller. The narrator of *The Investigation,* Joe Peters, is attached to the Queens County District Attorney's Investigating Squad, and his problems with internal and external politics, his concern over the possible failure of his marriage, and his willingness to play dirty in the in-fighting within the squad, all contribute to the suspense that probably accounts for the popularity of the book.

Collin Wilcox is unique among procedural writers in his use of the first-person narrator for an entire series, the stories featuring Sergeant (later Lieutenant) Frank Hastings of the San Francisco Police Department, which began with *The Lonely Hunter* in 1969. One result of the use of Hastings as narrator is that the reader gains an in-depth perception of the man, including not only his feelings about his job and the people he works with, but the pain he continues to feel as a result of his broken marriage and his battle with alcoholism.

Wilcox achieved another "first" among procedural writers in his collaboration with Bill Pronzini in *Twospot* (1978), in which Hastings shares an investigation with Pronzini's private detective. We will discuss this novel more fully when we match the approach of the police procedural with that of the private-investigator story, because it offers several bases for comparison and contrast.

Surely one of the crustiest of policemen is Detective Superintendent Andrew Dalziel, introduced by Reginald Hill in *A Clubbable Woman* (1970). Dalziel's foghorn voice and dyspeptic temperament are legendary among his colleagues and subordinates, and his tendency toward violent physical response gives pause to criminals and would-be criminals who may be tempted to provoke him, as the owner of an antique shop in *Ruling Passion* discovers when he attacks Dalziel and has his shop wrecked during the ensuing efforts of Dalziel to arrest him.

The tensions and anxieties of the Republic of South Africa have produced a body of distinguished fiction during the past three decades, including the series of procedurals by James McClure beginning with *The Steam Pig* in 1971. McClure's detective team is composed of Lieutenant Trompie Kramer, of Afrikaner descent, and Sergeant Mickey Zondi, a Bantu policeman. The racial combination of the team offers a variety of narrative opportunities, partly because the gifted Zondi must by local custom be regarded as an inferior, but even more so because Kramer knows Zondi to be indispensable as an assistant and also values him as a person of dignity and integrity.

Besides the faithful rendering of the South African scene, the McClure novels are distinguished by a pervasive suspense. A bizarre opening scene is the hallmark of the stories, like the one in *The Caterpillar Cop*, in which a love-making couple in the woods find themselves almost literally on top of the naked body of a murder victim.

The second woman detective to be featured in a procedural series was Norah Mulcahaney, who first appeared in Lillian O'Donnell's *The Phone Calls* in 1972. Norah begins her career in that story as a uniformed patrolman, is promoted to homicide detective third-grade, and within four years has made sergeant. She also marries her superior, Lieutenant Joe Capretto, and thus becomes a member of the first New York husband-wife police combination in procedural history.

The Mulcahaney series is especially rich in that quality that has distinguished the police procedural, the portrayal of the lives and concerns of policemen as private persons. Norah's and Joe's marriage turns out to be a perilous venture, jeopardized in part by the predictable conflicts between the two strong-minded detectives, and not ameliorated by the presence in the stories of Norah's Irish father and Joe's Italian mother, each of whom has quite decided ideas of how a marriage should work.

Olle Hogstrand is another Swedish procedural writer whose work has come to be well known in the United States. The first book in his series, *On the Prime Minister's Account* (1971), features Detective Jan Olsson of the Security Police (the notorious "Sepo," of which the readers of Sjowall and Wahloo can have no high opinion) and Lars Kollin, head of the Homicide Squad. The stories are strong in police methodology and insights into the police mind, but the picture of police motivations is uncomplimentary at the very best.

Lawrence Sanders has written two books featuring Captain Edward X. Delaney, NYPD, *The First Deadly Sin* (1973) and *The Second Deadly Sin* (1977), both enormous best-sellers. Neither was favorably received by reviewers, who almost unanimously criticized them as over-inflated, cluttered, too detailed to be viable as mysteries. What the reviewers apparently missed was that Sanders, especially in the first book, was undertaking the development of a theme that transcended the usual scope of a mystery.

Neither story begins as a procedural, and *The First Deadly Sin* does not become one until the plot is far advanced. In that story Delaney is pulled off the case for political reasons and is not placed in charge until three hundred pages later, at which point the novel moves into the standard procedural pattern. *The Second Deadly Sin*, which is much closer to the procedural formula, moves more quickly into the business of investigation, without the heavy thematic development of the first story.

Rex Burns' *The Alvarez Journal*, which was published in 1975 and won the Mystery Writers of America Best First Novel award in that year, introduced Detective Gabriel Wager of the Denver Police Department. The quality of Wager most likely to attract immediate attention is the fact of his descent: he is half Chicano and half Anglo, with the result that he is passed over for promotion because of his Mexican blood and at the same time regarded as a traitor to his Mexican heritage by others of Hispanic descent. This inner conflict, however, is not the determinant in Wager's character. He is also a canny cop with a strong sense of professionalism, more than a tinge of social-political conservatism, and a tough resourcefulness.

Burns is another series novelist who refuses to let himself be drawn into a tight, inflexible formula. Each book in the Wager series is a little different from the others, in theme, characterization and structure. The change is accomplished in part by a change of assignment—Wager starts out in the Organized Crime Division, moves to narcotics and then to homicide—and partly by the methods employed, from physical pursuit to empirical deduction to infiltration.

During 1975 Nelson DeMille published three paperbacks featuring Sergeant Joe Keller, NYPD: *The Cannibal, The Smack Man,* and *Night of the Phoenix.* Keller is tough, incomparably tough, incredibly tough, almost unbearably tough. The series was mercifully terminated after these three titles.

The first Danish procedural writer to be translated into English is Poul Orum, whose detective team of Jonas Morck and Knud Einarsen made their appearance in 1975 in *The Whipping Boy* (U.S. title, *Scapegoat*). Orum is another writer capable of considerable versatility. *The Whipping Boy* comes close to qualifying as a "pure" procedural, with the suspense sustained almost entirely through the questioning of witnesses and the use or threatened use of police clout, but *Nothing but the Truth* (1976) is essentially a psychological novel, with explorations of ego-mania and mother-fixation, neurosis and erotic obsession.

Most reviewers and critics have never been quite sure what to make of Janwillem van de Wetering, whose atypical series began with *Outsider in Amsterdam* (1975). A businessman who grew up in Rotterdam during the German occupation, has lived on six continents, spent more than a year as a monk in a Zen monastery in Japan, was for several years a member of the Amsterdam Special Constabulary, and prefers the surrealist writers of fiction, van de Wetering draws upon all of these elements in his books, with the result that the stories may seem a little odd and off-key to the reader of more conventional mysteries.

Actually, van de Wetering is a writer of considerable courage, whose stories demand more than an ordinary degree of commitment to be understood. One key to that understanding lies in the levels of awareness he assigns to the three members of his police team, the un-named commisaris, Adjutant Henk Grijpstra, and Sergeant Rinus DeGier, which translate into three levels of meaning in the stories themselves.

Yet another Swedish writer who has attained considerable popularity in the English-speaking world is K. Arne Blom, whose *The Moment of Truth* was published in the United States in 1977. The police in this novel work as a team, with no stars and no policemen characterized in depth. The theme of the story is police violence and its results, in the treatment of which Blom shares with Sjowall and Wahloo and with Hogstrand some rather sharp criticism of the police mentality and the police approach.

Besides these authors of series, we should mention two other writers who have produced single procedural stories. Frank De Felitta, author of *Audrey Rose* and other fiction, published *Oktoberfest* in 1973, featuring Chief Inspector Martin Bauer of the Munich police and distinguished chiefly by its treatment of the sense of guilt among Germans regarding Nazi atrocities. Dan Greenburg (probably best remembered for *How to Be a Jewish Mother*) produced *Love Kills* in 1978, chronicling the efforts of young Max Segal, NYPD, to solve a series of particularly sensational murders.

Like other kinds of popular fiction, the police procedural has responded to and capitalized upon current readers' interests generated by stories in other fields. The novels of John Le Carre and Ian Fleming, for example, produced a public hunger for tales of international intrigue during the 1960s and '70s, and it is not surprising that, in this period, several writers of procedurals sent their policemen abroad on investigative missions which, although they did not normally involve undercover operation, had at least a flavor of international stealth. Sjowall and Wahloo's Martin Beck, for example, spends considerable time in Budapest in *The Man Who Went Up in Smoke*. Beck conceals his identity as much as possible, though the Hungarian police soon identify him and work with him. Freeling's Van der Valk is a notable international operator, especially in *The King of the Rainy Country*, which takes him into Germany, Austria, France and Spain. The investigation in *Tsing-Boum* requires that he travel in France and Belgium, and *Over the High Side* (U.S. title, *The Lovely Ladies*) takes him to Ireland. Of course European cops must because of the nature of geography cross frontiers more often than those in America, and we may disregard the number of times the Swedish police run over to Copenhagen, or the Dutch cops into Germany and Belgium. It is unusual for an American policeman to go abroad on a case, though Virgil Tibbs in *The Eyes of Buddha* follows clues into Hong Kong and Nepal, not under cover but not advertising his identity either. The one story in which policemen operate abroad in a genuine secret-agent style is van de Wetering's *The Japanese Corpse*, where the commisaris and De Gier travel under carefully devised cover.

The public taste for the occult and supernatural has also made itself felt in the procedural, producing the witchcraft theme in Knox's *To Kill a Witch*, satanism in Wilcox's *Long Way Down,* clairvoyance in Greenburg's *Love Kills*, and overt haunting in McBain's *Ghosts*.

One fact that should emerge from this review of the series writers is that the police procedural does not have the geographic orientation of the older traditions of detective fiction. Howard Haycraft points out that the classic tale of logical deduction is customarily thought of as "English" in tone, while the hard-boiled private-eye story is typically "American."[13] The procedural, on the other hand, has a universal quality that adjusts itself to America, Britain, Sweden, Denmark, Holland and South Africa. There are, as we will see in Chapter 9, some atmospheric differences between approaches in America and Europe, but the fundamental methodology and attitude is much the same throughout the world.

Chapter 3

The Trouble with Cops

MOST DETECTIVE STORIES are written about crimes, and wherever there are crimes there are policemen. Consequently, the role of the cop is the most pervasive one in detective fiction, whether the story belongs to the classic school and features one of those brilliant, eccentric amateurs, or the hard-boiled variety where the detective-protagonist is a private investigator. The policeman's part in the drama is usually a minor one: often he is merely part of the scenery, occasionally his function is to impede the work of the gifted genius who is better at deduction than an ordinary cop could be, and quite frequently he is there chiefly as a foil whose ineptness serves to highlight by contrast the brilliance of the hero-sleuth. In one type of story he *is* the hero-sleuth, in which instance he rises to a height of attainment not ordinarily granted to the servant of society.

In this chapter we will take a look (necessarily brief) at policemen in mysteries outside the procedural school, with two purposes in mind. First, we will try to determine an image of the policeman who appears in the classic formal-problem tale and also the hard-boiled story, as background for the picture of the procedural cop. We will also be on the lookout for any important changes in the image of the policeman that have taken place during the almost century and a half of detective fiction and will ask, if there have been any changes, what they tell us about the changing public perception of the policeman.

Our review begins properly with the first of Poe's Dupin stories, "The Murders in the Rue Morgue." The Paris police are on the scene before Dupin begins his incisive inquiry, and the first newspaper evaluation of their activities is that they are "entirely at fault," though the reporter charitably adds that their perplexity is "an unusual occurrence in affairs of this nature." Most of the picture of police activities reaches the reader through Dupin's estimation of their effectiveness: they are "cunning, but no more," "there is no method in their proceedings, beyond the method of the moment," their perceptions are "hermetically sealed" against the possibility that those windows, apparently nailed shut, had ever been opened. Dupin does not miss the opportunity to take a cut at Francois Vidocq, celebrated policeman of the earlier generation, who, according to Dupin, "was a good guesser, and a persevering man,... but without educated thought." The police in "The Murders in the Rue Morgue" are shadow-figures who never really get into the story except to sharpen Dupin's brilliance, though the Prefect is quoted at the end as making some comments about the propriety of people minding their own business.

At the beginning of "The Mystery of Marie Roget," however, the Prefect G---- is sufficiently recovered from his pique (and is also feeling the pressure of public disapproval over lack of progress on a case that has dragged on for three weeks) to drop in and see if Dupin has any ideas. The rest of the story is the account of Dupin's review of the evidence and his analysis of the case, together with several predictable strictures upon the inadequacies of the Paris police. The narrowness of the police view, according to Dupin, stems from habits of inflexible thinking: having recognized the possibility of several modes and motives for the crime, they exclude the possibility of others. He takes them to task especially for their inability to recognize the implications of the simplicity-complexity principle, which holds that the more unusual ("*outre*" is Dupin's pet term) a case the simpler the promise of solution, and vice-versa. The police are defeated by the unusualness of the case which—and this should be especially noted—"to a properly regulated intellect" should have pointed the way to its solution.

By the time of "The Purloined Letter" the Prefect has not only recovered from his annoyance at Dupin's meddling but has developed a grudging admiration for his powers, thus becoming the precursor of all those other resentful policemen of the classic tale who first despise the precosity of the intellectual genius, then stand in open-mouthed wonder at his deductive powers, and finally become his devoted admirers. The Prefect has a problem that is at once "simple and odd," giving Dupin the opportunity to suggest that it is the very simplicity of the matter that has clouded the view of the solution. In this story Dupin pays several restricted compliments to the police: they are exceedingly able in their own way, competent in the knowledge their duties demand, persevering, ingenious and cunning; their methods are "not only the best of their kind, but carried out to absolute perfection." Their deficiency proceeds from their narrow view of possibilities: their resources, in Dupin's opinion, are a Procrustean bed to which the Prefect adapts his methods. If the Minister D---'s method of concealing the letter had lain within the Prefect's principles of investigation, "its discovery would have been a matter altogether beyond question." In short, the methods of the police are quite satisfactory in *most* cases (by implication, almost all those ordinary cases outside the present story), but not in *this* case, which is *outre*, seemingly complex but quite simple, its ingenious ambiguity placing it beyond the scope of ordinary police investigation and into the realm of Dupin's unique perceptions.

In these tales we get our only assessment of the Paris police from the somewhat supercilious Dupin, who critizes them on two counts, their restricted view of the problem and their unorganized, undisciplined habits of thought. The narrowness of their perceptions prompts them to use methods ill adapted to the case at hand and to try to fit the problem to the method instead of the other way around. The same kind of criticism applies to their lack of logic, according to Dupin, especially their inability to define and analyze. At the same time, he is generous in his praise of their tenacity, their vigor, and their cunning. In most cases, he gladly admits, the methods of the Prefect and his men are superior to his own.

Police figures much better known to the lover of mystery fiction emerge in the Sherlock Holmes stories of Conan Doyle, especially in the familiar figures of Inspectors Gregson and Lestrade, and also Athelney Jones, Alec MacDonald, and the promising young Stanley Hopkins.

Admittedly, these are not admirable policemen; Anthony Boucher probably voices the consensus when he calls them "dunderheaded clods."[1] We must recognize, though, that at least part of the bad press of Gregson, Lestrade, and the others results from the bias of Dr. Watson, who seems to enjoy characterizing them as "conventional" or "ferret-like." In "The Adventure of the Norwood Builder" he resents Lestrade's overbearing manner, and in *A Study in Scarlet* he observes how Gregson rubs his hands "in a self-satisfied way" when he reports to Holmes the progress he and Lestrade have made, which turns out to be no progress at all (iii). Later, though, (in *The Hound of the Baskervilles*) Watson condescendingly concedes that Lestrade has learned a great deal since their first case together. Holmes, by the way, in the same story refers to Lestrade as "the best of the professionals" and is glad enough to have his assistance in the climactic confrontation on the moor (xiii).

The policemen in the Holmes stories show four kinds of mental limitations that were eventually inherited to one degree or another by succeeding generations of cops in the classic stories, the most crucial being their obvious lack of imagination. This deficiency manifests itself when Lestrade fails to see the significance of the sailor's-knot in the string binding the packet in "The Adventure of the Cardboard Box," and when Gregson fails to ask the crucial question in his telegram of inquiry in *A Study in Scarlet* (iii). Holmes frequently complains about the way the police neglect possible alternatives and other lines of inquiry, and when (in "The Norwood Builder") Lestrade seizes upon an obvious conclusion, Holmes laments, "You do not add imagination to your other great qualities."

Their second shortcoming, which they share with the Prefect G-- of the Dupin tales, is their distrust of theory. Being practical men, they prefer to stick to actualities and to avoid abstractions. "Facts are better than theories," Athelney Jones tells Holmes in *The Sign of Four*, but a moment later when Holmes shows him one of his "facts" is an error and promises a workable solution, Jones snaps, "Don't promise too much, Mr. Theorist!" (vi).

Then there is their inferior level of education, which may prompt nothing more serious than a conversational gaffe, as when Inspector MacDonald in *The Valley of Fear* identifies Jonathan Wild as a character in a detective novel (ii). The handicap may actually limit their perceptions in an investigation, however, as it does when MacDonald in the same novel misses the significance of the Greuze painting in Professor Moriarity's study (ii), or when in the better-known episode in *A Study in Scarlet* the police assume the German *Rache* to be the incomplete spelling of a name (iii).

Finally, there is their complacency. As a rule they seem to be quite satisfied with their normal pedestrian police routines and unwilling to vary approaches to fit a new and different situation.

Even the bright young Stanley Hopkins falls victim to this defect in "The Adventure of Black Peter" in his failure to look for possible alternatives and to guard against chance.

Like Dupin, Holmes is quite willing to give the police their due, though sometimes his praise of their good qualities is discouragingly equivocal. He commends their courage, their cunning and their energy, and at no point does he ever suggest that they are dishonest or corruptible.

We should also note the way in which Holmes' personal regard for the police improves as the saga progresses. He becomes more tolerant of them as people, though he remains critical of their lack of acumen. As in the Dupin tales the police reciprocate the master-detective's regard, partly because they recognize that he is no professional threat to them. This growing esteem between the transcendent genius and the official police was to become a pattern for later writers of the classic school who, within the framework of a single novel or over the series, transform the attitude of mutual distrust into one of reciprocal respect if not personal regard.

One of the "dunderheaded clods" who bear the stamp of Conan Doyle's policemen is Inspector Japp, who figures occasionally in the Hercule Poirot stories of Agatha Christie, and whom Earl Bargainnier assigns to the "comically stupid" category of Christie's policemen.[2] At his first appearance in *The Mysterious Affair at Styles* Japp reveals his cultural level (he greets Poirot as "moosier") and his failure to recognize the simplicity-complexity formula: he dismisses the case as "pretty clear," whereupon the more perceptive Poirot gravely begs to differ with him (vii). It is perhaps not an over-simplification to characterize Japp's approach to detection as "physical" in contrast to Poirot's "cerebral" style: we are told (in *Death in the Air*) that Japp dislikes and distrusts the word "psychology," (vii) and in a particularly revealing scene in "The Market Basing Mystery" Poirot takes a sparing breakfast at the beginning of a case in order to avoid replenishing the stomach at the expense of the brain, while Japp cheerfully orders a double portion of eggs and bacon.

Sergeant Ernest Heath, the series policeman in S.S. Van Dine's Philo Vance novels, is a competent and resourceful cop, and we get the impression that if Heath ever had the opportunity to tackle a case not involving Ming pottery, or the breeding of scotties, or

Egyptian scarabs, he could acquit himself with credit. Upon his introduction in *The Benson Murder Case* the narrator (who shares his hero's snobberies) condescends to observe that Heath accords with the conventional notion of the detective and even confesses a liking for the sergeant "despite his very obvious limitations" (iii). Heath's most obvious limitation in Vance's estimation, is his substitution of energy for thought, and he asks District Attorney Markham, "How do those robust lads ever succeed in running down a suspect?" (iv).

There is also a strong flavor of Dupin's complaint against the Paris police when Vance tells Heath, in *The Greene Murder Case*, "Sergeant, you should thank your Maker that you are not cursed with an imagination" (viii). Heath shows up worst as a logician, a role in which his powers suffer in contrast with those of the masterful Vance, who demolishes Heath's theories as fast as the sergeant can devise them. Heath's personal relationships with Vance follow the standard series formula: he is contemptuous of Vance's esoteric approach to detection in the first novel, then admits a grudging respect as a result of Vance's sensational achievements, and later becomes his devoted admirer.

The same pattern appears in the case of Sergeant Thomas Velie, of the Ellery Queen series. Skeptical at first, the sergeant later begins to register amazement at Ellery's deductions and calls him "Maestro." "Bulky and rather blockheaded" is Francis M. Nevins' characterizations of Velie,[3] which he undeniably is, especially in contrast to the mental powers of The Great Man. At his first appearance, though, in *The Roman Hat Mystery*, Velie shows himself to be systematic and thorough, quickly restoring order at the murder scene, sealing off the area, and identifying witnesses for questioning (i). Velie is not stupid, though a little later in the story Inspector Richard Queen finds it necessary to caution him against making a premature arrest (xv).

Probably the most familiar policeman in classic detective fiction is Inspector L.T. Cramer, NYPD, in Rex Stout's Nero Wolfe series. As in the cases of other police detectives we have mentioned, Cramer's feelings toward Wolfe move from skepticism (more often, outright hostility) to open admiration, but the transition takes place within the framework of a single novel instead of being spread over the series. In the typical Wolfe story Cramer appears fairly early on the stoop of the old brownstone on West Thirty-Fifth Street, red of face and furiously chewing an unlighted cigar, stalks past Archie Goodwin with a grunt or no greeting at all, into Wolfe's office where a stormy confrontation takes place, during the course of which Cramer threatens at least once to take Wolfe and Goodwin down to headquarters or to lift their licenses, or both. At the end of the story, following a series of demonstrations of Wolfe's superior deductive powers, Cramer stands quietly by while Wolfe confronts an office full of witnesses and suspects, until the mystery is solved and it is time to clap the handcuffs on the culprit. Then, at the beginning of the next story there is Cramer back on the stoop, red of face and furiously chewing an unlighted cigar, and the pattern is ready to be repeated.

Those qualities which Wolfe finds most objectionable in Cramer are his tendency to intimidation, his lack of imagination, and his distrust of theory. As a policeman Cramer has official clout (one of the most important differences between the fictional policeman and other detectives), and he does not hesitate to use it. In *The Mother Hunt* (vii) Wolfe taxes him with harassment of his clients, and in *The Final Deduction* he accuses Cramer of having been a policeman so long and having asked so many impertinent questions that it has become spontaneous with him (xi). The accusation of lack of imagination stings Cramer in *The Red Box*, where he admits that he is "too damn dumb to be eccentric," (v) but it is verified in "Death of a Demon" when Cramer's narrow practicality prevents his recognizing the significance of the murder weapon. Like most of his predecessors in fiction, Cramer distrusts theory. "I'll leave you to your deductions and assumptions," he tells Wolfe in *The Final Deduction* and storms out of the office ready to take overt action (xi).

On the other hand, Wolfe finds much to praise in the Inspector's conduct as a policeman. Cramer is tenacious and thorough: his conclusions in a case are based upon a thorough and prolonged inquiry by an army of trained policemen, and on several occasions Wolfe refuses to initiate a search for a piece of evidence the police have been seeking, because, according to Wolfe, if Cramer's men haven't found it, it can't be found. Nor does he deny Cramer's competence. In nine cases out of ten, Wolfe admits, the official police are better equipped to handle a case than Wolfe is, a concession most important to the basic myth of the classic detective story. Finally,

Cramer is honest and incorruptible, as Archie Goodwin could testify in *In The Best of Families*, when Archie implies that the Inspector might be in the pay of Arnold Zeck, and Cramer's response is to take two swings at him (ix).

Any assessment of Cramer's failings and successes as a policeman must be conditioned by two aspects of his role in the series. First, he is a considerably more complex personality than Poe's Prefect G--- or Conan Doyle's Gregson and Lestrade, with the result that he can not be categorized as either a cunning fox or a dunderhead. The other is that we get our entire impression of him through the satiric eyes of Archie Goodwin, the narrator of the series, who is not usually inclined to charity toward anybody, especially cops.

Lieutenant Tragg (Los Angeles Homicide Division) in the Perry Mason series by Erle Stanley Gardner follows the same pattern as Cramer in his repeated transformation from distrust to admiration in each novel. The formula is illustrated in *The Case of the Queenly Contestant*. Sarcastic and officious, Tragg bursts into Mason's office unannounced and warns him about tampering with law-enforcement. On the witness stand he is all smugness and smiles under Mason's cross-examination, but then when Mason has ruined his case, Tragg goes with him to his office, where Mason puts him on the right track by pointing out a clue Tragg has overlooked (xiv-xviii). This model, repeated in almost every story in which he appears, has the natural effect of making the lieutenant look foolish, but he is still a policeman who knows his job and does it well. In *The Case of the Careless Cupid*, for example, it is suggested that Tragg might have overlooked a piece of evidence hidden in a dark corner during a search, to which he replies that in a police search there aren't any dark corners (xx).

A more recent example, and certainly one of the best in terms of police excellence, is Hugh Lanigan, Chief of Police at Barnard's Crossing in the Rabbi stories of Harry Kemelman. We learn two things about Lanigan when he is introduced in *Friday the Rabbi Slept Late,* the first of the series. He has a reputation as a policeman of integrity who would, according to one of the Barnard's Crossing residents, arrest his own son if he were guilty (xxiv). He is also a just and decent man who refuses to pin guilt for a murder on Rabbi Small, in spite of the fact that a Jewish scapegoat would be a convenient solution to public pressure for the arrest of a suspect. Chief Lanigan's handicap as a fictional police detective is the one he shares with his predecessors in the classic formal-problem story: his attempts at deduction suffer sharply in comparison with the logical powers of the Rabbi, who knocks down one after another of the Chief's hypotheses, just as Philo Vance did those of Sergeant Heath and Perry Mason did those of Lieutenant Tragg.

We have purposely passed over two well-known policemen in the classic tale of detection, Inspector Richard Queen, father of Ellery, and Chief Inspector Charles Parker, who becomes the brother-in-law of Dorothy Sayers' Peter Wimsey, because, as members of the family of the transcendent sleuth-protagonist, they bear a special relationship to the story that places them outside the category of the typical cop.

Clearly, the first thing we should say about the policeman in the classic tale is that, except for a few genuine dunderheads, he is not stupid. He is competent as a policeman, and in normal cases he can do better than the genius who has the starring role. He is tenacious, thorough, energetic, and if he can not find a culprit or a piece of evidence, neither can the brilliant protagonist and his associates. He does occasionally slip up on the routines of an investigation, but his procedures are usually as good as can be expected for run-of-the-mill police work.

At the same time, it is axiomatic that his perceptions are not capable of rising to the level of those of the detective protagonist. He can perceive patterns on a practical level but is not good at theory. Because his approach tends to be "physical," he has trouble understanding things like the simplicity-complexity principle, and his imagination tends to be limited. It is important to remember, though, that the policeman's handicaps customarily apply only to the present case—the story in the reader's hands, which is complex, abstruse, unique—and present little or no problem in the host of other crimes he deals with.

His cultural background is usually limited and often superficial, making him look especially bad in comparison with the transcendent genius who has put aside his researches in organic chemistry (Holmes) or his translations of the fragments of Menander (Vance) to help on the case. As a result, he may appear embarrassingly cloddish and boorish, but worse still he may overlook important clues that lie outside his scope, especially if they relate to those fields that lie exclusively within the scope of the detective hero.

Almost invariably, he is honest and incorruptible. His severest critics—like Dupin and Holmes—never accuse him of dishonesty. The cop who will take a bribe or frame a suspect is not to appear until the advent of the hard-boiled detective story.

In Chapter 8 we will have more to say about the mythic elements in detective fiction. We must not leave the discussion of the policeman in the classic tale, however, without at least a mention of his place in the myth of the formal-problem story. The interpretation offered by W.H. Auden in his essay "The Guilty Vicarage" holds that the interest in the (classic) detective story is "the dialectic of innocence and guilt," and he represents the progression from the peaceful state before the murder, through the invasion of the community by the criminal, through the discovery of guilt by the detective, to the peaceful state after the murderer is apprehended, as an analogue to the steps of classic Greek tragedy, beginning with the state of false innocence, proceeding through discovery and catharsis, to the condition of true innocence.[4] The deliverer from outside the community (in the mystery story, the detective), having dispelled chaos by discovery of guilt, gives the purged society back to its members, and true innocence is restored.

The picture we have seen of the policeman in the classic tale of detection is in harmony with the Innocence-Restored myth. The police must be generally competent, able to maintain order and security outside the present context, because that is the state of innocence which must be restored. The presence of corrupt or incompetent policemen would be disturbing in a world where all must be serene after the "genius from the outside"[5] has purged the community of the present threat. In a sense, the protagonist-deliverer hands the cleansed community back to the regular police at the end of the story. At the same time, the police must be incapable of handling *this* case (the loss of innocence), because they are part of the community, which is incapable of cleansing itself.

A special case of the classic school of detection is the story in which the detective-hero is a policeman. The list of these policemen includes some of the most illustrious personages in mystery fiction, such as Gaboriau's M. Lecoq, Green's Ebenezer Gryce, Simenon's

Jules Maigret, Biggers' Charlie Chan, Marsh's Roderick Alleyn, Tey's Alan Grant, James' Adam Dalgliesh, Rendell's Chief Inspector Wexford, and Keating's Ganesh Ghote. The impressive gifts of these men place them in a class that is closer to August Dupin and Sherlock Holmes than to the cops of the procedural stories, so that they may be properly designated as the Great Policemen of detective fiction.

The main difference between these men and the procedural cops is that the Great Policeman solves the case himself; the other police in the story help him with the accumulation of evidence, but in the resolution the Great Policeman is a solitary figure. Moreover, he typically withholds the solution or partial solution from the reader, though he may confide it to a close associate. In *Overture to Death*, for example, Roderick Alleyn has solved the mystery seventy pages before the end of the story; he apparently tells his close associate, Inspector Fox, but nobody else, including the reader (xx). The final explication is made to a newspaper man whom Alleyn has used for various tasks in the case (xxvii).

As a rule the Great Policeman works closely with one person, usually a fellow policeman like Alleyn's "Br'er Fox" or Gryce's mysterious "Q," but this associate may be a civilian. His work with other policemen is usually minimal, except as he sends them on errands or uses them to collect information. The other policemen may operate as a team, but the Great Policeman is not part of it.[6] Sometimes he works not only alone but under cover, as Charlie Chan does in *The Chinese Parrot*, where Charlie not only conceals his identity from the local police but misleads them regarding the true nature of the mystery. M. Lecoq does substantially the same thing in *File No. 113*.

Quite frequently the Great Policeman does not enter the story until after the mystery has been defined and a provisional analysis has taken place, and after the main characters have been established. The story is fifty pages along before Adam Dalgliesh arrives on the murder scene in *Shroud for a Nightingale*. Charlie Chan does not enter the story until halfway through *Charlie Chan Carries On*, nor does Roderick Alleyn in *Killer Dolphin*.

The setting of the story and personal qualifications of the protagonist also place the Great Policeman closer to the Dupin-Holmes tradition than to the procedural story. Notice, for example, the number of instances in which these policemen solve cases with which they have come to be associated by accident (Alan Grant in *The Singing Sands*, Jules Maigret in *Maigret in Vichy*), a thing that almost never happens in the police procedural but happens often in the classic tale. Quite frequently, also, especially if he is with Scotland Yard, he will be sent to a remote village, thus becoming the "genius from outside" instead of a member of the guilty community. Notice also how often the settings of these stories have an exotic or picturesque atmosphere in contrast to the ordinary settings of the police procedurals: a rural English village in Marsh's *Overture to Death*, complete with squire, rector, and woman of mystery; a Victorian mansion in James' *Shroud for a Nightingale,* complete with ghost.

The Great Policeman is usually not distinguished except as a detective, though Roderick Alleyn does have an Oxford degree, and Adam Dalgliesh is a published poet. In contrast to the minor policemen in the classic stories, though, he is richly endowed with imagination and a level of perception far above that of the ordinary cop. Even Keating's Ganesh Ghote, who is painfully reminded of his own humility, is capable of a brilliance of imagination in *Inspector Ghote Trusts the Heart*, when a flash of insight directs him to the kidnapped child just in time for a hair-breadth rescue (xv).

By and large, the cultural level of the Great Policeman is above that of the run-of-the-mill cop, as his conversation, his reading, and his taste in art will testify. Probably the extreme example is Josephine Tey's *The Daughter of Time*, in which Inspector Grant, recovering from an injury, becomes interested in the case of the allegedly maligned Richard III, does intensive reading on the subject of Richard's purported crimes, and ultimately, using his considerable deductive powers, proves him not guilty. If you want to see a really sharp distinction between the qualities of the Great Policeman and those of the procedural cop, try to picture George Gideon confined to a hospital room working out a vindication of a fifteenth century monarch.

Our examination of the policemen in the private-investigator hard-boiled school will be directed to the novels of three acknowledged masters of the craft, Dashiell Hammett, Raymond Chandler and Ross Macdonald.

The private eyes of the hard-boiled detective story use the

methods of pursuit and infiltration, in contrast to the ratiocination of the transcendent sleuths of the classic school. Thus it seems appropriate that the Continental Op, in Hammett's first novel, *Red Harvest*, goes to the town of Personville ("Poisonville," as he fittingly calls it) to clean up corruption by singlehandedly starting a gang war between rival factions. "Poisonville" is totally depraved, and the policemen in the story are distinguished only by their share in the local corruption.

Those in *The Dain Curse*, however, are distinguished by their incompetence, which looks especially bad in contrast to the expertise of the Continental Op. Young Pat Reddy, inexperienced in the game of man-hunting, takes his eyes off Mrs. Leggett just long enough for her to pull a gun (vii). Deputy Sheriff Rolly, whose vague response to any unusual development is "tch, tch," does not want to get too deeply involved in the investigation because so many of the possible suspects are his relatives (xiv). Sheriff Feeney, whose commitment to law enforcement is largely perfunctory, impatiently breaks off an interrogation just as the Op is about to ask a vital question (xvi). The only policeman in *The Dain Curse* capable of much action is the dull, pompous Marshal Dick Cotton, who draws and fires at a suspect as soon as he opens the door; the Op has to push Cotton's arm to make him miss (xvi). Just about the only redeeming feature of the police in this novel is their willingness to cooperate in the Op's investigation.

Hammett begins to differentiate his policemen in *The Maltese Falcon,* where we meet two detectives who are the prototypes of policemen that will appear in the stories of Chandler, Macdonald, and a host of other writers of the hard-boiled school. There is the friendly rival of the private investigator, Detective Sergeant Tom Polhaus, usually courteous and respectful toward Sam Spade, whom he treats as an equal and in whom he is even willing to confide. Then there is the hostile opponent, Lieutenant Dundy, who has no use for private investigators in general and Sam Spade in particular. The contrast is especially sharp in that early scene in which Polhaus and Dundy interrupt Spade's conference with Brigid O'Shaughnessy and Joel Cairo. Dundy roughs up Cairo and clips Spade on the chin; Polhaus pushes himself between them to prevent further violence (viii). Later, over lunch, Polhaus apologizes to Spade and begs him not to tell the District Attorney he has leveled with him (xv). At the end of the story, when Spade turns Brigid over to the police, Polhaus is conciliatory, Dundy silent (xx).

The most completely developed policeman in Hammett's novels is Lieutenant Guild in *The Thin Man*, and he is also the most professional. Guild is friendly and cooperative toward Nick Charles and even suggests he would like to see Charles work on the case "on the right side" (xi). Guild does not believe in rough stuff: he does threaten to slap a reluctant suspect (xxvi), but he also threatens to kill one of his subordinates who has severely beaten another suspect (xxix). Like many another policeman in fiction, Guild feels the force of pressure he is getting from the Commissioner's office (xxv), but he tries to play fair with Nick Charles and to look at every angle (xxvii). In this novel, which is celebrated for its sparkling dialogue, Guild's cultural level manifests itself in his repeated "ain't's" and "he don't's."

Hammett does not stereotype his policemen as the writers of the classic school so often do. Instead, he chooses the cops to fit the stories. In *Red Harvest* their corruption contrasts with the honesty of the Continental Op, and in *The Dain Curse* they are generally incompetent in comparison with the Op's competence. Polhaus and Dundy of *The Maltese Falcon* are two sides of the coin, serving to emphasize the moral ambiguity of the novel. Lieutenant Guild of *The Thin Man* is capable and professional, and he is substantially lacking in the sharpness of Nick Charles. It is worth remembering, especially before we move on to Raymond Chandler, that *as detectives* Hammett's policemen are all inferior to the private-investigator-protagonists.

The seven novels of Raymond Chandler contain a considerably larger number of policemen than do Hammett's book-length stories, and as in Hammett they are considerably more heterogeneous than those in the classic story.

The first policeman we meet in *The Big Sleep* is Detective Bernie Ohls, the District Attorney's chief investigator. Ohls is the friendly rival of Philip Marlowe in much the same role as that of Tom Polhaus in Hammett's *The Maltese Falcon,* though he is a much more capable and intelligent policeman than Polhaus. It is Ohls who puts Marlowe in touch with General Sternwood for the commission that starts Marlowe on the investigation in this novel; Ohls and Marlowe exchange information, and Ohls takes pleasure in ribbing the private investigator when Marlowe makes a mis-cue. The good-natured rivalry is continued in Ohls' other appearance, in *The Long Goodbye,* where he saves Marlowe's life and then kids him about almost getting killed (xlviii). Marlowe, whose feelings toward policemen are never cordial, at one point describes Bernie Ohls as an old friend, as both bulldog and bloodhound, a wise old cop (xli).

Two policemen in the Marlowe series are automatically hostile toward private investigators but not physically violent in the handling of Marlowe. Captain Cronjager in *The Big Sleep* accuses Marlowe of playing his cards too close to his chest and of interfering in police business, and he comes close to exercising the clout that official policemen always hold over private eyes, getting Marlowe's license revoked (xviii). Sergeant Green in *The Long Goodbye* is another private-eye-hater. He does not use his fists on Marlowe, but he shows approval when another cop does (vi).

The only genuine incompetent among Chandler's cops is Lieutenant Nulty, the "lean-jawed sourpuss" in *Farewell, My Lovely.* Nulty is an ineffectual paranoiac, full of self-pity and hungry for credit. His fear is that the case will be taken out of his hands, and he suggests to Marlowe that it would not do the private detective any harm to have a friend in the Department (iii).

The largest category of policemen in Chandler is that of the competent professionals. This group would include Lieutenant Randall in *Farewell, My Lovely,* who knows his business. Randall asks the right questions, and his reponse to Marlowe's habitual wise-cracking is sharp but unruffled. It would also include Lieutenant Breeze in *The High Window,* who is firm but not brutal, who gives Marlowe twelve hours to clear himself of coverup in the murder (xvi) and keeps his promise when Marlowe does so (xxiii). There are two good cops in *The Lady in the Lake,* each of whom undergoes a drastic change of role during the story. Jim Patton, who first appears as a caricature of the dumb rube, turns out at the end to be quick enough to save Marlowe's life. In the same novel, Captain Webber makes his first appearance as something of a hostile brute but proves later to be an honest, capable cop. The list of competent professionals must also include Captain Hernandez in *The Long Goodbye,* another keen officer who knows how to ask the right questions and is fair in dealing with Marlowe, and Captain Alessandro of *Playback,* who is not only capable and honest but also courteous.

There are several hints of police corruption in Chandler, but three of his cops can be definitely identifed as corrupt. Sergeant Galbraith and "Mister" Blane in *Farewell, My Lovely* are tied into the rackets of Bay City, prompting Marlowe to say that the law in that town seems to be pretty rotten (xxviii). The other is Lieutenant Degarmo in *The Lady in the Lake,* who is a murderer.

A number of the police in the Marlowe series are sadists, not just brutal cops but men who inflict pain for trivial reasons or no reasons at all. Lieutenant Moses Maglashan of Bay City lashes Marlowe across the face with a heavy glove in *The Little Sister* in response to one of Marlowe's gibes (xxiv). The most sadistic cop in Chandler is Captain Gregorious in *The Long Goodbye*, who orders a subordinate to put the handcuffs on Marlowe hard enough to make them bite, throws a coffee cup at his head, hits him with his fist, and finally spits in his face (vii). Detective Dayton in the same story hits Marlowe twice. Cooney and Dobbs, a couple of patrolmen in *The Lady in the Lake*, administer a severe beating without reason while placing Marlowe under arrest (xxv).

We should also mention Lieutenant Christie French in *The Little Sister,* who is not so easy to classify. Tough but not sadistic, French tells Maglashan to keep his hands off Marlowe (xxiv), but later in the story he hits Lieutenant Beifus when Beifus tries to keep him from hitting Marlowe (xxix).

heterogeneous in the sense that it is impossible to find common traits among them as in the classic tales of detection. The categories in which we have placed them do not constitute a hard taxonomy, which we have placed them do not constitute a hard taxonomy, because they tend to move from one characterization to another, most notably in *The Lady in the Lake*, where the apparently lazy, stupid Patton turns out to be a fast gun, the hostile Webber proves to be competent, and the apparently competent Degarmo turns out to be a murderer. Even the loathesome Galbraith of *Farewell, My Lovely* becomes friendly toward Marlowe, explaining why it is that cops get caught up in the corruption of the system (xxxiii). "That's the trouble with cops," says Marlowe in *The Long Goodbye.* "You're all set to hate their guts and then you meet one that goes human on you" (vi).

Also, like Hammett, Chandler seems to choose his policemen to fit the tone of the story. This technique is best illustrated in *The Lady in the Lake,* where the shift of character of the three policemen reinforces the theme of appearance versus reality. The same kind of reinforcement is apparent in *The Long Goodbye,* in which Marlowe's repeated beatings at the hands of the police dramatize the theme of his loyalty to his client.

One other observation should be made with regard to Chandler's policemen. *As detectives,* most of them are not inferior to Marlowe. They know their business, and they are by and large as capable as those in any of the procedural series.

The reader accustomed to thinking of fictional policemen in terms of the corruption of Hammett's "Poisonville" or the viciousness of Chandler's Bay City may be surprised by the police in the Lew Archer series of Ross Macdonald. Macdonald's police are neither corrupt nor stupid, says Peter Wolfe, and Archer has a good working relationship with them. They judge wisely, avoid bribes and graft, and neither fake evidence nor beat up witnesses. "A crooked policeman appears no more often in [Macdonald's] work than, say, a crooked doctor or lawyer." The one really notable exception, according to Wolfe, is Sheriff Ostervelt in *The Doomsters.*[7]

This is not to suggest that the police accept Archer in a spirit of fraternal amity. As a rule he must earn their confidence, and he does so by being honest with them, especially in regard to the exchange of information. The pattern is set in the first Archer novel, *The Moving Target,* where a deputy threatens to arrest Archer for resisting an officer (actually, he believes Archer is involved in the crime), holds a gun on him, threatens to slap him. When Archer gives him some information vital to the investigation, the deputy puts away his gun and becomes conciliatory (xix). Later in the story Sheriff Spanner arrests Archer for withholding information and threatens to get his private-investigator license lifted; Archer gives him a lead on a situation the sheriff does not know about, and the arrest is canceled with the assurance that it will be remembered if the lead proves false (xxvi).

Much the same relationship appears in the later stories. Captain Dolan and Sergeant Shantz in *Sleeping Beauty* are perceptive cops who are professional in their dealings with Archer, even when he declines to give them information that might violate the confidence of his client. In *The Blue Hammer* Sheriff Brotherton is sharp with Archer but not hostile, and he cooperates with Archer even though he suspects him of holding back on important information. Captain Mackendrick in the same story gives an impression of superior competence as a policeman, though his slowness to act makes Archer impatient. Archer understands, though, that the policeman must work under rules different from his own; Mackendrick is the power of law in the city, but he is under political constraints to use that power as the city tells him.

The big exception to the pattern of police integrity is Sheriff Ostervelt in *The Doomsters*, whom Wolfe calls "the scurviest person in the [Macdonald] canon."[8] Ostervelt uses his hold over the wife of a suspect in an old murder to force her sexual compliance, promising to keep her husband's confession quiet if she will "be nice to him" (xiv). When Archer calls him a Keystone Kop (a mild characterization, in light of Ostervelt's real nature), the Sheriff strikes him across the face with his gun and would give him a pistol-whipping if he were not restrained by a bystander (xv).

Otherwise, Macdonald's policemen are much more "sympathetic" characters than those in Hammett and Chandler. One explanation lies in the personality of Archer, who is considerably less abrasive in his dealings with the police than are Sam Spade and Philip Marlowe, though not less so than the Continental Op. Archer shares Marlowe's acid tongue and can speak as sharply to the police, but his gibes are usually accompanied by an offer to deal with respect to the fair exchange of information.

The big difference between the policemen in the hard-boiled story of the Hammett-Chandler-Macdonald tradition and those in the classic tale of the Poe-Conan Doyle-Stout tradition is the degree of diversity in terms of quality and integrity. The constants in the case of the police in the classic story are their honesty and their lack of imagination. In the hard-boiled novel the scope is much broader. In terms of police competence, it ranges from the professional capability of Bernie Ohls to the self-abasement of Lieutenant Nulty; in honesty from the probity of Lieutenant Breeze to the corruption of the "Poisonville" police; in social attitudes from the fairness of Lieutenant Guild to the blatant sexual harassment of Sheriff Ostervelt.

As fictional characters, they also play a much wider diversity of roles. Sometimes the role of the policeman is that of a foil, contrasting the ineptitude of the cops in *The Dain Curse* with the decisiveness of the Continental Op, or the stolidity of Lieutenant Guild with the sharpness of Nick Charles. Occasionally the function of the cop is that of obstacle, as when Marlowe's loyalty to his client is impeded by the wanton brutality of Captain Gregorious, or Archer's impatience by the slowness of Captain Mackendrick. On rare occasions the policeman may serve as a confidante to the private investigator, as do Tom Polhaus and Bernie Ohls, and sometimes he even serves the function of aide. In a few instances, as we have seen, the writers use their policemen to reinforce the theme of the story, as in the cases of the ambiguity of Chandler's *The Lady in the Lake,* corruption in Hammett's *Red Harvest,* and moral relativism in *The Maltese Falcon.*

As the official representatives of order in the community, the policemen have power (clout) that gives them an advantage over the private investigator. They can arrest him, get his license revoked, and make deals with him or not, much at their own discretion. Of course this is also true of the police in the classic story, but the transcendent super-sleuth typically puts himself beyond their reach with his formidable powers of ratiocination, which leave them open-mouthed. Moreover, the private investigator of fiction works according to his individual sense of justice, which is frequently at variance with the socially accepted code; the classic sleuth shares with the police the community's assumptions regarding order and justice.

The real difference between the policemen in the stories of the Poe-Conan Doyle-Stout tradition and those of the Hammett-Chandler-Macdonald tradition is to be found in the difference between two sets of assumptions regarding the nature of society. "In the devastated society of the hard-boiled novel," says George Grella, "crime is not a temporary aberration, but a ubiquitous fact."[9] If this interpretation is acceptable, the Innocence-Restored myth of the classic tale does not apply to the hard-boiled landscape. Here the police need not be simply competent and thoroughly honest, as in the classic tale, because the cleansed community is not handed back to them by the private investigator at the end of the story. The police are part of the "devastated society" where crime is a "ubiquitous fact." Sheriff Brotherton puts the point simply when he goes with

Lew Archer in search of the missing young woman: "I've got a daughter of my own."[10] The purging is never complete, but must be done over and over, as Lieutenant Christie French explains to Philip Marlowe: just as the police think they have things under control, the phone rings and they have to get up and start all over.[11] In this respect, as we will see a little further along, the police procedural is closer to the tone of the hard-boiled tradition than to that of the classic formal-problem.

"The private detective," says George Grella, "always finds the police incompetent, brutal, or corrupt, and therefore works alone."[12] What he really finds is that the police are diverse, varying, hard to categorize (cf. Marlowe, "the trouble with cops"), much like the rest of society. It might be argued, indeed, that *most* of the people in Hammett, Chandler and Macdonald are confused, maybe lost, often suffering, but not inherently evil. As far as the police and their society are concerned, "Poisonville" is not the world.

Does the change in the nature of fictional policemen from the classic tale (unimaginative but honest) to the hard-boiled (sometimes brutal, sometimes corrupt, sometimes incompetent) reflect a change in the public perception of the police in real life? The answer must be no, for several reasons.

In the first place, the classic school and the hard-boiled do not represent chronologically successive periods; although the private-eye story emerged much later than the formal-problem story, the latter is still going strong. After all, Chandler's sadistic Lieutenant Maglashan and Captain Gregorious are contemporaries of Lieutenant Tragg of the Perry Mason stories, not his successors. Rather, the change represents a difference in literary tradition instead of an altered perception of real-life police. The image of the unimaginative-honest cop serves to reinforce the image of the transcendent classic super-sleuth, whereas the sometimes incompetent or brutal or corrupt policeman serves as a foil to the private investigator, "who is not himself mean, who is neither tarnished nor afraid."[13] Finally, the myth of Innocence Restored demands cops who can handle nine out of ten cases, to whom the purged community can be re-committed. The Desolated Society, on the other hand, includes all kinds of cops who will never complete the cleanup because they share the communal guilt.

As we move into an examination of the policemen in the

procedural stories, one thing we will notice is that they are not radically different from the cops of the older traditions of detective fiction, with the exception of the giants of the Great Policeman school, whose powers of detection they can seldom match. In other words, the procedural writers did not invent a newer set of personalities for their detective-protagonists. The detectives in the police procedurals are, rather, the literary descendants of the policemen in both the classic and hard-boiled stories: they have a practical competence that does not usually rise to the level of abstract theory; their social-cultural backgrounds are limited; most of all, they are a highly diversified group of characters who refuse to conform to almost any stereotype.

The difference lies rather in the assignment of roles. What the procedural writer has done is to pull all those Heaths, Velies, Guilds and Randalls out of their subordinate functions and make them responsible for solving the mysteries. This is a plausible shift in emphasis because, in our society, criminals are apprehended not by gifted geniuses from outside who step into the scene just long enough to work out the puzzle, but rather by the people to whom the community has assigned the job of enforcing its laws. The procedural writer performs an act, not of transformation but of displacement, whereby the police detective, not really superior to most of us, becomes a personification of the community's need for security.

Chapter 4

The Special Case

THEY ARE CALLED "police procedurals" or sometimes just "procedurals," or occasionally "police-routine" stories. These are prosaic names in comparison with the dignity of "classic" as applied to the tales of the Poe-Conan Doyle tradition, or the evocative ring of "hard-boiled" for those of the Hammett-Chandler school. Although "police procedural" is a somewhat drab designation, it does have the advantage of description, because that is what these stories are: accounts of detective work carried on by policemen using the procedures or routines normally available to policemen. John Dickson Carr objected to "the glib term, 'police procedural'," as suggesting a story in which the "investigation moves in a machinelike way, with lever or cogwheel predominant."[1] Meanwhile, though, the label has stuck, and it does at least serve to distinguish this type of detective story from the others.

It will be the purpose of this chapter to describe and qualify the kind of novel we are discussing in this book, not to undertake an authoritative definition of the procedural story. Definition suggests label, and it is always hazardous to attach a label to any story, because we may pigeonhole it in such fashion as to ignore the purpose the writer had in mind. The arts, moreover, do not need the tight taxonomies of science, and any attempt to categorize a certain kind of fiction by setting up criteria whereby *this* class includes only *these* stories and excludes all others, would be not only futile but also self-defeating.

At the same time, we need some kind of broad agreement with regard to the kind of fiction we are discussing, and in this case we can insist upon two absolutes: First, to be called a police procedural, a novel must be a mystery story; and second, it must be one in which the mystery is solved by policemen using normal police routines.

The procedural tale belongs in the mystery-detection tradition, along with the classic formal-problem story and the hard-boiled private-eye story. There are certain stories—not mysteries—written about policemen and even using police procedures as an element of narrative interest, but we will not deal with them in this discussion because they are outside the mystery genre. This will exclude from our consideration the police novels of Joseph Wambaugh, and also a novel like Dorothy Uhnak's *Law and Order*. In these books the policemen are uniformed, not detectives, and hence the stories lack the element of mystery and detection.

Not only does the story contain a mystery, but the mystery is solved by policemen. This condition will also eliminate novels in which much—or most—of the narrative interest is centered on the detective activities of civilians, including committed amateurs and private investigators, with the result that, even though the cops do make the final arrest, most of the solution has been achieved by non-policemen. Thomas Chastain's *Pandora's Box* has been called a police procedural,[2] and it is indeed a mystery story with a policeman in an important role, and one in which some police routines are used. The novel has three narrative elements: 1) the involvement of Private Investigator J.T. Spanner, who instigates police action and is in on the resolution; 2) an elaborately planned and executed caper, which is the real center of suspense; and 3) the activities of Chief Inspector Max Kauffman, NYPD, who almost exclusively represents the police involvement. Although *Pandora's Box* contains elements of the procedural (including such conventions as the hostile public and the overworked police), two things would exclude it from our consideration: the involvement of Spanner in the investigation and solution, and the weight of suspense borne by elements other than the participation of the police.

The essential qualities of the procedural tale can be represented in terms of certain elements of plot-development and of the nature of the detection used in these stories.

With regard to the development of plot, the most obvious element of the procedural is a corollary of the second "absolute" outlined above, that the mystery must be solved by the police. In terms of narrative, this condition implies that police work, rather than the predicaments and involvements of outsiders, is the center of interest in the story. In the Norah Mulcahaney stories of Lillian O'Donnell, the eye of the reader is almost exclusively on Norah and her fellow policemen as they investigate and solve a crime. By way of contrast, one of O'Donnell's pre-Mulcahaney mysteries, *Death Blanks the Screen*, keeps the thrust of the story with the television-motion picture group, who are victims and suspects; the police play almost no part until the end of the story, when an inspector gives a long, expansive explanation of the solution.

The second element of plot-development that characterizes the police procedural is the use of police routines as the method of resolution, in contrast to the ratiocination of the classic story and the pursuit and infiltration of the private-eye story. One of the favorite devices of the older tradition of detection is the application of the three-fold criterion of Motive, Means, and Opportunity, around which a writer can build a frame-work of clever analysis and suspense, to the almost inexhaustible delight of the puzzle-fan. Such cerebral sports are essentially denied to the policeman, however, as Steve Carella of the 87th Precinct knows: Motive, Means, and Opportunity become meaningless catchwords when a corpse is staring up at a policeman.[3] At the same time, the policeman is usually denied the frantic variety of the private investigator of fiction, who seems to move through a story in a succession of mounting excitements, whereas police work is ninety per cent repetition, going over and over the same ground. The writer of police procedurals, though, finds compensation in a reasonably good bag of devices that are valid police routine and at the same time interesting and suspenseful. One of these is the practice of role-playing during an investigation, the assumption of "good guy" and "bad guy" functions for the purpose of harassing a suspect and at the same time tricking him into a confidential relationship. Such devices are legitimate to the "realistic" procedural, and they are suspenseful means to the solution of the mystery.

The nature of plot-development that also characterizes the police procedural is the use of multiple protagonists, the police team, instead of the single superior detective. In most of the procedural series, attention does admittedly tend to focus on an individual, like Martin Beck in the Sjowall-Wahloo series or Christie Opara in Uhnak's series, but the work of detection is being carried on by a group of policemen working as a team, and the resolution of the problem is seldom the result of the work of one outstanding individual. Of all procedural writers Ed McBain has been the most successful in building his plots around the efforts of an entire detective squad: Steve Carella figures more prominently than the others (for reasons explained in Chapter 2), but it is a rare 87th Precinct story in which Carella is not working closely and constantly with one of the others.

This would seem to be a good point at which to amplify the distinction between the police procedural and the Great Policeman story discussed briefly in Chapter 3, because the essential difference lies in the fact that the Great Policeman solves the mystery on his own, whereas the procedural policeman shares the honors with his fellow cops.

The contrast is apparent in two novels by Michael Gilbert: *Close Quarters,* the first Inspector Hazlerigg story, an example of the Great Policeman school, and *Blood and Judgment,* the first Petrella story, a police procedural. Hazlerigg is credited with a first-rate brain, and he is the finest chief inspector at Scotland Yard, gifted with the power of selective concentration. Petrella is young, hard-working, possessed of a sense of justice, and planning to leave the service as soon as the current case is finished. Hazlerigg's range of methods is limited: one technical, one practical. Petrella employs a half-dozen approaches, technical and practical, including the use of informants. Approaching the resolution in *Close Quarters*, Hazlerigg sits up alone late at night working out the problem with an approach that is individualistic and almost abstract. Petrella in *Blood and Judgment* also stays up for a late conference with the director of prosecutions and the detective chief superintendent, reviewing the case. At the point of arrest, Hazlerigg and one of his aides hide and nab the suspect when he falls for Hazlerigg's staged ruse. Petrella and the chief constable, at the same point, follow the suspect but ignominiously hit the dirt when he reaches into his pocket. (He pulls out his pipe.) The explanation at the end of *Close Quarters* is typical of the classic school, long and complicated, directed by Hazlerigg with some minor assists by others. At the end of *Blood and Judgment* Petrella makes a brief explanation to the assistant commissioner; nothing further is needed, because solution and explanation have already developed through the action of the story. As far as narrative thrust is concerned, *Close Quarters* is Hazlerigg's show. While Petrella is the main character in *Blood and Judgment* (largely because his sense of justice can not abide a false conviction), he shares investigation and solution with his fellow policemen. Both men are policemen, but they are heirs of different literary legacies: Hazlerigg with his superior mental powers belongs in the Sherlock Holmes tradition, while Petrella, with his energy and his mistakes, would be much more at home with Harry Martineau or one of the other procedural cops.

Before undertaking a characterization of the police procedural in terms of the nature of detection, it will be necessary to define the Game, which sets the limits on the methods that are allowed to police detectives. All detective fiction has some game-elements, but in the procedural story the rules are different. The basic rule is: The solution, no matter how logically or aesthetically satisfying, is of no value unless it will lead to the conviction of the guilty party. "Court positive" is the term fictional policemen use to describe a case that will stand up before a jury, every step of the way, under cross-examination, free of the single flaw that could wipe out all their gains. The slow-witted Lestrade would win the applause of all procedural policemen when he says to Holmes in "The Boscombe Valley Mystery," "Theories are all very well, but we still have to deal with a hard-headed British jury." There can be no lapses, no leaps of intuition, no unsupported assumptions. The chain of evidence must be complete and firm from the time the crime is discovered until the actual trial begins. The rules of the Game, moreover, deny to the policeman that device so well loved by the eccentric super-sleuth of the classic tale, entrapment, and the one so often used by the private investigator, enticement.

We need next to turn our attention to the nature of the detective work carried on in the police procedural, taking special note of those elements that distinguish the procedural story from the other kinds of detective fiction. Here we will be concerned not with narrative techniques but with actual content, in terms of the way policemen carry on the business of detection.

Certainly a basic difference between the police detective and the private investigator or the consulting detective is the fact of the policeman's clout. The overt manifestation is, of course, the authority inherent in his position as official representative of the community, which allows him to make arrests, to invade premises denied to the civilian detective, and even to have access to information that would otherwise be considered confidential. Often it is not even necessary to exercise his clout, because the fact of his authority creates a vulnerability among criminal classes, especially ex-convicts who know he can put them back in prison if they refuse to cooperate. The vulnerability also extends to law-abiding citizens, who have a natural fear of policemen and to whom the phrase "routine investigation" is a source of uneasiness. Sometimes all the policeman needs is to suggest that he might undertake to make bad matters worse for a reluctant witness: the threat to obtain a warrant is usually effective, especially when accompanied by the hint that the extra work will make the policeman more irritable than he is now. Bartenders are particularly vulnerable to the mere suggestion of placing a couple of uniformed patrolmen outside the bar, and building superintendents to the threat of reports of all kinds of code violations, real or imagined. If these devices do not produce results, there is always the possibility of the frame, not too difficult for the police, especially if the subject has a record. Then there is the ultimate clout available in the case of a suspect whose guilt can not be proved: kill him in such a way as to make it look like just another hoodlum operation.

Later we will have more to say about informants as adjuncts of the police sub-culture, but we must at least mention them here as important components of the special nature of detection in the police procedural. Of course there are a great many people in the other mystery traditions who are willing to give (or sell) information to the consulting detective or private investigator, but the informant ("stool pigeon," as he is sometimes called, or "nark" in Britain) has a special role in the procedural. First, he is indispensable: his availability is the backbone of any successful police department. Without informants, a detective is as good as dead; with a few, he looks like a genius. Moreover, he is not too hard to recruit by a cop who knows his business. His inside information is usually available for reasonable pay, especially if the policeman is in a position to slap him with a felony rap if he proves unco-operative.

The policeman's efforts at crime-prevention represent another break with the other traditions of detective fiction. Prevention, in the opinion of George Gideon, is ranked with detection as a constituent of the policeman's task.[4] The big difference between the procedural and the other traditions is that it is not just the policeman's job to solve the mystery; he should try to keep it from developing in the first place.

As for detection itself, the policeman has a signifcant advantage over other fictional detectives in the accessibility of information and the availability of fairly sophisticated technology. The policeman is not entirely dependent on the observations and memories of taxi-drivers and railway attendants (whose prodigious capacities are parodied by Robert J. Casey in his delightful satire on some of the excesses of the classic tale[5]), because he has access to mountains of information, always filed and now usually computerized. Neither does he need to be a chemist like Holmes or a biologist like Thorndike in order to analyze evidence. The police lab does that for him.

Finally, we should take note of the existence of the unsolved case in the procedural, probably the ultimate break with mystery tradition. As we will see in Chapter 8, major unsolved cases are not permitted in the stories themselves, but the references to the large numbers of them keep the reader reminded that in police work most mysteries are *never* solved.

It is the nature of the detective work that really characterizes the police procedural, not the atmosphere of the story or the form of the crime. Procedurals have acquired a reputation for dealing only with grubby crimes committed by commonplace criminals under prosaic circumstances, but it is not this quality that makes them police procedurals. It is rather the way the policeman handles the case, his use of automatic authority, his access to police information and to his informants. We can illustrate the difference by reference to one story that has many of the classic earmarks of the older tradition but belongs in the procedural category because of the nature of the detection that leads to the solution of the mystery.

John Ball's *Five Pieces of Jade*, one of the Virgil Tibbs stories, has strong overtones of the Golden Age mystery. The problem is bizarre and exotic in respect to the method of the murder, the Oriental mystique of the situation, and the atmosphere of opulence that surrounds the setting. The list of suspects is limited, and clues are even concealed from the reader in the spirit of an Agatha Christie novel. Tibbs himself, moreover, performs at least one feat of ratiocination of which Sherlock Holmes would not be ashamed (ii). We can call *Five Pieces of Jade* a police procedural, however, because of the way Tibbs operates. In the actual work of detection, it is his policeman's clout that makes the difference in the solution.

Tibbs has a policeman's authority and he uses it, once to gain access to information that would not otherwise be available (ix), once to extract a favor in the interests of the administration of justice (xiii), and finally to arrest a suspect for a relatively minor infraction in order to hold him for a more serious charge (xv).

In terms of general tone and intention, as well as narrative technique, we have an unusually good opportunity to compare the police procedural with the private-investigator story in the novel *Twospot*, co-authored by Bill Pronzini and Collin Wilcox. In *Twospot* the investigation is shared by Pronzini's nameless private detective (who is only called "Bill" in the book) and Wilcox's Lieutenant Frank Hastings of the San Francisco Police Department. The divergencies between the approaches of the two become apparent early in the story: Bill accepts a job as bodyguard because he needs the money; Hastings gets involved because he is on call at headquarters. Bill is not allowed to work on a homicide case; Hastings not only can but must. Bill, having discovered the complicity of one person in the murder plot, realizes that he has no power over the man except to report him to the police; his own obligation, meanwhile, is to protect his client (xvii). Hastings, on the other hand, uses his clout to make a deal with a criminal he has caught, in order to get information the police need (xi).

The most pointed contrast comes at the end of the story, when Hastings is thinking about the differences between himself and Bill. If the private investigator gets into trouble and is attacked by a criminal, there will be no partner to help him or fleet of squad cars to rush to his aid and hunt down his attacker, nor will he get hazard pay or sick leave. If he is killed on the job, there will be no full-dress funeral, no volley fired or taps played over his grave, as there will be for the policeman. The private eye is a loner, with his individualistic sense of loyalty, while the policeman is both servant and guardian of the public. At the conclusion the two men part, Bill to go home and catch up on his sleep, Hastings to get back to the squad room and answer the questions of the reporters who are waiting for him.

We have described the police procedural as a mystery story in which police work is the center of the reader's interest, in which police procedures are employed as the method of resolution, and in which police teams, rather than a single superior protagonist, solve the mystery. We have also described the procedural as a story in which the nature of the detection is limited to plausible police methodology, like the use of the policeman's clout, heavy reliance on informants, and dependence on police information and technology. Having done all this, we must at once remind ourselves that we have been speaking in terms of general qualities, not tight criteria, and that actually relatively few stories have *all* these qualities in undiluted form. If we look for examples of "pure" procedurals, we can place Waugh's *Last Seen Wearing*--- on the list, along with Jobson's *The Evidence You Will Hear*, Procter's *I Will Speak Daggers* and Orum's *The Whipping Boy*. Some series hew fairly close to the line, including Bill Knox's Thane-Moss stories and most of Ed McBain's 87th Precinct series, with the exception of those novels in which the Deaf Man steals the show from the police.

We should certainly not exclude those stories in which the police interest is divided between the policeman as detective and the policeman as a private person and member of a family, because the writers of these stories usually seek to give depth to their protagonists by portraying them as human beings who do not cease to live when not about the business of detection. Thus in the Sjowall-Wahloo series we get a strong sense of the effects on Martin Beck of a ruined marriage, and in the Freeling series the effect on Piet Van der Valk of a happy one. Burns' Gabriel Wager and Ball's Virgil Tibbs have to contend with the problems of being non-white, Uhnak's Christie Opara and O'Donnell's Norah Mulcahaney with the disadvantages of being women. The spotlight, though, is still on the police and is not shared with gifted amateurs, private investigators or criminals.

Chapter 5

Procedures in the Procedurals

JUST TO MAKE UP a list of the methods, procedures, routines used by the police in the novels discussed in this book, with a one-paragraph description of each, would require a volume of encyclopedic dimensions. The frequency is not surprising, because these are after all *procedural* stories in which police methods substantially replace the detective styles used in other kinds of mysteries.

One problem that every writer of police procedurals must face is the necessity for making cop-work, the ordinary routines of tailings, stakeouts, lab analysis, and the like, so enthralling and suspenseful that the reader will follow the action with the same degree of interest generated by the legal acrobatics of Perry Mason or the hard-fisted penetration of Mike Hammer. Most of the writers we are discussing have shown a real talent for keeping their readers' attention by a skillful handling of police techniques that are at once plausible and fascinating.

Some of the accounts in the procedural stories are detailed to the degree that they substantially supply a layman's knowledge of the subject. One of the most memorable is the description of the work of the police artist in Ed McBain's *Lady Killer*, with drawings supplied in the text, to show how the artist works up a usable identification picture of a perpetrator from the accounts of witnesses (x, xvi). Then there is the fourteen-page report in John Ball's *Johnny Get Your Gun* of how the police handle an angry crowd in such a way as to prevent a riot: this account, by the way, proposes some do's and don't's for policemen, some drawn from the field of social psychology, some from the hard experience of the Watts riots (xi). We might also mention the use of the Gas Chromatograph in Bill Knox's *Pilot Error*, a device for checking alcohol content in the blood, which gets a three-page description (i). In none of these instances does the writer interrupt the story to deliver a lecture: each is developed as the narrative progresses and becomes part of the suspense.

In the interests of brevity we will list the topics under which the police methods may be grouped, merely to suggest the scope and variety of procedures employed in the novels:

COMMUNICATION

The most ordinary kind of communication is the intra- or inter-departmental flyer, used to alert all precincts to be on the lookout for a wanted criminal or to locate a missing person or stolen property. More sophisticated technology is represented in the Muirhead Transmitter, on which a picture of a thumb-print can be circulated, or by two nation-wide systems for circulation of information, the Law Enforcement Teletype System and the National Crime Information Center. The most exciting kind of communication used by the police, however, is the network set up for spotting and tracing persons or automobiles, especially when the reader is allowed to stand by at the command center.

CRIME-PREVENTION

We have mentioned this police activity in Chapter 4 as one of the major breaks in the procedural with the older traditions of detection, the principle being that it is more efficient to prevent crime than to apprehend criminals. Consequently, some departments carry on a program of crime-prevention-education, a good example being Meyer Meyer's lecture to the students of Amberson College in *Hail to the Chief* on how to deal with a rapist (vi). More often, though, the police use the news media to inform the public regarding a specific danger, as Scotland Yard does in *Gideon's Power* when a child-kidnapper is menacing the neighborhood (vi).

EVIDENCE

The collection of evidence represents another one of those ambivalences in police work, the professional spirit versus the need to get a job done as quickly and effectively as possible. On the one hand is the demand for evidence that is not only collected by legal means but will stand up in court, like the photographs of a crime scene with a detective or medical examinar in each picture in order to establish the identity of witnesses at the location. On the other hand is the practice of bugging—almost always acknowledged by the police to be illegal even when they are setting it up—to get leads that will be used in the investigation but can not be presented to a jury.

FILES AND INFORMATION

This is an area in which the policeman has a significant advantage over other fictional detectives. Everything that happens must be recorded and filed, the resulting documentation ranging from the Occurrences Book carried by every British policeman to the formidable cross-file on a case, containing every scrap of information, all indexed and cross-referenced. The number and variety of files maintained by even a fair-size department is overwhelming: the Lousy File (known criminals), the Known Muggers File, files of known sex-offenders, files on street gangs, and scores of others, including the discouraging Open File of unsolved cases. If the information is not available in the department, the chances are that it can be found at the Missing Persons Bureau, the Department of Motor Vehicles, the Ballistics Bureau, or one of those national or international respositories like the FBI, the Scottish Criminal Records Office, Scotland Yard, or Interpol. During recent years computerized information has begun to show up in the stories, with mixed results. Roger West is pleased by the new system at Scotland Yard that will permit him to press a button for a dossier on a suspect and have it in his hands seven and one-half minutes later.[1] In Holland, the computer does actually "remember" the alias of a criminal, but by the time the information comes back the police have already gotten it from an informant.[2]

FORENSIC MEDICINE

The policemen in the series by Bill Knox have an advantage in this field, in the person of Andrew MacMaster of Glasgow University, who serves as consultant to the department. MacMaster's abilities are not limited to human beings; in one of the stories he makes a discovery in the field of veterinary medicine that vitally affects the solution of the mystery.[3] In almost every series the police are heavily dependent on autopsy reports (already well known to readers of all kinds of detective fiction) and analyses of blood and bone fragments on murder weapons, but a figure gaining increased prominence in the procedural story is the police psychiatrist, who can deliver a creditable psychological profile of an unknown criminal from an analysis of the nature of his crimes.

IDENTIFYING CRIMINALS

The police are divided in their estimate of the value of that time-honored method of identification of a perpetrator by witnesses, the lineup. Legally it is supposed to be reliable, especially in a "fair lineup" in which the subjects are of approximately the same height, coloring, and build, and wear the same kind of clothes. Theoretically it works, but there is at least one occasion in which a witness identifies a detective who has been pressed into service to fill out the lineup,[4] and another in which witnesses refuse to make any identification at all.[5] The police also have mixed feelings about the reliability of the Identikit, the device used by the police artist to make a drawing of a perpetrator with the guidance of witnesses. In *Leisure Dying*, Norah Mulcahaney marvels at the ability of the artist to create a really good likeness, and she considers the Identikit an important police tool (vi). Martin Beck, on the other hand, wonders in *The Man on the Balcony* if it has any value in the search for the man they want (xxii).

INFORMANTS

We are not concerned here with the occasional "snitch" who for revenge or some other motive gives the police information that will lead to the apprehension of a criminal, but with the regular pro, usually himself a criminal or a person with criminal involvements, who sells information to the cops. Customarily he works for only one policeman, who considers the informant his private property and will give him a degree of latitude in his own operations but will not protect him if he gets into trouble with another policeman. He is paid from the departmental discretionary fund, but the pay is not large because his usual primary motivation is to keep himself out of jail. He is customarily "recruited" as a result of having committed some infraction the policeman is willing to forget if he cooperates; if he is a three-time loser and hence liable to life imprisonment, his continued participation as informant is assured.

His value in law enforcement is considerable, as witnessed by the number of stories in which the mystery could not be solved without his assistance. In one of Michael Gilbert's stories we are told that the second largest number of people caught are those given away by informants (the largest number being those who are apprehended trying to dispose of stolen property).[6]

INTERROGATION-INTERVIEW

One of the policeman's most difficult problems is that of getting a suspect to talk, and the police in the procedural stories have developed an impressive number of techniques, most of them involving one form or another of intimidation. There are two basic approaches: one is to keep asking questions over and over, covering the same ground in different contexts, without giving the suspect time to recover, in the hope of provoking contradictions; the other is to give the impression that the interrogator already knows all the answers and that the suspect is trapped. Policemen usually work in teams during interrogation (as they do in almost everything else), and one of their most effective devices is that of role-playing, in which one of them takes the part of the bad-guy mean cop, while the other becomes the good-guy sympathetic questioner. The bad-guy cop goes after the suspect like a tiger, while the sympathetic one cautions restraint and asks questions designed to induce a sense of security. Later, of course, the good guy visits the suspect in his cell and opens up a flow of confidences. The technique is more effective with the young first offender than with the hardened hood, who is onto it. The old third-degree methods of hard fist and rubber hose have substantially disappeared from the stories, though it still may be helpful to have a tough patrolman wearing heavy leather gloves standing silent in the interrogation room. For interviewing subjects who are not themselves suspects but who may be reluctant to tell the truth, the police have also developed several intimidating approaches. One is to drop in on the subject unannounced, without giving him an opportunity to prepare himself. Another is to visit him at home where, in theory at least, he has his guard down and finds it hard to lie. For approaching possible witnesses who may or may not know anything and who probably have no cause to lie, the most productive technique is simple courtesy, and it is to the credit of policemen in the procedural stories that this is the approach they customarily use.

INVESTIGATION

In the case of a homicide, which most of these novels involve, investigation begins at the murder scene. The police no longer chalk or tape the outline of the body, to the disappointment of newspaper photographers who used to get their most dramatic pictures from that practice. Instead, they take polaroid shots, which are faster and also supply the necessary supporting detail. As the investigation proceeds and the quantity of accumulated data mounts, it becomes increasingly necessary to keep everybody on the case involved in the business of assimilation and interpretation: the methods most frequently used are the processes of brainstorming (free association of facts and ideas) and snowballing (accumulation of possibilities). Above all, throughout the investigation, is the necessity for detailed documentation, the accumulation of a file into which every scrap of evidence must go, whether it seems relevant or not.

LABORATORY AND OTHER TECHNOLOGIES

The use of the police lab is not unique to the police procedural. Readers of other kinds of mysteries have waited through many pages for reports on bloodstains, fingerprints, and footprints, but the laboratory and the other technologies available to policemen play a much more important part in the procedural. Part of this increased role is the result of improved methods for identifying perpetrators. The police are no longer completely dependent on fingerprints and blood-types; technologies have been developed for classification and identification of hairs from the head and body, semen, and even dandruff, which can be typed like blood. Neither are the collection and analysis of clues dependent upon the encyclopedic knowledge and deductive powers of the super-genius who could recognize the origin of dust on the hem of a skirt or the inkstain peeping through the rip in a glove. He has been superseded by the expert lab man, the best of whom is Captain Sam Grossman in the Ed McBain series. In a small wad of "glopis" (Grossman's term) that had been stuck to a shoe, he is able to separate and identify ten different substances picked up in places where the subject had walked.[7] Outside the lab, detection is no longer at the mercy of the vagaries of nature: snowed-over footprints are recovered by first using a blower to scatter the surface snow, then a red aerosol spray to bring out the best contrast on photographs. Then there are the awesome files maintained by large departments that can be used in the identification of laundry-marks, tire treads, gift boxes and typescripts.

NEWS MEDIA

As in so many other respects, fictional policemen have divided opinions regarding the usefulness of newspapers, radio and television. On the one hand the news media can hinder investigations by getting in the way at a crime scene or ruining a good lead by premature publication of the story. At the same time they can provide valuable assistance, by bringing in witnesses, helping to locate kidnapped children, or instilling a false sense of security in a wanted criminal. On several occasions the police even borrow the device used by Dupin in "The Murders in the Rue Morgue" and release a false story to force a culprit's hand.

SECURITY AND CONFIDENTIALITY

The police are a paramilitary organization, and their security measures are as tight as those of most military units. The general rule is, Don't discuss anything with anybody outside the squad; the greater number of people who know anything, the greater the chance of a leak. Policemen protect their sources, and confidential information is not discussed outside the department. Apparently, however, the one communication system against which security has no defense is the "bush telegraph," the highly efficient grapevine maintained by policemen's wives.

STAKEOUTS

The familiar panel truck with the name of an innocent civilian business painted on the side, filled with photographers and parked at the end of the block, is disappearing from the stories along with several other police methods that the criminal world has caught onto. There seems, however, to be no method of surveillance to replace the effectiveness of a plainsclothesman sitting for long hours in an unmarked squad car or crawling around in the shadows, especially if he has a walkie-talkie to help co-ordinate his efforts with others on the same stakeout.

TAILING
    Neither has any instrumentation been developed for replacing the policeman following a subject on foot, or even making his job easier, but the police have devised several techniques for guarding against being spotted by the suspect or losing him as a result of unpredictable circumstances. The cops in Procter's Granchester, for example, have been known to use a team of four, dressed according to various social levels, so that one of them can follow the subject into whatever place he enters without being conspicuous.[8] This is a variation of the rotating or "leapfrog" tail, which eliminates the danger of always keeping the same person close to the subject. Another variation is employed by the Swedish "Sepo": the subject discovers himself being tailed by a clumsy "amateur" (i.e., a cop in that role), shakes him and is lulled into a sense of false security, whereupon the real job is taken over by another policeman.[9] Following a suspect in a vehicle without being spotted can be accomplished by a "rolling tail," in which several cars, linked by radio, alternately follow and turn aside.

TRAINING
    We do not get much information on the pre-service training of the police, because most of the detectives in the stories are long out of the Academy and have little to say about it except that a number of life-long friendships started there. The training must be exacting, however, if we judge it only by the "Window Washer Bit," a tricky situation used to test powers of observation and memory.[10] A reader wanting a detailed account of on-the-job training will find it in Ball's *Police Chief*, in which Jack Tallon plans and executes a program for shaping up a seedy small-town department.

VEHICLES
    Automobiles used by suspects are vulnerable to a number of investigative techniques, some involving plain common sense, some using advanced technology. Fred Fellows, for example, locates a hideout by reading the mileage on a new automobile.[11] The Scottish police, on the other hand, make it possible to follow a suspect by concealing a homer device (battery life twenty hours, range up to two miles) in his car.[12] As far as police vehicles are concerned, the main problem is to conceal their identity. The

familiar black-and-white with flashing colored lights is satisfactory for uniformed patrolmen but much less than useful for detectives. Consequently, Scotland Yard maintains several taxis equipped with police radios.[13] The Scottish Crime Squad does not wash its vehicles: clean automobiles attract attention.[14]

WITNESSES

Unfortunately for the police, people who see crimes committed or get a good close look at perpetrators are not always much help at supplying reliable data. Policemen are trained to report what they saw, but civilians are more likely to remember what they *think* they saw. Consequently, most departments employ various aids to memory, the most common being the "mug file," a collection of pictures of known offenders. Scotland Yard, which seems to have developed maturity in dealing with the unreliabilty of the public, also maintains a file of every type of key to assist in the recognition of a key once seen but not now available.

In addition to these specifics, there are a number of maxims that show up in various contexts and comprise a set of General Principles that might constitute the basis of a manual for the rookie detective:

1. Routine breaks cases. Police work is ninety percent repetition, a matter of following from one thing to the next.
2. Leave nothing to chance, no stone unturned. Never neglect the obvious. Touch all bases. Check out every tip.
3. Don't try to fit facts to theories.
4. Never let personal feelings affect judgment.
5. A policeman can never have too much information at his fingertips.
6. It is better to know something ahead of time than to have it pointed out later.
7. Look for the lowest possible motivation; it is probably right.
8. Hunch—instinct, the ability to judge intangibles—is part of a good detective's equipment.
9. Pit suspects against one another; encourage them to talk about each other.
10. If the perpetrator in this case is not caught, you will probably nab him in a later case of the same type.

11. When facing danger, take the initiative and exert authority. Never surrender the advantage of cover.

12. Draw your revolver only to shoot, then shoot to kill.

The policemen in the procedural stories employ two broad types of procedures, both based on experience. The experience of science, especially applied science, has given them such sophisticated tools as the voice-print for identification of anonymous callers, the spectrometer for analysis of a flake of paint, the polygraph for lie-detection, and the computer for instant recovery of needed information. The other kind of experience is the one that has been accumulated and passed on by successive generations of policemen and is often re-learned the hard way by the detective on duty, which is common, applied "cop sense." Procter's policemen know how to eavesdrop on a conversation in a crowded pub without attracting notice: they sit at a nearby table, one detective playing patience while another watches, the card game giving them an excuse for silence and concentration.[15] Steve Carella of the 87th Precinct has a practical method for determing whether a suspect spoke with a dialect, when all the elevator man heard from him was the number of the floor: Carella pronounces the word "nine" five different ways and gets the elevator man to identify the one closest to the suspect's pronunciation.[16] Colin Thane of the Millside CID knows that one of the best and most reliable sources of information is the patrolman on the beat, who builds up a supply of contacts over the years and is in the best possible position to collect favors and exact revenge.[17] Although the better detectives can draw upon either kind of experience according to circumstances, the stories also represent a contest between technology and common sense, which is reflected in the attitudes of the new-style science-oriented detective and the old-style canny type.

The best opportunity for comparison of the two attitudes toward police work is presented in the first procedural series, Lawrence Treat's stories featuring Mitch Taylor, who is the traditional slogging precinct cop, and Jub Freeman, who is the laboratory-oriented police scientist. When they first find themselves working on the same case in *V as in Victim*, they warily size each other up, not sure whether the different points of view they represent can be harmonized. Mitch Taylor is a stoic who knows how to be aggressive, and he has become adept at passing the buck and avoiding unnecessary work. Jub Freeman, who got tired of pounding a beat as a patrolman, applied for and received an appointment to the police laboratory, where he taught himself the methods of research and inquiry.

Mitch goes after the first suspect in the story with shrewd, patient questioning, hinting at favors to be granted for co-operation but also using the methods of provocation and intimidation. Jub has come into possession of what he considers an important piece of evidence (a flake of paint from the hit-and-run automobile), and he wants the case to be solved in the lab. He is outraged when the first suspect is arrested (as the result of Mitch's work), because her arrest contradicts the evidence of the spectroscope (I, v). Mitch reads but does not understand half the medical examiner's report (II, i), a fact that disturbs him not at all. He does, however, admit a grudging respect for science and concedes that most policemen do not use the lab half enough (I, iv). The mystery is resolved, partly as a result of Mitch's patient searching, but chiefly because of Jub's brilliant technology.

Mitch Taylor substantially disappears from the series for a period of time (largely as a result of having disgraced himself in the New York Police Department), and the scene shifts to an unnamed city where Jub Freeman serves as civilian consultant to the local police.

Mitch re-enters the story in *Big Shot*, where he continues to develop his technique for doing as little as possible, for holding a steady job and staying out of trouble. Things do go right for him, but as a result of luck rather than expertise in police science. Jub, in the same novel, saves Mitch from another disgrace by use of the comparison microscope to establish the identity of a bullet (xiv).

The contrast between Mitch and Jub is primarily between two attitudes toward police work and only coincidentally between two sets of personal qualities. It is true that Mitch likes to call it a day at five o'clock, whereas Jub will voluntarily stay up all night working out a problem in the lab, but Mitch can be energetic and aggressive when the occasion demands. The big difference between them lies in their attitudes toward the empirical foundations of police investigation, with Mitch's faith centered on accumulated cop-wisdom, Jub's on the growing competence of applied science.

A person who reads many procedural stories and takes note of the formidable array of techniques for catching criminals at the disposal of the police may wonder how any perpetrator ever escapes apprehension and conviction. The answer is lack of time and lack of manpower; the number of crimes with which they have to deal makes it impossible for the police to solve more than a small per cent of their cases, in spite of the mass of accumulated wisdom and the variety of technical resources available to them.

Chapter 6

The Cop and the System:
The Police Sub-Culture I

IT IS NOT POSSIBLE to make any kind of adequate interpretation of the fictional police detective unless we consider him or her as a member of the police sub-culture and then in turn consider that sub-culture in relation to the whole of society. As a member of the community the policeman is not only responsible for the preservation of the order and security of society, but he is in turn affected by the common condition, because he and his family share the fruits of security or suffer the dangers of disruption felt by the rest of the community. He is, moreover, by the nature of social organization, the servant of the community that pays him, judges him, and ultimately controls his success or failure as a law officer. The roles thus denied to him are that of the lonely solver of mysteries who works in isolation from mankind and that of the solitary knight-errant who sets his own priorities.

In this chapter we will consider the police sub-culture as it affects the lives and operations of its members, and in Chapter 7 we will examine that sub-culture as part of the total social ambiance.

The police in these stories usually refer to it as the System, by which they mean not only the department, the squad, or the broader complex of police organization, but the total of customs and folkways that make up the whole of the police environment.

The first step in understanding the System is to recognize its paramilitary nature. The police force, we are told, is a small army; criminals are the enemy, orders are to be obeyed no matter how ridiculous, and the team always comes first. The degree of influence of the military spirit naturally varies according to circumstances, but it is never completely absent, all the way from the strict line-and-staff of the big city department down to the rank-pulling in the most informal team. It manifests itself not only in formal structure but, most particularly in the lower ranks, in the ways the cops find to subvert it.

Military organization naturally implies regulations, and it is apparent that everything a policeman undertakes is governed by the vapid, often unintelligible prose of the Police Manual and the Criminal Code, which are designed to systematize police efforts but serve more often to hamstring law enforcement. Consequently, one of the strongest motivations on the police sub-culture is to find ways of getting around regulations without actually getting caught breaking them. Judicious bending of the rules comes to be a special skill of the lazy cop for getting out of work or avoiding responsibility, but it also a well-developed ability among conscientious policemen who find that the regulations interfere with performance of their duty.

Police work has a military flavor in its strong emphasis on rank and channels. The art of pleasing one's superiors is essential to success, and a wise young cop does not argue even when upstaged and humiliated. A mature police detective must be an advocate who is able to persuade his superiors, but he does not argue with the boss even though he may consider him a fool. Channels are sacrosanct: going over the head of one's superior can cause a world of trouble and is to be avoided, as George Gideon is reminded in *Gideon's Drive*, when a Scotland Yard detective declines to report directly to him: Gideon is Commander at the Yard, but the detective insists upon reporting to his superior, who will in turn report to Gideon (xv). Channels are also a source of personal security, however; when Patrolman Jason is not sure about the importance of an incident he has observed, he reports it to the detective in charge, whereupon it becomes the dick's problem, not his.[1]

There is a special kind of channel, unofficial and unauthorized, that as a result of its effectiveness has become a part of the System. This is the pipe, e, which can be extraordinarily efficient when a policeman has a personal friend strategically located in a position to supply accurate information without being subject to the normal official red tape. The pipeline can be especially effective when the repayment of a favor is involved and information is needed in a hurry. It is not recognized in the Police Manual, but it is one of the most useful channels.

Rumor becomes a police folkway, as widespread among cops as

the familiar "scuttlebutt" of the military. There is no way to control it, as Roger West discovers in *Alibi* when a chance phrase overheard by a constable touches off the rumor network of the entire Metropolitan Police (xi). The rumor mill is a subversion of the need for confidentiality essential to investigation, and consequently a denial of the spirit of professionalism, but it is so deeply ingrained as to constitute an aspect of the police sub-culture.

The principle of territoriality is another fetish of the police world. The smart cop stays out of the other guy's province, and he guards his own with fierce jealousy. The principle has a geographical reference, as in the case of a captain to whom the precinct is *my* world, or in the case of an already overworked squad happy to discover that a crime happened outside *our* division, in which instance it can be forgotten. More often, though, the territory is organizational, with reference to function instead of geographical space. People who have been working on a case do not enjoy having outsiders come in and break it, and a person heading a squad is certain to be infuriated if he learns that outsiders are making periodic phone calls to the members of his team. Anybody who finds it necessary to step into another's territory had best make sure of two things: proper authorization from up the line and correct observance of the amenities, which may amount to nothing more than a courtesy conference with the person or team whose territory is being infringed upon.

Military organization is built upon hierarchies, hierarchy involves rank, and rank implies the opportunity for promotion. In the police sub-culture of the world of the procedural, there seem to be three basic principles with regard to promotions: 1. They are as dependent upon internal politics and subservience to one's superiors as upon merit, often more so. 2. The power of promotion is a prime source of administrative intimidation. 3. The person wanting a promotion must attract the attention of his or her superiors while at the same time preserving the spirit of modesty and humility in the presence of colleagues. Departmental politics, personality conflicts, and internal feuds can effectively block the promotion of a good policeman, as they did with Matt Anders in the early years of his career.[2] Frank Hastings, who has reached the rank of lieutenant, knows he will never make captain on merit alone, without the proper degree of servility toward selected persons in influential positions.[3]

The nature of the power-structure, moreover, gives people in administrative positions an especially potent kind of clout with respect to promotions, as Assistant Chief Constable Ilford is aware when he hands a difficult assignment to Detective Chief Inspector Colin Thane in *Pilot Error,* reminding him at the same moment of the upcoming meeting of the Promotion Board (i). The ultimate power of the administration in the case of an insubordinate or otherwise undesirable cop who cannot be dismissed outright is to get him assigned to something like the Organized Crime Unit, which is not even taken into account in figuring departmental promotion quotas. The person eligible for promotion (and of course needing the higher pay) finds himself squeezed by the power of his superiors, whose attention he must attract and hold, and by the very considerable pressure of his peer-group, who may reject him if he gives the appearance of bucking for promotion and stepping on other people's toes. This is another of those spheres in which the policeman's position is dominated by ambivalence: there is a formal structure for determining fitness for promotion, but there is also a set of folkways that are at variance with authorization.

No public institution is immune to pressures and influence from outside, and in the police department the pressures of influential civilians become part of the System. Breaking up a narcotics ring on a campus may call for tactful handling, for example, when "somebody's" son or daughter is involved. Obvious signs of wealth and prestige are warning signals to go easy: Frank Hastings is not eager to arrest a man who drives a Cadillac,[4] and Roger West is pointedly advised against antagonizing the president of an industry, who might be in a position to raise objections when West's next promotion comes up.[5] Quite often, though, the pressure comes from people who think the police are not moving fast enough in the investigation of a case, and on occasion it can have beneficial results, as it does when an influential local man in *The Heat of the Night* insists that Virgil Tibbs be retained on the case in a small Southern town where the white policemen resent him.

All institutionalized bodies, including military units, university faculties, and police departments, are subject to internal politics. The two police procedurals with fullest development of the political theme are Lawrence Sanders' *The First Deadly Sin* and Dorothy Uhnak's *The Investigation.* One of the policemen in the Sanders story characterizes the New York Police Department as a "school of barracudas" (III, iii), with its cliques, cabals and factions, and the strategies developed for undermining an undesirable superior officer include the use of such rough tactics as espionage and infiltration. In *The Investigation* departmental politics becomes involved with an upcoming city election, with resultant double-crossing and throat-cutting, performance of favors, and revenge. It is important to notice though that Edward X. Delaney in *The First Deadly Sin* and Joe Peters in *The Investigation,* each of whom is deeply involved, both take the politics in their stride, assuming it to be neither unusual nor reprehensible. Both of these stories have their settings in big city departments, but politics is never absent from the small police force, where people with seniority and those on the right side get the posh assignments, while those out of favor get transferred all over town as the result of somebody's whim.

Policemen's relations with one another naturally shape themselves within the framework of the organization, with the result that their attitudes toward other cops become part of the System. Like military personnel, they develop patterns of horseplay and banter, modesty and egotism, favors and revenge, that are inherent in the folkways of the police sub-culture.

Horseplay and banter are a type of communication that establishes a level of camraderie among policemen. It is customarily rough (demonstrating the ability of participants to take it as well as dish it out), good-natured (intended to sting but not to do serious damage), and manly (oriented to the world of male aggressiveness; when a policewoman is involved in it she knows she is really accepted). As group communication it serves several ritualistic functions. Most often it is a device for exorcising the horrors and other tensions of the job. When the policemen of the 87th Squad in Ed McBain's stories arrive on the scene of a particularly gruesome murder, their first act is to engage in a chafing exchange with the detectives from Homicide, as antiphonal and rhythmic as the chanting of a cheering section; after two or three pages of mutual insults, pretended misunderstandings, and hurt feelings, the cops go to work with a restored objectivity.[6] Horseplay and banter also serve to strengthen the solidarity of the team: when Christie Opara and her male colleagues are setting the trap for a rapist in *The Bait,* they first engage in a round of straight-faced gags about the poor marksmanship of members of the team, designed to pull them together and to make them aware of each other as persons (xvii). Anther function of this kind of communication is to reduce the distances between ranks, and it is especially useful in cutting an arrogant medical examiner down to size, as when the members of the Lund force in *The Moment of Truth* are mercilessly unsympathetic to the tax problems of the physician assigned to their case, joyfully referring to him as a tax-evader (29). As might be expected, rough horseplay serves as an initiation rite. Two older cops take young Max Segal to the morgue for the avowed purpose of contributing to his "education" as a policeman; their real intention is to find out how long it will take to make him vomit.[7] Whatever the purpose of the ritual, though, the victim knows he must not take offense, because his turn as aggressor will eventually come. Sometimes the banter can become rough and insulting, as it does when the men of the 87th Squad make some broad jokes about the sexual preferences of Meyer Meyer's wife, which Meyer endures with stoic calm. After all, Meyer had it coming, in repayment for his own bawdy observations when Steve Carella returned from his honeymoon.[8]

As we have seen in connection with promotions, one of the fictional policeman's most difficult problems in adapting to this sub-culture is that of maintaining an acceptable balance between modesty and egotism. Policemen, we are told, have their own pride and hate being laughed at. Trompie Kramer in *The Caterpillar Cop* has seized upon an important clue in a murder case, but he is reluctant to check it out because of the danger of making a fool of himself (ix), and Edward X. Delaney in *The First Deadly Sin* asks a reporter not to refer to his passion for logic in a newspaper story because Delaney would never live it down (II,ii). The hazards of seeming to be superior are not imaginary, because section chiefs don't want their people to get the idea that they are supercops. The Swedish National Police Commissioner, already suffering from acute paranoia, dislikes talking to Martin Beck, who has received a little too much publicity over the years,[9] and Joe Capretto, who has also attracted too much attention for his own good, knows that the brass is cool on folk heroes in his department.[10] The brass in some departments has developed singularly effective devices for taking the starch out of a hero, like assigning him to an all-night stakeout in February in order to re-establish a proper sense of humility. At the same time, there is a protocol within the System that provides for awarding credit where credit is due; a policeman who has made an important discovery is the one to phone in the report and get the recognition. The cop's trick is to be a good policeman and to know he is a good policeman without sharing this self-knowledge with anybody except his most trusted associates.

According to Captain Edward X. Delaney, who knows the police sub-culture better than most fictional cops, the system of favors is the cohesive force that keeps the Department from falling apart.[11] If there is a rule, it would be, Never miss an opportunity to do a favor, and never fail to collect on favors done. A good store of favors performed is like a healthy bank balance, which can come in handy in an emergency. Detective Joe Peters takes the opportunity of a desk job to do a few for people who are in a good position to repay when he needs a favor and can start calling in his IOU's (I,v). Eagerness to perform favors on the international level surprises Inspector Van der Valk in *Tsing-Boum*, when he sends a request for information to France and has back a reply within hours (viii). Civilians also get in on the system, making it clear when they help the police that they will expect reciprocation the next time they get into trouble. The Department, in Delaney's opinion, also functions on vengeance.[12] Revenge is a weapon that can be wielded by many hands, as the Assistant Chief Constable of the Strathclyde Police discovers after he gets into a quarrel with a forensic lab assistant director: the lab man orders the executive washroom closed for a week because of "suspicious germ cultures" he has conveniently found on the walls.[13] The system of favors and revenge seems to provide a kind of catharsis for the fictional policeman. Once a favor has been repaid it can be forgotten, and when vengeance has been wreaked there is no need for continued resentment on either side.

This, then, is the System, its official, authorized version manifesting itself in regulations, in hierarchies and territories, in law, in intimidation. Underlying this formal structure, though just as much a part of the System, is the whole world of the police folklore, expressing itself in one-upmanship, persiflage, role-playing, and the art of the psych-out.

Where there is a system there are ways of beating it, and the fictional police have learned this lesson as thoroughly as have college students and military personnel.

One way of beating the merit system, for example, is to have a "rabbi"—in this context not an expert in Talmudic law but a well-placed person with influence in the Department who takes an interest in a policeman, guides his career, and eases his advancement through the ranks. Mitch Taylor's rabbi is a distant relative for whom Mitch does an occasional favor and who in turn "takes care" of Mitch. It must not be supposed that only inept cops have rabbis: the highly professional and capable Edward X. Delaney has one of the best, no less a personage than New York's deputy commissioner.[14]

As we will see in Chapter 8, it is part of the procedural formula that police cover for each other and especially that they protect their subordinates from discipline or re-assignment, and of course this convention represents another way of beating the System. Covering for each other is practically automatic between people of the same rank, part of the network of favors, but a superior will go to considerable lengths to protect a member of his squad from outside authority. He can be harshly authoritarian in dealing with his subordinates, but the spirit of the team forbids that any external power come between him and them. This is the problem of Lieutenant Kramer in McClure's *The Sunday Hangman*. Kramer's faithful and competent assistant, Sergeant Zondi, is suffering from a wound that might get him retired or at least re-assigned, and because Zondi is a Bantu he could expect little consideration from the white authorities. Throughout the novel Kramer resorts to all kinds of subterfuge to conceal Zondi's handicap, even making him walk five painful kilometers to demonstrate his fitness (v).

The very rigidity of the formal structure of the System offers an opportunity for beating it. The principle is that the policeman carries out his orders to the letter and thus avoids the responsibility of making decisions. Patrolman Kvant in the stories of Sjowall and Wahloo has reduced the practice to a formula: See nothing, hear nothing, but if you do see or hear anything, report it.[15] Joe Peters in New York has developed the same wisdom. His superior has put him to work digging out information that might be useful in a political campaign; Joe is dubious of the propriety of the assignment, but if the boss tells him to spend his working hours in this way, that is exactly what he is going to do (II,ii).

The System demands that, once a case has been placed in a policeman's hands, he must carry it through to resolution. In response, the policemen in these stories have developed a methodology for a) getting a case off one's own hands and b) avoiding taking a case off somebody else's hands. Christie Opara, on her way to an important assignment in *The Bait*, is forced to make an arrest which, if followed through, will tie her up for the better part of the day and delay her appearance where she is needed. She tries to turn her "collar" over to the first patrolman on the scene but without success: he knows that, having once accepted the responsibility, he will be compelled to follow through. Christie is stuck with her perpetrator (iii).

The figure of the policeman on the take is a recurrent one in the procedural stories, the seriousness of the corruption ranging from a financially hard-pressed cop's acceptance of a free lunch, through the practice of "skimming" (taking part of the drugs confiscated), to blatant theft of whatever the burglars have left behind. Mitch Taylor distinguishes between "clean money" and "dirty money," the clean variety being whatever comes into a policeman's hands by way of normal petty graft, the dirty kind coming from outright theft.[16] Not unnaturally, there is a strong correspondence between professionalism and susceptibility to graft. Conscientious detectives like Steve Carella and Roger West take pains to avoid the appearance of corruptibility, but those of lesser integrity accept the rakeoff as part of a policeman's way of life.

Policemen also on occasion break laws. Sometimes this infringement of the System is done for the sake of preserving the System, as when a scrupulous detective learns that he must on occasion break some laws in order to enforce others. The necessity manifests itself most clearly in the case of the illegal search; policemen needing evidence against a suspect are quite skillful in "tossing" his apartment without leaving any sign of their own activities. More often, though, the cop simply accepts the right to commit minor infractions as part of his immunity as a policeman, like illegal parking, or buying a bottle of wine after closing hours, or tossing a sandwich wrapper out of a car window, usually to the accompaniment of some light remark about bending the law a little without breaking it, or the special privileges of being a police officer.

Then there are ways of beating the work schedule. Courtesy, we are told, requires that a relieving officer appear on the scene fifteen minutes before the beginning of his shift, which means that a detective whose shift begins at 6:00 a.m. should show up at 5:45. Detective Andy Parker of the Eight-Seven, one of the most notorious goof-offs in the business, takes care of this inconvenience by getting himself assigned to a plant in a grocery story that does not open until 6:30. (It should be noted, however, that poetic justice is done in Parker's case: he gets shot during a holdup in that store.)[17]

A joke on one's superior officer, as long as it doesn't backfire, is a satisfying way of striking back at the Establishment. Sergeant Joe Keller, frustrated by the abrasive feud he has been carrying on with Lieutenant Piscati, gets at least partial revenge when he registers in a house of prostitution in *The Smack Man* (in line of duty), using Piscati's name (xii). Sergeant Dutton, on the other hand, almost gets himself put on report when he fails to remove an insulting sign directed at Chief Inspector Philip Hunter. Dutton wants to get the pleasure of Hunter's seeing the sign, but press photographers see it first, and Dutton's laugh at the expense of his superior is cut short by the cold wrath of the Inspector.[18]

Beating the System is more often a symbolic gesture than a response to practical necessity. The Police Establishment is almost always authoritarian and frequently tyrannical to the extent that the detective must subvert it to protect himself and his professionalism, but most of the cops in the procedurals seem to strike back at the System because it's there. The contest is a game, not a rebellion.

To be quite truthful, we get the feeling that the policeman finds it easier to empathize with the criminal world than with the Police Establishment or the public he is paid to protect. His affinity with the criminal arises partly out of the fact that his social orientation and his methods are much like those of the criminal, partly out of a natural sympathy with people who encounter many of the same problems as himself, and partly from an aggregate of shared understandings and values.

Freeling's Inspector Van der Valk is especially conscious of the affinity between cops and criminals with respect to their mutual adjustments and methods. On one occasion, Van der Valk tells himself that a policeman can feel sympathy for a lawbreaker because he is so nearly a criminal himself, and in another story he sizes up a con man as a potentially good policeman, of the kind who will accept a bribe.[19] The identification becomes especially sharp in the case of a corrupt policeman, whose guilt is a demonstration that cops are no different from crooks; as the informant Fat Willy tells Gabriel Wager in *The Farnsworth Score*, pinning a badge on a crook and calling him a cop does not change anything (xiii). Part of the resemblance lies in their mutual dependence on violence as means to achieve their ends. One reason for Lennart Kollbert's resignation from the police is his sense of guilt over having accidentally killed a policeman; as he sits across the table from a murderer he thinks of the other man and himself as a killer and a policeman who had killed.[20] In part, the similarity is based on personal qualities: Mitch Taylor is cheerful and untroubled, the perfect temperament, he tells himself, for a cop or a murderer.[21]

Curiously, policemen can feel sympathy for criminals— especially young people in trouble with the law—for the same reasons as they empathize with the victims of crime. Most of them are family people who have children of their own and who can visualize their own kids in the same kind of trouble as the youngsters they handle in line of duty. George Gideon has a hard streak in him, but his toughness comes close to giving way to sentimentality in *Gideon's Week* when he confronts a young woman who is a friend of his daughter Pru and is about Pru's age (iii). Bill Decker in *F as in Flight* is one of the toughest cops in procedural literature, but while questioning a young woman suspect he is constantly aware of her similarity to his own daughter. This kind of identification is another reminder of the status of the cop as a member of the community, sharing the common guilt and the common danger.

We are not surprised, on the other hand, to learn that policemen think like criminals. Cotton Hawes in *Fuzz* feels a symbiosis with a junkie he is questioning, a secret bond that affirms the interlocking subtlety of crime and punishment (iv). Cops and criminals often share the same value-systems, both holding, for example, that sex offenders are worse than murderers. In an investigation this mutuality can give a policeman a considerable practical advantage. Gabriel Wager knows a former convict is lying, for the reason that he speaks the ex-con's language better than anybody else would be able to.[22] Despite the running warfare between police and violators, criminals even occasionally participate in the system of favors. When Colin Thane is about to leave the old Millside Division, one of his former antagonists slips up in the dark to inform Thane that an automobile is shadowing him, a piece of knowledge that presently saves Thane's life.[23]

The conception of the affinity between policemen and criminals must not be stretched so far as to imply any habitual gentleness between them. They are opposing players in a rough game, played according to harsh rules that are well understood by both sides. They are much alike in their methods, and they have the same kind of respect for each other that team players customarily have for the opposition, but they are out to get each other. The game analogy must be limited, however, because neither side wins. Society (symbolized by the Law), moreover, intervenes like an unreasonable referee in a sandlot football game, limiting the police side to a degree of clean play that inhibits a really decisive mop-up.

On the police side, the score is expressed in terms of numbers of "collars" made, a day being considered good or bad in relation to the number of scalps garnered. The best and most professional of police can maintain an unbiased objectivity toward the game and a stinting respect for the other side. Patrick Petrella insists that he is not shocked by crime any more than a doctor is shocked by disease,[24] and as Steve Carella remembers all the people he has sent to the penitentiary, he thinks of them as "business associates."[25] None of this objective spirit keeps the cops from playing dirty when the Referee is looking the other way, and the opportunity presents itself most easily when a criminal is being placed under arrest. Thus a hoodum beaten up during arrest is reported as having tripped and fallen, or having accidentally run into somebody's elbow. The use of weapons by policemen is limited (especially outside the United States), but this regulation does not prevent an arrestee from being clubbed by a metal bar that "just happened" to be in the patrol car. Police brutality is always a subject for public concern, but it should be remembered that criminals also play dirty: the thug who "ran into somebody's elbow," for example, had struck and kicked the arresting officer.[26] Finally, the rough rules demand that the police take advantage of mistakes made by the opposition. The Strathclyde Police in *Pilot Error* shed no tears over any casualties incurred during a fight among "neds" (Glasgow slang for hoods) as long as no outsider gets hurt (iv).

Although the game is rough, the police in these stories are capable of being considerate and even gentle with criminals as a group or as individuals. One way of playing ball with the criminal world is to stage periodic "showcase" cleanups of narcotics, prostitution, or gambling, information regarding which is supplied in advance to designated participants, usually through selected police informants who thereby earn for themselves some credit in the underworld. Much more often, though, the police expend their compassion on the down-and-out who, although technically lawbreakers, need help rather than punishment. The rural sheriff in van de Wetering's *The Maine Massacre* is a tough law officer, but he arranges to have a carload of drunks taken home instead of locking them up for the night (x). At another time he holds the town drunk in jail until he can send some prisoners to cut wood for him, knowing the man will freeze to death if he sends him home now (xi).

Although he is capable of pity toward criminals, the policeman is customarily resentful of any manifestation of softness on the part of society. He is especially scornful of lenient judges who grant bail too freely, of the probation system that releases a perpetrator after he has served half his sentence, and of the practice of plea-bargaining. American cops almost universally resent the Miranda and Escebedo decisions, which established safeguards for the rights of persons under arrest. In the opinion of many cops, Miranda-Escebedo serves only to confuse the business of law enforcement, making the job tougher and the criminals bolder. The English equivalent of Miranda-Escebedo is the Judges' Rules, which govern the manner in which the suspects can be interrogated;[27] CID men do not seem to resent them as sharply as their American counterparts do Miranda-Escebedo, but neglecting to observe them can ruin a case, and they thus represent another straw on the load of a policeman's tensions and frustrations.

Most cops have families, and in this respect they differ from the eccentric genius of the classic tale and the lone knight-errant of the private-eye story, who are almost always unmarried. The reason for the difference, as we have implied earlier, is that the policeman or policewoman is part of the community, not the lone genius from outside who enters the picture long enough to purge the guilty society and then withdraws into his isolation. Thus it is not merely the demand for "realism" that makes the cop a family person in contrast to the unencumbered detective of the older traditions, but rather the necessity for a useable fictional situation. A married Nero Wolfe, with a couple of Wolfe youngsters romping around the brownstone on West Thirty-Fifth Street, would be impossible for a writer to handle, as would a faithful Philip Marlowe who must call the missus from Bay City to tell her he is going to be detained for a few days. On the other hand, it is not only natural but essential for Luis Mendoza to have his kids crawling all over him as soon as he arrives at home; they are, as Mendoza so often says, his "hostages to fortune," part of his vulnerability as a member of the society whose security he tries to defend.

Consequently, most procedural policemen are married. Only a dozen or so of those who play major roles are single, like Ball's Virgil Tibbs, McBain's Cotton Hawes and Andy Parker, and Sjowall and Wahloo's Gunvald Larsson. Several marry during the the series: Shannon's Luis Mendoza, O'Donnell's Norah Mulcahaney, McBain's Steve Carella and Bert Kling, Treat's Jub Freeman, Linington's Ivor Maddox, Gilbert's Patrick Petrella, Procter's Philip Hunter. Two of them marry within the Department: Norah Mulcahaney to her superior officer, Joe Capretto, and Ivor Maddox to his subordinate Sue Carstairs.

A few are divorced, including Sjowall and Wahloo's Martin Beck, Burns' Gabriel Wager, Wilcox's Frank Hastings, and Waugh's Frank Sessions. Of these, Wager and Hastings suffer some emotional trauma as a result of their disrupted lives, but Beck and Sessions are glad enough to be relieved of earlier unfortunate marriages. Uhnak's Joe Peters is separated from his wife in *The Investigation*, but a reconciliation seems likely at the end of the story. Two are widowed: Uhnak's Christie Opara, whose policeman husband was killed in line of duty, and DeMille's Joe Keller, whose wife and son were murdered by the Mafia. Sanders' Edward X. Delaney is widowed at the end of *The First Deadly Sin* but is happily re-married at the beginning of the second novel.

Of the rest, the great majority are at least satisfactorily married, and some have partnerships that are almost ecstatically happy, like McBain's Steve Carella and Sjowall and Wahloo's Lennart Kollberg, whose wives are every man's erotic dream-mates.

Freeling's Van der Valk has the good fortune to be married to a Frenchwoman with exquisite taste in food and clothes. The wife of van de Wetering's aged and ailing commisaris is a tender nurse who eases his rheumatism with hot baths, orange juice, and small cigars. The norm, however, is the marriage troubled by problems, like the memory of the Gideons' dead child or the poverty of the Zondis, but the difficulties are customarily offset by more general satisfactions.

Only two have marriages that are total failures. Van de Wetering's Grijpstra is married to a slovenly harridan whom he avoids as much as possible, and Ørum's Einarsen to an adulterous lesbian, whom he plans to divorce.

The rule that most of the police marriages in these stories are at least satisfactory and at best blissful is nothing short of marvellous, when we consider the reciprocal strain between police work and family life. The policeman's low pay, the long hours he must work and the unpredictability of his schedule, together with the danger to which he is subject, create tensions at home that are not conducive to successful marriage or to good parent-child relationships. Conversely, pre-occupation with family problems can handicap a policeman in the performance of his duty, especially when he becomes aware that his vulnerability to danger can be easily extended to his family.

Two comments frequently heard in the procedural stories are first, that a policeman ought to stay single and second, that a woman is a fool to marry a cop. These comments are most often made in the context of the danger of violence to the policeman and his family, but the long hours and the low pay combine with the threat of danger to produce another familiar figure, the police wife who wants her husband to leave the force. The wish can take the form of a half-expressed attitude, as it does with the wife of young Constable Addis in *Gideon's River*, who is about to become a mother for the first time and secretly longs for her husband to leave his police job so he can be home at night (xvi). It almost wrecks the marriage of Roger West in *A Part for a Policeman*, whose wife is suffering menopausal symptoms and accuses her husband of deliberately working long hours to avoid being near her (v). The wish is answered for the wife of a Scottish policeman wounded on duty. When she hears that he may never be fit to return to duty, she expresses a sense of relief.[28]

The reciprocal tensions between home and job are especially obvious in the relations between policemen and their children. Most of the police fathers in these stories love their children, but their work keeps them away from home too much to establish really good associations, and when at home they are frequently too tired and irritable to participate in family life. The problem becomes especially acute when a son or daughter turns into a rebel or a dropout. Casey Reardon almost becomes completely alienated from his daughter in *The Witness* when she insists upon participating, against her father's wishes, in a non-violent demonstration. Barbara's idealism clashes with Casey's conservatism on a level that leaves room for reconciliation, but other policemen experience far more serious problems with their children. Martin Beck is concerned about his son Rolf, who at age thirteen was lazy and introverted, uninterested in school, and showing no promise in the development of talents or special interests. Years later, Beck has never established a good contact with Rolf and feels guilty about his lack of deep feeling for his son.[29] Henk Grijpstra has a more serious situation: his son is a school dropout and an army reject who sniffs cocaine and is apparently involved in criminal activities. Grijpstra's only hope is that he will be eventually picked up and sent to a reform school.[30] In each such case the policeman-parent is handicapped, because the very behavior against which he is conditioned is showing up in his family, but the approaches he uses in handling young delinquents will not work with his own son or daughter.

Inevitably, trouble at home hampers the policeman in the performance of duty. Knud Einarsen's suspicions regarding his wife make him dyspeptic, snappish, even brutal.[31] Norah Mulcahaney has a different kind of family problem: her father's determination to find her a husband (and get her out of police work) does not constitute a personal handicap, but it does in *The Phone Calls* almost get Norah killed when Patrick Mulcahaney's choice of a nice young man turns out to be a particularly unfortunate one. A family can also add to a policeman's vulnerability, especially when there is a young child whose safety may be threatened. Christie Opara gives a good account of herself when she confronts a hoodlum single-handed in *The Ledger*, but when he hints at a threat to her six-year-old Mickey, Christie begins to experience fear (xii).

To the happily married policeman, though, home is the Great Good Place, the antidote against the pressures of the job. The pattern was established in Treat's *V as in Victim*; whatever his faults, Mitch Taylor loves his Amy, looks forward to the end of the work-day when he can go be with her, makes her tastes and opinions his touchstone in judging people and situations. Van der Valk is as thoroughly attached to his Arlette: she is his resource against depression, and he is proud of his "Arlette-trained eye" in judging women's clothes.[32] It would be difficult, as a matter of fact, to find in popular fiction a more admirable group than the police wives in the procedural stories. Most of them (like Teddy Carella, Mary Thane and Kate Gideon) are good wives and mothers who are the central figures in homes that are cohesive and secure. One (Harriet Byrnes, wife of Lieutenant Byrnes of the 87th Precinct) is loyal not only to her husband but to the ideals of his profession. Another (Cessie Fellows, wife of Chief Fred Fellows) has a good, logical mind that helps her husband to define the problem he is working on. Miriam Zondi makes a good home for her Bantu husband in spite of the poverty and squalor to which race and social banishment have consigned them. Finally, there is Sarah Meyer, surely one of a kind, who can help Meyer Meyer over the rough spots but can also reduce him to size when necessary.

For most policemen, then, home is the context, the milieu, the frame of reference. A threat to society is not just an abstract problem for them to solve, because they and their families are part of the threatened order.

The socio-economic status of the police in the procedural stories is middle-middle and lower-middle class. All of them complain about the low pay, most of them barely get by on their salaries, and the only well-fixed cop among them is Shannon's Luis Mendoza, who inherited his wealth. One result of their meagre incomes is envy of the criminal classes, who seem to fare much better. Detectives Brown and Carella, observing the wall-to-wall carpeting in the apartment of a hood they are investigating in *Jigsaw*, decide they are in the wrong racket (iii). Neither are the feelings of Detective Eddie Maher improved very much when he discovers that a prostitute makes more in a single night than he does in a week.[33] Another result is the graft, a predictable development among poorly paid policemen in contact with well-heeled criminals. Most policemen, according to the stories, supplement their incomes with "tribute"; the prostitute whose good income annoys Detective Maher complains on one occasion that paying off the cops is one of the biggest sources of overhead in her trade.

The automobile-symbolism of the other traditions of detective fiction has carried over into the procedural story as a representation of social class. We remember Philo Vance's custom-built Hispano-Suiza, the Duesenberg driven by the early Ellery Queen, Mike Hammer's souped-up heap, Travis McGee's converted Rolls, Nero Wolfe's expensive but dependable Heron—each symbolic to a degree of the personality and social class of its owner. The automobile of the procedural policeman is typically a clunker that may or may not start in the morning, may or may not quit in the midst of rush-hour traffic, and should have been traded long ago.

The policeman's prejudices against minority groups are part of the instinct of their socio-economic class. Too many cops, we are told, are angry people with angry feelings toward non-whites, and neither training nor reprimand can make much headway against those prejudices.

The nature of police work binds policemen to middle-class values and subjects them to a vulnerability not shared by the rich or the poor. During the 1950s in Maurice Procter's Granchester, divorce or separation in a police family was frowned upon to the extent that, whether or not he was happily married, a policeman had to pretend to be, otherwise his career was in jeopardy.[34] Illicit sexual affairs are dangerous, because they leave the policeman or policewoman open to blackmail. Their precarious financial status also increases their vulnerabilty. It is easy for a policeman to get a loan, but cops in debt are cops in trouble. The policeman is locked into the tradition of middle-class respectability which he (or she) finds it difficult to assume, and which leaves him (or her) wide open to the threat of scandal and coercion.

Another kind of vulnerability effected by social status results from that component of the System mentioned earlier, pressure from the wealthy and the influential. Investigating a crime committed during a labor dispute, Roger West tries hard to be impartial between labor and management, but, as a labor leader reminds him, West had better not offend management, knowing which side his bread is buttered on.[35]

In spite of his meagre financial return, however, the policeman enjoys a security not granted to the gifted super-sleuth or the private investigator. His pay is not large, but it is at least regular. He will never be able to afford a brownstone on West Thirty-Fifth Street like Nero Wolfe or a two-story apartment "in" East Thirty-Eighth Street like Philo Vance, but neither will he be compelled to operate out of a fly-specked one-room office five floors up in a ratty office building. His financial security (such as it is) is not dependent on the solution of the current case; win, lose or draw, he will get his pay check. The police detective's promotion and consequent financial improvement are dependent upon his overall performance (including his ability as a politician) rather than brilliant performance in a given case. Thus each solution becomes part of the job and further accents the difference between him and the detectives in the other traditions of mystery fiction.

If we want to classify the fictional policeman ideologically, we can call him an anti-intellectual conservative. In view of his commitment to the preservation of order and his impecunious security, his conservative bias is not surprising, nor is his anti-intellectualism when we consider the degree to which his success is dependent on physical rather than cerebral ability.

People apparently do not expect policemen to think, and anyhow nobody wants to get intellectual in the squadroom. Detectives, Pete Friedman tells a suspect, do not waste time theorizing.[36] Consequently, they distrust experts whose conceptualizations are theoretical, especially psychiatrists, sociologists and criminologists. Psychiatrists, in the police view, are people who tell lies in court to gain acquittals for people the police have worked hard to put behind bars, and Friedman states that he has never found one who can second-guess the hunch of a good detective.[37] As for sociologists, the police take a dim view of their findings, especially those which deal with the police sub-culture. Criminologists, because their activities are so close to police work, are objects of special scorn. All they know is statistics, according to Adjutant Grijpstra, who is infuriated at their casual dismissal of the prevalence of cases of child-molestation.[38] What annoys Grijpstra is the scientific coldness of broad generalizations in contrast with the horror of crimes he must deal with on an immediate level, an opinion shared by the much more perceptive Van der Valk, who deplores the tendency of the behavioral sciences to make everything important but nothing really significant.[39] The improvement in opportunities for education among policemen may eventually reduce their anti-intellectual bias, but at present those cops with college training (especially those in the behavioral sciences) keep quiet about their degrees.

Consequently, the conservatism of policemen is more instinctive than ideological, expressing itself in their attitudes toward social reform and planned environmental change. We are not surprised at the attitude of a policeman like Paulsson of the oppressive "Sepo" in Sweden, who distrusts long hair, liberals and blacks,[40] or those of the whites in the South African stories of James McClure, where reactionism is the social norm, but policemen in other environments are almost consistently skeptical of welfare programs, civil rights movements and modern education, especially those that seem to encourage permissiveness toward delinquents. Slurs on "bleeding hearts" and "do-gooders" show up frequently, along with distrust of social workers, and nobody has a good word for the American Civil Liberties Union. Many policemen are unhappy about the directions of public education, especially if they have children at or approaching school age. Luis Mendoza, for example, distrusts current public education to the extent that he has bought his four-year-old twins a set of McGuffey primers.[41] Dislike of urban renewal and other visionary changes in the environment makes itself felt everywhere. In Denver, Gabriel Wager is saddened by the disappearance of the neighborhood where he grew up and by plans to raze his favorite eating place, the Frontier Restaurant.[42] The Stockholm police are exasperated at the efforts of government to revise the face of their city, Gunvald Larsson asking at one point why they don't blow up all of Stockholm at one time and start over instead of wrecking the place piecemeal.[43]

One feeling almost universally expressed among policemen and their families is a concern over the decline of morality and social standards in general. Understandably, much of this anxiety is directed toward the disintegration of the home as the basic unit of society and toward increasing sexual permissiveness. The reason people are unhappy, says Detective Canelli in San Francisco, is that there is no family life any more,[44] a sentiment echoed by Inspector Van der Valk in Amsterdam, who believes that the permissive parents in Holland are in for trouble and deserve what they will get.[45] As for sexual misconduct, Roger West thinks social callousness has developed to the point where even rape is no longer below the level of public acceptance.[46] Knud Einarsen describes downtown Copenhagen as a "gigantic whorehouse," taken over by porn shops and junkie prostitutes.[47]

This decline in standards of decency has fostered a tendency toward violence and a rise in the rate of crime. If violence has become a way of life, Edward X. Delaney asks himself, who will even care about one more murder?[48] Even the traditionally peaceful areas are no longer secure. People in the Highlands, says Sergeant Francey Dunbar of the Scottish Crime Squad in *Live Bait*, used to leave their doors unlocked; they lock them now, as a result of the invasion of "civilization" (v). Roger West blames the plight of society on a succession of wars that have bred into people an acceptance of violence for its own sake,[49] but the father of a killer cop in Sweden has a broader explanation, the lack of anything to believe in. If he had known what society was coming to, says the elder Erikson, he would never have fathered any children.[50] Deputy Commander Laidlaw, in one of Gilbert's stories, blames the breakdown of fundamental religion: if people don't have any fear of going to hell, they will commit all the crime they can get away with in this life.[51]

Anxiety over the trends and tendencies of twentieth century life tends to engender in the policeman a feeling of alienation from the mainstream of life, with the result that he withdraws progressively into the company of his own sympathetic associates and thus becomes the victim of what Lennart Kollberg calls the policeman's occupational disease.

Twenty-three years on the force have made Kollberg incapable of maintaining normal relations with the outside world. Police work is not a normal job, because it throws a person into abnormal contacts with abnormal people. As a result, Kollberg thinks, policemen who get outside their usual circle of associates feel ashamed of their profession. The ultimate condition, which he feels himself approaching, is paranoia resulting from the constant encounter with fear, distrust and contempt.[52]

Kollberg's sense of alienation is more intense than the one experienced by other policemen, but most of them share his qualms, if only to a lesser degree. Part of their isolation is engendered by the nature of the job, which puts them into contact with the worst in people and leaves them jaundiced and cynical. All men are liars; nobody is to be trusted. It is the nature of the job to be suspicious of everybody and everything, with or without justification. A policeman, in the opinion of Frank Hastings, is a lonely hunter among nondescript, hostile strangers until they all become strangers—every one of them.[53] Consequently, says Van der Valk, he becomes as stunted and blunted as a prisoner, because both his dignity and his personal esteem are under attack.[54]

Many of the police in the procedural stories feel a loss of identity, a sense of ceasing to be a person. Jonas Morck, watching a couple on a lonely quay at night, tells himself that there is not a soul besides them, not counting himself, who is not a soul but a policeman,[55] and Detective Pollock, sitting in church, is struck by a possible incongruity: Do police officers have souls?[56] Steve Carella voices the loss of identity automatically when a telephone supervisor tells him she can not give out unpublished information to just any person: "I'm not a person," Carella replies, "I'm a cop," and wrinkles his forehead for a second over the implication of what he has said.[57]

One of the causes of the policeman's occupational disease is the stress inherent in his job. Stress-related diseases, according to Burns' *Speak for the Dead*, are the number-one cop-killers, with the result that the life-expectancy of a policeman is only fifty-seven years (v). Stress makes cops react even more violently than necessary, using fists and saps as expressions of their frustrations. At home, as a result, they may shout at the children, push them away, or give short answers to their questions.

The policeman's work exposes him to physical danger, a hazard that adds to his anxiety and sense of alienation. Trompie Kramer will not marry because he is unwilling to take on the responsibility of a family in the face of the imminent danger of being killed.[58] Every cop's wife lives with the dread of news that her husband has been killed or wounded, to the extent that a phone call from headquarters or a visit by another policeman is often greeted with panic. Policemen are very poor insurance risks; they have their own insurance system, because regular companies will not handle them.

We should also mention the tedium and boredom most

policemen feel on the job, a manifestation of what Pete Friedman calls the "dullsville security of civil service,"[59] and George Gideon "the needle of romance in the haystack of routine."[60] Opinions vary with respect to the nature of the tedium, but not with regard to the extent. Half the life of a policeman, says Adjutant Grijpstra, is spent hanging around and waiting.[61] Detective Carella's estimate is that half the time is spent on the telphone, the other half typing up reports in triplicate.[62]

The universal complaint of the procedural police is the unrelenting overwork, which exacerbates the tedium, danger, stress, alienation, anxiety and the rest of the manifestations of the policeman's occupational disease. Unlike private detectives, the police are never off duty; a policeman customarily carries his gun, and if he runs into a crime while not working his shift, he is obligated to at least begin the investigation. His "off days" are frequently spent catching up on the leg-work and paper-work he did not have time to do during his assigned work period. Saturdays, Sundays, legal holidays, and religious hoidays are like all other days, because law enforcement must go on regardless. He has assigned vacations, but the stories are full of holidays necessarily postponed or interrupted because of a sudden rash of crime or a shortage of manpower. The understaffed department is the norm, with the result that everybody must carry a heavier caseload than could be reasonably expected. Here is another of the basic differences between the procedural cop and the heroes of other kinds of detective fiction: very rarely can he devote his attention exclusively to the case in hand. In the normal scheme of things, the case in the present story is one of a half dozen or so, all of which are demanding his attention. Consequently one case is not finished before he must turn his efforts to another one—or two or three.

Overwork affects the policeman in several ways, none of them good. First, of course, is the fatigue, which ruins his health, makes him irritable and causes him to over-react and to make mistakes that should be avoidable. The overwork of the policeman is the most common source of family troubles, especially when a wife resents the necessity for her husband to be away from home so much of the time. Finally, an overworked policeman is vulnerable to accusations of negligence and inefficiency, as every sharp defense lawyer knows.

One of the most familiar figures in the procedural is the policeman unsure of himself, his ability and his motives. Generally the uncertainty expresses itself in terms of lack of confidence in one's fitness as a human being. Martin Beck dislikes some of his colleagues, has no high opinion of certain others, but he most especially has no high opinion of himself.[63] Van der Valk knows he does not have any big talent; he has a small talent, and it is not enough.[64] More specifically, they experience guilt over their failures to perform adequately in a current case. Roger West blames himself for forgetting to provide protection for a witness and for failing to assign more men to guard a critical site.[65] Christie Opara in *The Ledger* feels strong self-reproach after she allows a suspect to make her lose her temper (ii). On a broader professional basis, they experience uncertainty about their ability to deal with their fellow policemen and with criminals, as when Norah Mulcahaney in *The Phone Calls* feels subsequent guilt over getting out of line with her lieutenant (vi), or when Seved Olofsson in *The Moment of Truth* worries about whether his predecessor could have done a better job than he is doing (51). Most importantly, though, the police frequently feel uncertainty about their motives. More than once Steve Carella finds himself strongly attracted to a sexy suspect or witness, and his sense of guilt always bothers him, especially when he has to face his wife Teddy. In a different context, young Bill Knight, working under cover, experiences moral conflict regarding his relations with the family he has been assigned to observe.[66]

These self-doubts create tensions between the police detective's uncertainties about his abilities, performance and motives on one hand and his sense of professionalism and his pride in his own personal standards on the other. This tension, however, is not a completely personal internal conflict.The policeman is neither a lone hero nor an isolated victim. Whatever he does, and however he feels, finds expression in the context of the police sub-culture in relation to the whole of society.

Chapter 7

The System and Society:
The Police Sub-Culture II

BEFORE WE CAN GET an adequate picture of the police sub-culture in relation to the whole of society, we must raise two questions about the Police Establishment. First, to what degree is the detective squad typical of the community in terms of representation by ethnic groups and sex? Second, what is the status of police work as a profession?

The squad with the broadest mixture in respect to ethnicity and sex is found in the 87th Precinct stories of Ed McBain. The 87th Squad, we must remember, is located in McBain's "imaginary city," which is not New York City but is obviously so close to New York in geography and social composition as to be practically indistinguishable from it. In the late 1970s, the characters with major or secondary roles in the stories belonged to the following groups: four Anglo-Saxon males (Cotton Hawes, Bert Kling, Andy Parker, Hal Willis); two Jewish males (Sam Grossman, Meyer Meyer); two males of Italian descent (Steve Carella, Richard Genero); two of Irish descent (Peter Byrnes, Bob O'Brien); one black male (Arthur Brown); one male of Puerto Rican descent (Alexiandre Delgado). One white woman cop (Eileen Burke) played an important role early in the series, and another (Alice Banion) a minor one. Of the other American series, the ones by Elizabeth Linington (including those under the pseudonyms of Dell Shannon and Lesley Egan), and those by Lillian O'Donnell and Dorothy Uhnak, show a broad ethnic and sexual mix, which seems plausible in view of the fact that they set their stories in large metropolitan areas. Equally credible, however, is the composition of Hillary Waugh's squad in the Fred Fellows stories, solid Anglo-Saxon male, which is what we would expect in "Stockford," Connecticut, with a population of 8500. In British stories, the squad is almost invariably composed chiefly of white males, with a few roles assigned to women. The Swedish stories of Maj Sjowall and Per Wahloo, not surprisingly, feature a squad composed exclusively of Swedes, but there are more policewomen in at least intermediate roles than we find in most series. Finally, we should mention the "Trekkerburg" squad in McClure's stories set in the white-dominated Republic of South Africa, in which it is the responsibity of the Bantu sergeant, Mickey Zondi, to cope chiefly with black problems.

We will deal more fully with the special characteristics of ethnic and women detectives in Chapters 10-13, but it should be at least noted at this point that, when we speak of the police sub-culture in the procedural stories, we are not dealing with a group that is a microcosm of society. It is, rather, a population usually dominated by males of the local ethnic majority.

Is police work a profession? The people in the procedurals sometimes speak of it as one, or think of themselves as professionals, or talk about the professional approach in law enforcement. The answer to the question depends, in part, on the sense in which the word "profession" is being used. If we compare police work with the learned professions like medicine or engineering, applying such criteria as financial security (in service and after retirement), lengthy, intensive training, the enforcement of a code of ethics, and the existence of a body of scholarly literature, our answer must be negative. Police work in almost no sense approaches the professional status of such well-established vocations.

The characters in these stories, as we might expect, are using the term in a broader, looser sense, as Philip Hunter does when he refers to himself as a specialist in a profession in which the uniformed police (who are not detectives) are merely practitioners.[1] When the police use the word "profession" to describe their work, they customarily place it in one or more of four contexts: confidentiality, objectivy, vigilance and dignity.

Confidentiality is part of the spirit of professionalism: a real pro does not discuss police work outside the department or even outside the squad. When Jack Tallon, newly appointed chief of a small-city department, discovers that members of the city council have heard what has gone on in a departmental meeting, he resolves upon a lecture to the loose-mouthed one: talking out of school is unprofessional.[2] Objectivity is another criterion: the first rule of detection, Roger West reminds himself, is never to let personal feelings affect one's judgment.[3] The same rule applies to departmental politics, in which Edward X. Delaney does not want to get involved because he thinks of himself as a professional policeman.[4] The third criterion is vigilance: policemen suspect everybody, says Van der Valk, characterizing this quality in the same breath as part of their "professional deformation."[5] Finally, they equate professionalism with dignity, the projection of an image consistent with the public expectation of a policeman's bearing. When the members of the District Attorney's Special Investigations Squad give way to unseemly clowning in the squad room, Stoner Martin, only half humorously, calls them to order with the reminder that they are expected to act like professionals.[6]

There are indications in the recent stories that law enforcement is moving in the direction of real professionalism. Joe Peters is a little disturbed by the way the New York Police Department is replacing experienced people with college-educated men and by the frantic scramble for officers in service to take courses at John Jay College of Criminal Justice.[7] There is even some promise of the development of a body of professional literature. Edward X. Delaney, we are told, has written a series of three articles for his department's monthly magazine. The first, "Common Sense and the New Detective," is a conventional treatment of the exercise of good judgment during an investigation. The second, entitled "Hunch, Instinct, and the New Detective," deals somewhat less conventionally with the importance of the subconscious in the cultivation of insight. The third article, which unfortunately was never published, sounds like a real breakthrough: in this one Delaney develops the thesis of a "sensual," "Dostoevskian" relationship between policeman and criminal, going so far as to suggest the necessity for the policeman to enter the physical being and the psyche of his quarry in order to bring him to justice.[8] Little progress is apparent, however, in the improvement of a professional code of ethics. It would appear that, in the procedural stories, police work is making some headway toward becoming at least semi-professional.

At the same time, certain ingrained attitudes constitute real obstacles to the professionalization of law enforcement. Two of the biggest advantages of the police detective are his access to a tremendous amount of information compiled chiefly from reports, and the availability of a highly sophisticated technology, but most cops, particularly the older and more experienced ones, almost automatically resent the paper work involved in their jobs and the intrusion of technology, which negates the common-sense approach.

Report-writing is part of a policeman's job. There are mountains of paper at every stage of an investigation, with three, five, seven copies of everything required. Policemen, oriented as they are to physical rather than cerebral activity, tend to resent report-writing. Inspector Van der Valk is good at writing reports but has never got over detesting them, and he estimates that they require seven-tenths of a policeman's time.[9] Chief of Detectives Martin Holmberg complains that paper work makes him feel like a clerk or a secretary.[10] As we have seen in the discussion of police methods, the awesome quantity of information available to policemen, most of it derived from their reports, gives them a decided advantage over the private detective, but they continue to resent paper work. Most professions require a great deal of record-keeping (as any hospital patient knows who has tried to get the attention of the nurse at the desk), and it would appear that something will need to change the bias of policemen against paper before law enforcement can become truly professional.

Prejudice against technology is not as nearly universal as the antipathy toward paper-work, but it is as intense, especially among experienced policemen who are convinced that good cop-sense is more reliable than anything the lab can come up with. The stories abound in sarcastic references to the work of the police laboratory as "crossword-puzzle-solving" and "Sherlock Holmes stuff," and to "the Great Computer in the Sky." Anything smacking of science is likely to be scorned: Patrick Petrella says at one point that instinct can be a better vehicle than science,[11] and, in the opinion of "Buddha" Ilford, the Glasgow Scientific Bureau (one of the best) is staffed by "damned jumped-up plumbers."[12] The point hardly needs belaboring: no profession in the twentieth century can subsist on horse sense.

Here is a point that will bear watching in the procedural stories of the next few years. It is possible that improved educational requirements will produce more young men and women who will be better prepared to handle report-writing than the two-fingered squadroom typist of the past, and who will more readily accommodate to the advances of police science.

Meanwhile, the evidence is that police work is not sufficiently advanced, as a profession, to permit policemen to think of the public as client or patient. They are too deeply involved in the community to develop the attitude of impersonal detachment that engineers are supposed to feel for their clients, or physicians for their patients, or professors for their students. The lack of such detachment engenders in the police an ambivalent attitude toward the public and intensifies a sense of alienation and susceptibility to the policeman's occupational disease.

The relationship of the police department to the public (usually characterized as "the public we are sworn to protect") is at best ambiguous and at worst paradoxical. Unlike the private detective of the other traditions of mystery fiction, the policeman has no client; he serves an amorphous Master that is sometimes fearful of him, occasionally hostile to him, or most often indifferent toward him. His responsibility is to his lieutenant or chief, and his loyalty is to his fellow cops. As for the law-abiding public, they seem more alien to him than the hoods and thugs whose language he speaks and whose motives he understands.

The police expect automatic hostility from certain segments of society. Practicing criminals, and their families and associates, regard cops as the natural enemy, to be respected because of their power but never trusted. Policemen expect hatred from people who have grown up as tough street kids in harsh urban neighborhoods and who retain their early hostilties into law-abiding adult life. They expect it also from the young drop-outs from society, the Flower Children and the "beat" types, to whom the cops represent the power of the Establishment they have rejected. The police have become accustomed to the names assigned to them by members of these groups, "pigs," "fuzz," and "Gestapo," and they do not react to pointed remarks by individuals who claim the power to smell a cop a mile away.

In other segments of the community there is a covert, unmotivated antipathy toward the police that seems to be almost instinctive. It manifests itself in the reaction of a small boy in

Johnny Get Your Gun (viii), who automatically thinks of the police
as "goddamn cops," and it is described by Fredrik Melander in *The
Laughing Policeman* (xix) as a latent hatred of police that exists in
all classes of society and needs only an impulse to set it off. The
reason for such compulsive hostility may be the public
misconception of the police detective as a big, tough man who
carries a gun and is easily provoked into gunplay in the street.

Or, it may be due to people's natural fear of policemen. Most
people feel nervous and even guilty, we are repeatedly told, in the
presence of a cop, searching their memories for infractions they
have committed. They are not reassured by being told that the police
are conducting a "routine investigation," because those innocent
words strike terror to their hearts. A psychiatrist in *The Con Game*
explains the fear as a result of the feelings of guilt most people
experience, which are triggered into panic in confrontation with a
guardian of law and order (vii).

Many people, for various reasons, simply do not want to get
involved in police business. Few citizens, Virgil Tibbs reflects, will
come forward to help the police when a serious crime has been
committed;[13] people will not even report offenses because the police
will then be involved, and the result is trouble. Some witnesses will
not cooperate, in the opinion of Harry Martineau, because police
investigations are long and thorough, and they can take up a lot of a
civilian's time.[14] Then there are those who, like a milk deliveryman
in the 87th Precinct, worry about the financial loss involved in
taking time off to help the police locate a murderer.[15]

Snobbery toward policemen is not uncommon, often set in the
context of the cops' middle-class position on the social scale.
Receptionists, themselves middle-class, seem to delight in
identifying with their upper-class employers and keeping the police
waiting an inordinately long time before admission to the boss'
office. Among the most commonly used civilian snubs are the Pat-
on-the-Head Gambit (What's a nice boy/girl like you doing in a
business like this?) and the Public Servant Syndrome (I pay your
wages.). Condescension to a black policeman can be especially
cutting, as when a white woman sends her maid with the tea back to
the kitchen with the pointed reminder that Virgil Tibbs is not a
guest,[16] or to a policewoman, as when a woman apartment
superintendent is surprised at the presence of Norah Mulcahaney

on an investigation: she knows there are women policemen, but she thinks they act as file clerks and such, who do not actually go out and detect.[17]

Another reaction policemen come to expect is the Perpetual Grievance, which is motivated by either of two opposite conditions. First, there is the civilian who once got a ticket for speeding and becomes forever after a cop-hater. Then there is the one-time victim of crime who greets every policeman with "Where were you when my house was robbed last year?"

Finally, there is the Robin Hood Myth, the inclination of the public to side with the underdog in the contest between policemen and criminals. George Gideon is especially annoyed when, after an especially embarrassing coup perpetrated by a band of hoodlums, the law-abiding public will grudgingly admire the daring of lawbreakers and hope they at least get a sporting chance.[18]

The one time people appreciate the police is when they need them. Fredrik Melander, who does a great deal of theorizing about the place of police in society, is of the opinion that the public considers policemen a necessary evil who on occasion are the only ones who can help them. What does a professional burglar do, Melander asks, when he wakes up during the night and hears somebody in the house? He calls the police, of course.[19] Even in New York, where people fiercely guard their privacy and resent the threat of interference, Policewoman Audrey Ochs finds herself during a crime-wave the most popular tenant of her apartment building, which has no security employees.[20]

One condition apparently unknown to the public is the degree of friction, rivalry and outright hostility in the police world, between squads within a department, between departments and between the police and the other public services. We are reminded once again of the paramilitary nature of the police force, because these rivalries recall the traditional ones between army, navy, air force and marines. They exist at all levels: within the department (squad versus squad, plainclothes detectives versus the uniformed branch, precinct versus precinct); between departments (city versus city, urban versus rural); and between the police and other services (police versus the fire department, public welfare, corrections and the like).

To a great extent the rivalries are instinctive, like the familiar hostilities between soldiers and sailors. The uniformed branch is automatically suspicious of detectives, and policemen in general are contemptuous of firemen and social workers. The friction also has a very real basis, however, in the fact that all branches and services are in competition for budget funds and for recognition and credit. Competition for funds is likely to produce chauvinistic jealousy for the reputation of the department when the police have to compete with forty other agencies for budget allocations, and during periods of financial restriction (which is most of the time, according to the stories) each department poaches on the other's manpower. The converse of the need for funding is the need for credit and reputation; in Britain the intrusion of the Criminal Investigation Department into a case is usually resented by the regular police, who know the CID will get the credit for a successful solution.

One result of this resentment is the need for diplomacy in dealing with other organizations, which is felt especially by people in the upper levels of command. Roger West is particularly careful in giving instructions to the local police because he is aware of the rivalry between Scotland Yard and the provincial forces, and he does not want to tread on sensitive toes.[21] In the same situation, Philip Hunter avoids being critical of the disposition of forces by a local chief, pointedly reminding himself that the local commander's procedure is none of his business.[22]

The emotional basis of friction-rivalry-hostility is the team spirit. Toward the public, as we have noted earlier, policemen tend to adopt an attitude of stoic resignation, and toward the criminal world a feeling of grudging kinship. Within the team, the rule is mutual defense, with the result that members of the same squad will suffer the danger of physical harm for each other, and will lie or otherwise violate regulations to cover up each other's mistakes. Let an outsider from another squad, department or service intrude on the scene, however, and the sparks begin to fly. Lennart Kollberg and Gunvald Larsson detest each other, but as members of the Swedish Homicide Squad they refrain from criticism of each other, especially in public. All such tact disappears in their dealings with other services and squads: Larsson sharply corrects a member of the fire department who calls the police "the fuzz" and tells him to shut his mouth; Kollberg purposely refuses to identify himself to a uniformed patrolman at a murder scene, traps the patrolman into threatening arrest, and then humiliates him by pulling his rank.[23] It is important to notice that, in each of these confrontations, there are three factors operating in addition to the obvious one that the antagonists belong to different services or squads. The first is status: Larsson outranks the fireman and Kollberg the patrolman. The second is territory: the nature of the crime has involved the fire department in a police case and has placed patrolmen to guard an area where plainclothes detectives are conducting an investigation. The third is personal: Larsson and the firemen are strangers, and so are Kollberg and the patrolman.

These three components very largely determine the degree and intensity of hostility between members of rival services, departments and squads. Status in the hierarchy naturally sets the tone for relationships between people from different organizations. Plainclothesmen delight in pulling rank on patrolmen, as Kollberg did; captains and lieutenants love to chew out lower-grade detectives from other precincts. The worst rank-pullers of all are medical examiners, who almost invariably put down all cops from the lower echelons. On the other hand, when equals or near-equals from different services or squads come into contact (lieutenant versus lieutenant, lieutenant versus medical examiner, detective versus lab personnel), they usually kid or amiably insult each other. The principle of territoriality, which we have already seen as a condition of fierce jealousy, becomes especially intense in contacts between rival outfits. In many cases, territories necessarily overlap, as they do when the narcotics squad becomes involved in precinct business, or when Scotland Yard is called in on a local problem. In such cases, there is customarily a give-and-take of profane and obscene insults, horseplay and banter, which serve to establish a framework for at least temporary cooperation. When there is a case of actual invasion of territorial space, however, as when members of a precinct get involved outside their own geographical boundaries, the result is more like open warfare, with threats of unfavorable reports, demotion or outright violence. There is, however, a third factor, personal relationship. Policemen who know each other or have worked together and maybe attended the Academy together will (sometimes maliciously) tolerate violation of status and territory, while strangers almost automatically square off against each other.

Policemen, as members of a tightly organized hierarchy, are extremely rank-conscious, and that sensitivity is nowhere more apparent than in the case of inter-squad rivalry. Even normally humane superiors like George Gideon, who are not oppressive in dealing with members of their own teams, almost automatically enjoy the privilege of pulling rank when they come into confrontation with a stranger from another branch. Gideon, who has stopped his car in London traffic to talk with headquarters on his radio in *Gideon's Day* is accosted by a constable who does not recognize him and who suggests that he is holding up traffic. Gideon, instead of immediately identifying himself and explaining his business, keeps the constable in suspense for a moment with a lofty remark about "talking to the Yard," chuckles over the uniformed man's discomfiture, then moves on (viii). Gideon is not a cruel person who enjoys putting people in their places, but the constable, an outsider of inferior rank, is fair game. The procedural stories are full of such episodes, the most extreme case being that of Detective Andy Parker of the 87th Squad, whose personal appearance is such that he may be easily mistaken for a hood, and who enjoys walking around other precincts in the hope of being stopped by an unsuspecting patrolman on whom he can pull his rank.[24] This kind of upstaging is naturally resented, and policemen develop a special nomenclature for superiors on the other side of organizational lines. Thus the state police, who are notorious rank-pullers, are "the supercops," and the desk man at another headquarters, taking a call from Martin Beck in *The Abominable Man*, refers to him as "that snob," making sure Beck hears him (xviiii).

A different kind of relationship comes into being when people of the same rank from different departments or squads are compelled to work together. Denied the privilege of rank-pulling, they play a game of mutual toleration, frequently expressed in terms of good-natured and irreverent insults. We have already mentioned the elaborate ritual that takes place in the 87th Precinct stories when members of the detective squad meet the pair from Homicide North or Homicide South at a murder scene. The two groups can not upstage each other because they hold comparable rank, and consequently the initial exchange takes the form of mutual kidding, ribald abuse, and accusations of ignorance. There is a beautiful example of the same kind of thing in one of Maurice Procter's stories, in which Harry Martineau of the Granchester CID has pursued a killer out into the county, into the jurisdiction of his old friend Superintendent Vanbrugh. When Martineau and Vanbrugh meet, they engage in a ceremonial exchange of insults, wherein the Superintendent accuses the Chief Inspector of heading an incompetent squad and the Chief Inspector accuses the Superintendent of running a lax district, all in good humor.[25] This sort of ritual serves as a safety-valve for emotions, asserts hierarchical status, and establishes a basis for a working relationship that is denied to people of unequal rank from different outfits.

Protocol demands that territorial limits be strictly observed, and policemen are usually scupulously careful to stay out of each other's provinces. There are, however, circumstances in which territories are not clearly defined, geographically in a case of questionable jurisdiction, organizationally in cases where services necessarily overlap, as when a specialized squad like homicide or narcotics must work inside a precinct. Territoriality is a much harder problem to deal with than rank in the persistent inter-departmental frictions, because territory is more sacrosanct than hierarchy. Thus Harry Martineau, who has no problem establishing a working relationship with his equal-opposite in the county, is told by a county police constable, "I don't take orders from you... You're off your manor."[26] Any question of jurisdiction is likely to generate heat on both sides, because it automatically raises two attendant questions: Who takes the responsibility? and Who gets the credit?

One of the basic principles is dealing with the System, as we observed in the last chapter, is that no policeman (or police team) ever takes a case off somebody else's hands, and the corollary is that nobody ever lets anybody else take over a case that is jurisdictionally his. The principle meets a severe test when Edward X. Delaney pursues a killer outside the city and runs into a confrontation with the New York State Police, who want to take over for the apprehension. Delaney beats down the State Police captain by pointing out the blunders the state man is making because of lack of familiarity with the case. The captain gets the point, especially after Delaney reminds him of the fiasco the State Police perpetrated at Attica. Botching an arrest would be bad enough, but messing up a pursuit almost successfully completed by another outfit would be disastrous.[27] The other principle involved in a territorial dispute is a question of credit. Policemen, as we have seen, are intensely conscious of the reluctance of recognition within the System and lack of appreciation by the public. No team is willing to lose status by surrendering its share of the action to an invading group, an axiom recognized by Harry Martineau in his confrontation with the constable who refused to take orders from him: the county man's concern, Martineau recognizes, is that he will be deprived of an opportunity to attract favorable notice. Even when geography is not involved, when the status of the invading outfit automatically confers jurisdiction, as when homicide moves into a precinct on a murder case, or Scotland Yard moves in on a county case, the locals are still jealous of their participation in the credit. Colin Thane, another policeman experienced in the perils of territoriality, takes pains to assure the local inspector that he and the "county lads" will get their proper share of the action, after which the CID and county men work harmoniously together.[29]

The other component that conditions the degree of conflict between services, departments and squads is that of personal relationships. People who know each other can cross territorial lines and work with each other, regardless of rank and status. We have already seen how quickly Inspector Martineau and Superintendent Vanbrugh could establish a basis for co-operation, even though Martineau was stepping into Vanbrugh's preserve. Besides the equality of rank, there is one other factor operating between these two: they are old friends who trust and respect each other. Christie Opara, who is aggressively professional in refusing to discuss her squad's business with any outsider, feels no qualms in calling up a former partner now working in another branch, who has some information she needs.[30] Neither does Trompie Kramer, who seeks the expert opinion of a friend in the fire department, in spite of the traditional mutual contempt between policemen and firemen.[31]

Among the local police there is almost automatic resentment against national secret and semi-secret security agencies. In the United States, it is the FBI, whom Pete Friedman calls "our natural enemies"[32] and whom Luis Mendoza compares with little boys playing at being James Bond.[33] In the Republic of South africa it is BOSS, the Bureau of State Security, whom Trompie Kramer

suspects of interfering in his case and whom he also accuses, in
private, of trying to be James Bond.[34] In Sweden it is "Sepo," the
National Police Board's Security Division, whose head man Martin
Beck takes delight in squelching.[35] Very rarely does any local
policeman in the procedural stories have anything good to say about
the national agencies; they are exasperated by the way the agents of
the FBI, BOSS and "Sepo" upstage the locals, refuse to share
information with them, and set their own priorities.

In view of the three factors that determine the nature and degree
of inter-service friction, it is not surprising that the regular police
feel hostility toward national agencies. Agents of the FBI, BOSS
and "Sepo" are conscious of their own superior status, and they
habitually pull rank. By the very nature of their work they are
invaders of territories. Finally, they are strangers. Considering the
nature of the status-territoriality-personal relationship syndrome,
clashes between them and the regular police are practically assured.

There is also no evidence in the stories that the public is aware of
all these rivalries at the departmental, system-wide, and nation-
wide levels, or that they would be much concerned if they were. The
question should be raised, then, whether competition between
outfits is harmful to the business of law enforcement. The evidence
is that these rivalries tend to sharpen efficiency and to build morale
by intensifying team pride and spirit. A squad will move fast, for
example, to get the job done before an outside group can come in and
hog the credit. Morale is improved when a specialized branch
(plainsclothesmen) enjoys the opportunity to feel superior to an all-
purpose one (the uniformed police) by sorting out the muddle the
inferiors have made of the case. Pride in one's own territory is
enhanced by comparing the crime-rate in the local precinct with
that of a rival department, an opportunity seldom missed by
suburban cops when they are confronted by city police. We are
reminded once again of the paramilitary nature of the police,
because their rivalries are morale-builders in providing the
occasion to feel superior to other groups, as soldiers feel themselves
superior to sailors, or vice-versa, and marines know they are
superior to eveybody else.

We have mentioned the use of informants as one of the
distinguishing features of the police procedural, and as one of the
instruments in the array of police methods. Now, however, we must

consider the informants themselves as elements in the police sub-culture. Ed McBain calls them "part of the family"[36] and rightly so, because they are very decidedly members of the System.

A useable informant has two qualifications: he must be so placed in the underworld as to have relatively easy access to information the police can use, and he must be dependable, which, as we will soon see, means that he must be vulnerable to police coercion. His position is a little like that of the scout in the Western story, in that he has feet in both camps, though he must conceal his anomalous position from the criminal camp. He is more like the "contact" of the secret agent in spy fiction, and his position is just as dangerous. A well-placed informant, however, is so valuable that there have been cases, so we are told, where a good policeman was sold down the river in order to protect a good informant. Essential as he is, however, his association with the department is never formalized. He is paid only when he delivers, the money coming from the "discretionary fund," which is also used for such purposes as narcotics buys.

The informant, as a matter of fact, is never used by the whole squad, but by a single detective who considers him private property and usually keeps his existence secret from his fellow cops. The affinity between them is naturally guarded but close, each knowing that he must trust the other. The trust, however, does not extend to other policemen; one cop's informant is still another cop's crook. As long as the informant is willing to play ball and does not get exaggerated ideas of his own power, the policeman will let him run, so long as he stays out of trouble with other cops. This freedom is the chief fringe benefit of the informant. He is permitted to practice his trade as bookmaker or in some other form of non-violent legal infraction, provided of course that he stays out of trouble and continues to serve as a source of information. He may be allowed to act as a double agent, supplying relatively harmless police information to the criminal community and thus cementing his relationships with the people on whom he will inform.

One thing he will not do is double-cross his police employer, because his recruitment as informer is based on his vulnerability as a criminal. Sometimes his susceptibility to extortion is limited, as when Gabriel Wager in *Angle of Attack* catches Jesus Quintana writing a false deposition in one case, which he promises to forget if

Quintana will inform in a more serious one (viii). Often, though, he is a permanent recruit because of his continued vulnerability: this is the case of Fats Donner, who cooperates with Hal Willis because he knows Willis has enough on him to put him away for twenty years. One other thing the informant will not do is to feed the police false or useless information, knowing that if he does he will be picked up within thirty minutes on a charge of indecent exposure. The police response to outright betrayal by an informant is drastic and ultimate. When Stoner Martin in *The Witness* discovers that Fat Man Carver has deceived him, he swears he will send Carver up if he must commit perjury to do so (xxiii).

Besides their vulnerability to arrest and the little pay they receive, what makes people become informants? In *Hideaway* Procter lists four motivations for informing: 1. The hope for a police "blind eye" toward their own petty infractions while they give information on the big ones; 2. Love of excitement and risk; 3. Love of sharing what they know with somebody else; 4. Spite or vengeance (vii). This last motive affects only a few, according to Procter, but it is strong enough for Birdy Merrick in *Gideon's Day*, whose daughter got hooked on reefers, turned to prostitution, and died at age nineteen (ii).

The pay is not large, and it is made out of unallocated funds that will not be audited, because taxpayers would undoubtedly take a dim view of such expenditures of public funds. Before the onset of double-digit inflation the rate was in the neighborhood of $10-$20 per job. In 1957 Steve Carella paid Danny Gimp $25, but only because Danny was broke, and in response Danny promised that the next one would be on the house.[37] At a critical moment in 1975 Hal Willis quickly agreed to pay Fats Donner $100, though when Donner regretted not asking for more, Willis cautioned him not to press his luck.[38] In London in the mid-1970s Patrick Petrella paid in the 10-20 pound range, and never more than 25 pounds.[39]

Informing, all the same, is a dangerous business. There is almost nothing, we are given to understand, that criminals will not do to an informant. When Harry Martineau tries to get information from Pot Eye Walker that will pin a theft on the notorious Dixie Costello, he discovers that Pot Eye, though brave, is not suicidal: to be the instrument of sending Costello to prison would be asking for premature and painful demise.[40] Statistics confirm the fear: of the twenty or so informants who play significant roles in the books we are discussing, four are killed as a result of their activities, and one, Birdy Merrick, who wanted to avenge her daughter's death, is beaten almost to death.[41]

Curiously, there is only one woman among the list of regular informants, a prostitute who is used by Virgil Tibbs.[42] There are cases where women come to the police with incriminating information, but only to spite a faithless lover or husband.

As a group, informants are shadowy figures out of the no-man's-land of society, without goals or loyalties. Many of them practice their trade because they lack the energy to make a dishonest living, and to judge by their names they tend to run to obesity: Fat Willy, Fat Man Tomlin Carver, Fats Donner. Their position in the System is paradoxical, since their activities are indispensable to law enforcement and at the same time covert and unauthorized.

Informants are, as a matter of fact, one component of a whole complex of unsanctioned and officially unrecognized methods and procedures used by the police in these stories for the propagation of justice and the maintenance of order. The Sub-Rosa System of justice, as we will call it, underlies the formal system of law enforcement and yet is not necessarily related to law because it is based upon the policemen's group interpretation of justice instead of statutes and ordinances. Most of the police detectives' efforts in the preservation of order fall into this context rather than the strict category of law enforcement. There is, among the policemen in the procedural stories, a kind of tacit mutual agreement that there are many situations where a cop must take matters into his own hands and administer justice according to his light, regardless of the law or police regulations.

The elemental manifestation of the Sub-Rosa System is what Lawrence Sanders calls "street justice," wherein the precinct policeman renders judgment and settles matters on the spot instead of making a formal arrest and filing a written report. In the case of a drunken brawl in which the parties are equally at fault, for example, he may give both a tongue-lashing, threaten arrest for disturbing the peace, and send them off in opposite directions. For every case that comes to court, according to Sanders, a hundred are settled by the administration of "street justice." Even if the case is more serious, and especially if a plainclothes detective becomes involved and charges are placed, it often happens that the charges are withdrawn and no warrants are issued, whereupon the detective fills out the proper forms and writes the required report, which will be stuffed into a file and thrown out later to make room for other paper.[43]

The Sub-Rosa administration of justice is an inherent part of the police sub-culture that must be condoned but not formally authorized. At one point in an investigation ex-Chief of Detectives Edward X. Delaney and Sergeant Abner Boone find themselves confronted by the padlocked door to the studio of a murdered artist, a door sealed by the Internal Revenue Service and not to be opened without incurring severe penalties. The Sergeant just happens to have in his possession a set of "picks," with which he speedily and expertly takes care of the padlock. Delaney compliments him and in the same breath observes that this is the first time Boone has made such an illegal entry. After this ritual obeisance to the sanctity of laws and regulations, the two policemen proceed with the practicalities of an unauthorized search essential to the solution of the mystery.[44]

Besides the instinctive desire of policeman to beat the System, there are at least two good motivations for maintaining the Sub-Rosa approach. The first is that it expedites justice in a way that would be impossible on the level of official authorization, by the simple expedient of keeping a lot of things from getting into the established channels. All police departments are badly overloaded, and one of the most troublesome sources of overwork is the mountain of paperwork that must be done for every case. If "street justice" and other short-cuts reduce numbers of arrests and the development of files and records, they more than justify their practice by keeping the system from breaking down under its own weight. The courts, as every policeman knows, have such crowded dockets that many criminals are allowed to escape retribution by plea-bargaining, and too many juvenile offenders are put back on the streets with a slap on the wrist. The Sub-Rosa System at least serves a useful purpose by keeping an enormous number of cases from ever getting to court, and besides it gives the police an advantage in the Game, which, when played according to the rules, requires that a case be not only logically satisfying but "court positive," invulnerable to attacks by defense lawyers.

At this point we should say a special word about the illegal search, widely practiced (and dangerously, because if discovered it may get an otherwise airtight case thrown out of court) in order to expedite the apprehension of criminals. Delaney and Boone are by no means the only policemen in the procedural stores who pick a forbidden lock to speed up an investigation. In special emergencies, according to Maurice Procter's *Exercise Hoodwink,* policemen make secret and illegal searches, breaking the law for what they consider to be the public good (xii). This activity is customarily carried on to the accompaniment of a ritualistic recognition of its prohibited nature. When Colin Thane in *Pilot Error* finds it necessary to have a look into an apartment, he sends away the two policemen working with him, "loids" the lock on the door with a plastic credit card, and when his fellow cops return he suggests that a break-in has occurred and they should investigate. One of them takes a look at the opened lock and asks, "Mice?" (vi).

The second motivation for the Sub-Rosa System is that policemen feel themselves justified in circumventing the law when they consider the law to be wrong. We have already observed their reactions to the Miranda-Escebedo formula, easy parole, and the permissive attitude of courts toward juvenile delinquents. The stories are also full of expressions of resentment against the principle of one law for the rich, another for the poor. A policeman should not raise questions about the law he is paid to enforce, but he can't help wondering why the laws are so scrupulous in their protection of the rights of criminals and the privileges of the wealthy and influential. It is not that the policemen in the procedurals are habitual lawbreakers, but rather that they give allegiance, collectively, to a sense of justice that occasionally transcends and may take precedence over statutory law. Private detectives in fiction, like Philip Marlowe, also habitually circumvent the law by re-arranging or concealing evidence, but always on the basis of their private ethical interpretations of a case in hand. For the policeman, subversion of laws and regulations is the result of a group consensus and is universally applied.

The policeman's clout makes it possible for him not only to make judgments of guilt and innocence but to follow up with punishment or absolution. It is relatively easy, for example, to frame a troublesome civilian, as Gabriel Wager does with the newspaper reporter Gargan in *Speak for the Dead*, after Gargan has written an insulting article that has made Wager an object of ridicule in the Department. Wager entices the newsman to a restaurant, plies him with drinks, feeds him a cock-and-bull story that sends him racing to the airport, then gets him picked up for drunken driving (xv). On some occasions a policeman can make judgments on whether or not to place charges after a serious crime. This opportunity is infrequent, because a police detective, unlike the consulting detective or the private investigator of other traditions in mystery fiction, usually works with other policemen who must share in the decision. The chance does present itself to Van der Valk in *Gun Before Butter*, however, when he has worked alone on the case and has apprehended the obviously guilty party. Van der Valk refuses to arrest the murderer, partly for reasons of personal sympathy and pity and partly on grounds that are almost metaphysical (207). Ultimately, the policeman's clout can even provide the opportunity to administer capital punishment. In two of Olle Hogstrand's stories members of "Sepo" consider the possibility, once for getting rid of a troublesome prisoner and once for disposing of a suspect.[45] The completely professional Edward X. Delaney even considers the advisability of shooting Daniel Blank when it appears that he may never be brought to justice.[46] Execution is not carried out in any of these instances, but there are other cases in which a policeman does exercise his ultimate clout. At the conclusion of *The Smack Man*, Joe Keller follows the killer of Policewoman Pamela York to Florida and kills him (218). Gabriel Wager, at the end of *Angle of Attack*, aware that Tony Ojala will not be convicted, passes word to a local gang that Ojala has betrayed them, knowing that they will do the rest (xvii).

The Sub-Rosa System is unsanctioned, but it is not effectively subversive. Policemen, who can empathize with criminals more easily than with respectable civilians, have developed a set of folkways for dealing with the criminal world, a moral code that is frequently at variance with the legitimacies of society. It is often brutal because the game is a rough one, and it sometimes puts the policeman in the position of lawbreaker. For the most part, though, it is represented in the stories as underlying and supporting the officially recognized enforcement of the law.

The whole relationship between the police world and society

seems to be set in a complex of contradictions, paradoxes and ambivalences, some of which can be understood by recognizing the nature of the police sub-culture, but others are rooted in the literary formula or in the myth, to which we will next direct our attention.

Chapter 8

Formula, Myth and Reality

Formula

LIKE ALL OTHER KINDS of popular fiction, the police procedural has developed a formula that is generally used by writers and has come to be expected by readers. Certain standard patterns, conventional situations, what John Cawelti calls "familiar shared images"[1] appear in these stories with such a degree of consistency that they substantially determine the frame of reference of the procedural tale. For example, one of the accepted conventions of the police procedural is that of the happily married policeman with family problems. In contrast to the older traditions of detective fiction, in which the detective is customarily unmarried, the expectation of the reader of the procedural is that the police detective will be a reasonably happily married man or woman; it is also part of the convention, though, that the policeman will be worried by some kind of difficulties at home, such as an unhappy spouse, an overstrained family budget or rebellious offspring. There is, of course, no reason why the policeman in any story should be unmarried, or should not enjoy a domestic life free of perplexity, but the convention of the happily married cop with some problems at home has established itself as part of the procedural formula and is consequently the rule rather than the exception.

There are several reasons for the prevalence of formula in popular fiction. One, as Cawelti points out, is that certain patterns, which have been tested and have proved successful, tend to survive as a result of audience selection.[2] Another is that conventional situations establish a common ground between writer and reader and thus become an accepted vehicle for a set of attitudes or a particular aesthetic effect (8-9). Moreover (and this one seems to hold special force in the case of the police procedural), the formula

112

answers a need for author and audience to share certain basic feelings about the world (32). We should especially mark the fact that the five components of the formula we are about to examine are stated in terms of limitations and handicaps, so that they collectively represent a conception of police work that is frustrating, unrewarding, surrounded by chance and by the probability of failure.

There are a number of other conventional frames of reference that contribute to the atmosphere and tone of these stories, like that of the happily married policeman we have just mentioned, but we will be concerned in this section with five that are employed so consistently that they may be considered as the components of the procedural formula, and they basically determine the mood of the stories and distinguish them from other types of mystery fiction:

The Ordinary Mortals: The almost universal assumption that police detectives, though usually competent in their jobs, are people of commonplace abilities, lacking both intellectual brilliance and cultural background, and incapable of heroic action.

The Thankless Profession: The conception of police work as an unrewarding job that anybody would be crazy to get into, which is scorned by the public and is humiliating to policemen.

The Tight Enclave: The image of police detectives bound together for mutual protection against the hostile public, the criminal world, and the Police Establishment.

The Fickle Breaks: The assumption that police detection, no matter how carefully practiced, is largely dependent upon sheer chance.

The Tyranny of Time: The supposition that time is always working against the police detective and that if a case is not solved quickly it will not be solved at all.

We can call these conventions the components of the procedural formula for two reasons. One is that they are practically universal, showing up in almost every novel as either stated axioms or tacit assumptions. The other is that they collectively represent the folklore of both the police and the public, generally accepted and rarely questioned.

An interesting thing happens, though, within the framework of a given story: the general assumption, stated as conventional wisdom, is contradicted by the immediate circumstances. "Everybody knows," for example, that policemen are stupid and are incapable of heroic action, but *this* policeman in *this* story is a gifted individual who is not only intelligent but capable of heroism when it is demanded. "Everybody knows," moreover, that success in police work is more often than not dependent on pure dumb luck, but the resolution in *this* story is never the result of luck alone. The paradox becomes evident in the case of each of the five components, with the single exception of the Tight Enclave, where, as we will see presently, there is no need for the immediate circumstance to contradict the convention. Otherwise, the convention states a generally accepted principle that seems to be entertained by the people in the stories, but in the current instance (the book in the hands of the reader) the assumption more often than not proves untrue.

The Ordinary Mortals

The formula dictates that the protagonists in these stories shall be policemen who are competent as cops but lacking exceptional ability or reputation. Sjowall and Wahloo pose the substance of the convention in this characterization of Fredrik Melander of the Homicide Squad in Stockholm:

He was generally known for his logical mind, his excellent memory and immovable calm. Within a smaller circle, he was most famous for his remarkable capacity for always being in the toilet when anyone wanted to get hold of him. His sense of humor was nonexistent, but very modest; he was parsimonious and dull and never had brilliant ideas or sudden inspiration. Briefly, he was a first-class policeman.[3]

The pattern varies, but this is the essential image: a practical orderliness, a disinclination to excessive zeal, a minimal sense of humor, an inclination to stinginess, and a lack of imaginative insight. In contrast to the transcendent genius of the classic formal-problem story or the knight-errant of the hard-boiled school, he would appear to be a commonplace figure indeed.

As we will see a little later, this dull image is the one the convention demands, but there is a reality beyond the appearance that tends to contradict the formula. Fredrik Melander is a good case in point: actually he has a memory that is not only "excellent" but would compete with the memory bank of a sophisticated computer, and he can at a moment's notice come up with a detailed case history of almost any criminal under investigation.

The self-image of the policeman in these stories, as we have noted earlier, is one of uncertainty and distrust of his own capabilities. If he is young, he wonders whether he will be able to measure up when he is put to the test. If he is older and more experienced, he may wonder if he is beginning to fail because his advancing age is robbing him of some of his ability. If he is in a position of responsibility, he often suspects that his decisions look bad in comparison with those of his predecessor. Often he is unsure of himself with respect to both his capabilities as a policeman and his performance as husband, father and citizen. On Ash Wednesday, when his wife Arlette goes to church to have her forehead marked and to be reminded that she is dust, Inspector Van der Valk goes to his office with the gloomy feeling that a policeman is reminded every day that he is dust.[4]

Public opinion generally concurs in this image. Most civilians are almost automatically either hostile and discourteous to policemen or indifferent to them. As far as the news media are concerned, the cops can do nothing right. If they are indulgent, they are clumsy and inept, according to the newspapers, and if heavy-handed they are brutal and provocative.

The policemen in the procedurals worry about the quality of their fellow squad-members. There are hundreds of good detectives at Scotland Yard, Roger West tells himself, but few outstanding ones.[5] Too many of the people who become policemen do so because they are not really fitted for more demanding professions, and police work does not have much to attract well-qualified applicants.

We see the sharpest image of the Ordinary Mortals when the policemen blame themselves for their inadequacies in the performance of specific duties. Being shaken on a tail-job by a not-too-experienced suspect; forgetting to supply protection for a vulnerable witness; overlooking an important clue; giving way to hatred and killing a suspect when violence is unnecessary—these are a few of the hundreds of causes for self-blame and loss of confidence.

Naturally it is part of the convention that policemen be stupid and uneducated, generally lacking in cultural background and civilized refinement. "All beef and no brains,"is what a policeman may hear muttered under the breath of a bystander, and he is not really surprised if a civilian asks him, "Did you ever go to school?" The image of the dumb cop is tacitly accepted by many of them, to the extent that even a real professional like Fred Fellows urges his son to get an education so he wont *have* to be a policeman.[6]

Finally, there are no heroes in police work. In contrast to the hazardous life of the secret agent, or the passionate world of the private investigator, the ambiance of the law officer is humdrum and shabby. Heroes, we are repeatedly told, are in short supply on a police force.

At this point a question seems appropriate: How can the authors write interesting stories about such uninteresting people? The answer is that they don't. The stories are interesting, right enough, but the policemen in them—the main characters, at any rate—are not dolts and dullards who never do anything intelligent or exciting. This sounds like a paradox, but what we want to remember is that the formula has two 'frames of reference. On the one hand, convention demands that the image of the policeman be one of insensitive, unimaginative ordinariness. At the same time, though, narrative interest requires that *this* policeman in *this* story be exciting, superior and gifted. The result is a double image, in which the protagonist perceives himself to be an ordinary cop who is only doing his job, but under the right stimulation he can perform on a level that may—and usually does—surprise himself.

Consider, for example, the reputations of the characters who have important roles in these stories. Five of them, on the basis of the testimony of other people in the stories, are already famous as detectives: John Creasey's Roger West, J.J. Marric's George Gideon, Hillary Waugh's Fred Fellows, Lawrence Sanders' Edward X. Delaney and Maurice Procter's Harry Martineau. Of the rest, the overwhelming majority are competent policemen who know their jobs and perform them well. A few are sub-standard but manage to get by, like Lawrence Treat's Mitch Taylor. The number of real incompetents is extremely small, and they are usually assigned minor roles in the stories. We are constantly reminded of the existence of these mediocre ones, and they represent the substance of the convention of the Ordinary Mortals, but the authors usually keep them in the background and bring them in only to create difficulties or to supply comic relief.

A more specific case in point is the image of the police detective who is mentally inferior, uneducated and culturally feeble. Cops in these stories don't habitually talk about their educational attainments, but we do know that Virgil Tibbs has a college degree, Frank Hastings is a Stanford graduate, Meyer Meyer has a law degree, and Max Segal finished a pre-law curriculum. Others have at least a partial university education: Vic Varallo had to drop out of Berkeley in order to support his family when his parents died, and Steve Carella was apparently maintaining a satisfactory record until "Chaucer got him." Some of them at least show evidence of a superior cultural level. Virgil Tibbs on one occasion cites a scene from *Tosca*, and Carella, for all his problems with Chaucer, can quote Shakespeare. Rinus DeGier has a good knowledge of surrealism, and Edward X. Delaney has a good enough acquaintance with painting to qualify as an "untrained amateur."

The disparity between image and reality shows up again in that part of the convention which ordains that heroes be in short supply on the police force. The actuality is that policemen are quite capable of heroism on occasion. In *Gideon's Week*, George Gideon grabs a tube of nitroclycerin just in time to keep a criminal from knocking it to the floor and killing himself and a number of policemen (xv). Frank Hastings in *Doctor, Lawyer,...* risks his own life to capture a suspect who must be taken alive (viii). Norah Mulcahaney offers herself as bait to trap the obscene-caller-murderer in *The Phone Calls* (viii). In *Hell Is a City* Harry Martineau is severely wounded while crawling along a rooftop to catch an armed criminal (IV,ii). What attracts our attention in the four cases, though, is the fact that the cops, while capable of heroism, shun heroics. "Funny thing," says Gideon just after he has retrieved that tube of explosive, "people live every day doing a job which would blow them to Kingdom Come if anything went wrong" (xv). When the newspaper reporters tell Hastings he has produced "a real macho performance, according to Lieutenant Friedman," Hastings' noncommittal response is, "If Lieutenant Friedman says so" (ix). Norah

Mulcahaney is equally modest about the operation in which she was almost killed: "I just stumbled my way through" (xv). Martineau never comments on his own heroism; his promotion to Chief Inspector speaks for itself. We get the impression that the story makes them heroes, but the convention of the Ordinary Mortals keeps them from admitting that they are.

Is there any identifiable reason for the double image, the policeman as inadequate bumpkin and the policeman as talented hero? There are two explanations, one historical and the other cultural.

The first policeman in a procedural story, Mitch Taylor in Lawrence Treat's *V as in Victim*, was conceived as a very ordinary mortal indeed, a cop who "uses most of his canniness to get out of work" and whose version of police work is casual, unsystematic and physically aggressive.[7] Mitch is a sufficiently interesting character in this story, but it is important to note that Treat substantially wrote him out of the series later, bringing him back for only occasional appearances, and transferring the narrative burden more and more frequently to the gifted police scientist Jub Freeman and the charismatic Lieutenant Bill Decker, neither of whom exercises Mitch's talent for gold-bricking, goofing off, and figuring the personally advantageous angles. Meanwhile, other writers were successfully using the competent, self-assured, even heroic policeman, like Procter's Harry Martineau, Waugh's Fred Fellows, and Marric's George Gideon. Mitch Taylor did not set the pattern for the procedural policeman, but his manner is still quite evident in the conventional outlook.

The other reason for the persistence of the convention of the Ordinary Mortals may be a product of our collective habit of thinking about all kinds of people who live and work in groups, such as policemen and enlisted military personnel. We tend to think of individuals in these groups as people who are Regular Joes, who are not "gung-ho," who don't step on each other's toes or try to do anything particularly brilliant. It is possible that most readers like to think about policemen in general as run-of-the-mill, live-and-let-live types, while at the same time demanding that *this* policeman in *this* story be a gifted, heroic type who can stimulate the excitement necessary to a good story.

The Thankless Profession

It is also conventional in the procedural that police work is almost unanimously regarded as a thankless profession. Most of the policemen in these books like the authority the badge confers, some of them believe that they are good cops with at least a satisfactory level of performance, and a few feel that they are contributing something to the stability of society, but when they talk about police work they are likely to speak of it as a "dirty, thankless job" and frankly admit that "you have to be crazy to become a cop."

We notice two things about these expressions of scorn. The first is that they are spoken by policemen to other policemen or to members of the family, never to outsiders (in keeping with the convention of the Tight Enclave). The other is that they come out most frequently at times of exasperation with the difficulties of the job, such as unproductive clues, overloads resulting from shortages of personnel, the permissiveness of courts that impose light sentences or set criminals free, and the prevalence of juvenile delinquency in what should be well-regulated neighborhoods. The total attitude of the fictional policeman, though, can be very nearly summarized as frustration, which is what Steve Carella of the 87th Precinct feels as he bends over the unconscious body of an attack victim in *'Til Death*: Carella has the impression of chasing specters, and he longs for a sport in which the rules are clearly stated and the opponent plainly visible, and he wonders, "Why the hell would anyone ever choose police work as his profession?" (xiii). Carella is not the only fictional cop who asks that question. Most of them feel the futility of a fight that can not be won, against an enemy not always easy to identify. This sense of frustration is heightened by an awareness of lack of appreciation that shows itself in their low pay, in the attitudes of the public toward them, and the senseless regulations that hinder them instead of making their job easier.

The assumption is universal, with concurrence from all kinds of policemen of various nationalities. "Being a policeman is not a profession," a Budapest policeman tells Martin Beck in *The Man Who Went Up in Smoke*. "And it's certainly not a vocation, either. It's a curse" (xvii). Judging from their own accounts, we must conclude that most of the people in the stories never wanted to become policemen in the first place but drifted into the job because of the influence of a trusted uncle or some other respected acquaintance who was a cop. Being in, they find two conditions that contradict their original expectations. The first is that police work is largely tedium and boredom, short on exciting chases and shoot-outs, long on filling out forms and filling in time, and chiefly following dull routines. The other disappointment is the lack of public appreciation for the status of the policeman, to the extent that they expect only hostility or indifference and are surprised when somebody from outside the police world even offers to be helpful.

Sociologists, who are not generally esteemed by policemen anyhow, can even present figures to prove that police work is no more dangerous than the jobs of construction workers, lumberjacks, taxi drivers or housewives. In *The Abominable Man* (x) Martin Beck takes a dim view of a sociological report that refutes the generally held belief that a policeman's lot is riskier and harder than any other. The reason policemen consider themselves as leading more dangerous lives than anyone else, according to the authors, is that no other professional group suffers from such strong "role fixation" or dramatizes its daily life to such a degree as policemen do.

One source of constant frustration is the whole complex of regulations which are supposed to regularize and facilitate performance in police work but which are almost universally regarded as senseless red tape that leads to duplication of effort and ties a policeman's hands. The consensus is that the tangle of regulations is getting worse and worse every year, with more and more bright bureaucrats creating work for other people to do and more and more forms to fill out. Some day, Harry Martineau predicts, there will be a form for going to the toilet.[8]

In view of the thankless nature of police work as it is represented in these novels, we might expect policemen to resign from the profession in large numbers. Actually, they do not, at least not the main characters. All policemen have ideas about quitting and trying something else, Jack Tallon tells his wife, but the real pros stay on because police work is their life.[9] This is the case with Roger West in *Alibi* (xvii), who turns down a job with a private security outfit at four times his present salary, and Colin Thane in *The Tallyman* (viii), who declines an offer from the Central Bank of Scotland at double his present pay, plus good hours and guaranteed vacations. The notable exception is Lennart Kollberg, an excellent policeman who has wanted to get out of police work for years and finally turns in his resignation at the end of *Cop Killer*. Others stay on for a variety of reasons: they like the job security of public service, or they like working under the superiors assigned to them, or—in a few cases—they honestly believe they are doing some good in the world. They continue to complain about the "thankless job," of course, but there are indications that the bitching serves a therapeutic function, like the ritual banter and horseplay.

Here is another instance where narrative necessity takes precedence over convention. Even the best of policemen complain about the thankless nature of the job, but the writers can not allow them to resign in any considerable numbers, because such turnover would ruin the continuity of the series. It is significant that Sjowall and Wahloo, even though they finally allowed Lennart Kollberg to quit the force, brought him back for a minor role in *The Terrorists*, apparently feeling that readers would miss him.

Of those policemen who do leave the force, most apparently take jobs in the private security sector. The characters in the novels are constantly running into former colleagues who are now working as industrial security police, porters or night-watchmen. The fact that these people have taken jobs that entail the same kinds of competence and predilection, without the long hours, the regulations and the paper work, may be an indication that what they really like is the benefits of the policeman's clout without the attendant frustrations.

The Tight Enclave

Another of the "familiar shared images" is the Tight Enclave, a conception of the police community whose members cover for each other's derelictions and infractions, who take a superior, exclusive attitude toward the non-police community, and who are ready to avenge at all costs any threat of violence to their fellow officers.

The basic motive for the solidarity of the Tight Enclave is the need for security in a dangerous job. There are only two places on earth where a cop feels safe enough to relax, says Burns' Gabriel Wager, home and the unit headquarters.[10] Consequently, as another policeman observes, they are like the inmates of a jail, banded together against the rest of the world.[11] The security available to the policeman operates in two contexts. On the one hand, he belongs to a vast and powerful organization that protects its members: even in his worst moments, surrounded by hostility, a policeman knows that he has only to put out a call for help and it will be immediately answered by overwhelming force. Within this formal structure, however, he is also a member of a fraternity of cops who return favor for favor and who will cover for each other in the face of the civilian world and the Police Establishment. Thus we have a double-walled fortress, the authority of the Department that will get a fleet of squad cars on the scene the moment a policeman is threatened, and the Tight Enclave of cops who will subvert the authority of the Department to protect other cops. They may not like each other, but they stick together.

Consequently they do not make accusations against each other, because their personal ties are stronger than the official ones. "The average cop," says Lawrence Treat's Jub Freeman, "if he happened to see an infraction on the part of another cop, kept his mouth shut."[12]

We get the impression, as a matter of fact, that the system of favors is the cement that holds the fraternity together. Where a minor infraction of the rules or dereliction of duty is concerned, it is routine for people of the same rank to cover for each other. Superiors also cover for subordinates. When Detective Superintendent Matt Anders discovers that one of his men has been suspended for unauthorized use of of a police car, Anders writes out a retroactive order that will remove the basis for the charge, the reason being that Anders needs him back on duty.[13] Preservation of the team takes precedence over formal regulations; almost invariably, a "good man" (or woman) is to be protected, even against the Police Establishment.

The test of the solidarity of the Enclave comes about in the case of a crime or suspicion of crime committed by a policeman. Here the cement that binds the Enclave is severely strained, because the fellow cops find themselves caught in an ambivalent position between natural sympathy and an ingrained sense of duty. When Detective Sergeant Micklewright in J.J. Marric's *Gideon's River* is accused of wife-beating, the attitude of half the Yard is, "Poor devil—shows coppers are human, too," and the other half, "He's let the Force down" (xviii). In most cases, however, the cops almost automatically cover for each other. When Detective Bert Kling and two other members of the 87th Squad go to arrest the murderer of Kling's fiancee, Kling attacks the man and beats him almost to death, while a fellow-officer is already mentally composing a report which would explain how the murderer was resisting arrest.[14] One problem in this connection is a public awareness that, when a policeman is accused, other policemen will automatically cover for him, and the sense of distrust between policemen and civilians is intensified.

It is almost essential to morale and the sense of professionalism that civilians be excluded from the police world. Admissions of weakness and shortcomings in the department are not permitted outside the group. Lawrence Sanders' Captain Edward X. Delaney is annoyed by the fact that young cops don't look like cops, but he would never tell a civilian that.[15] A county sergeant in Procter's *Hideaway* resents the way the CID pushes the locals around and hogs the credit: "Not that you'd let an outsider say it," a CID inspector adds, and the sergeant agrees (x). Civilians are not part of the code; they are messy, and they spoil the efficiency of the group. This is the reaction of Lieutenant Frank Hastings in *Power Plays*, when the daughter of a victim almost gets herself and him killed by an armed hoodlum: "It always happened, when civilians meddled in police business" (xx). Vigilante operations are not only a nuisance but an affront to the profession: "People playing at being vigilantes," George Gideon calls them in *Gideon's Power* (iv). Fundamentally, though, the real basis for exclusion is the fact of identity. "It's just that you're not a cop," Captain Delaney tells a reporter who complains that the police won't talk to him. "You don't belong. There's a gulf."[16]

One good device for building morale in a group is a sense of superiority to the outside world. It is better to be the lowest-ranking cop in the department than to be a simple civilian, because civilians are stupid, they can't be trusted, and they don't understand police work. When one of the cops in Procter's *Exercise Hoodwink* suggests that inquiries be made in certain mercantile establishments, he is immediately overruled: "No. You can't trust a civvie not to talk" (xiii). Just being accused of a civilian-level mentality is enough to bring the strongest-minded policemen around, as Detective Sergeant Norah Mulcahaney discovers when she refuses to enter the hospital after being attacked and chloroformed. "Oh, yes, you are," says another policeman. "You are going to behave like a mature, sensible police sergeant and not like a dumb civilian." That does it. Norah goes to the hospital.[17]

The extreme violation of the police community, and consequently the real test of the Tight Enclave, comes into being when a policeman is murdered. After a cop-killing, all other cases seem unimportant. A new sense of unity takes hold, since nothing can galvanize a police department like the knowledge that one of their own has been gunned down. Personal feelings toward the victim no longer apply; he may have been the biggest SOB on the squad, but his killer automatically becomes the Most Wanted Man. We are told, moreover, that the surest way to get caught is to kill a policeman; a great many cases may go unsolved, but never a cop-killing. Working hours and vacations are forgotten, with the members of the squad coming in for voluntary overtime or cutting short their treasured holidays. Professional objectivity becomes irrelevant. One of Gilbert's policemen in *Blood and Judgment* cares very little what happens ultimately to his victims, "unless they happened to have killed a policeman, in which case they ought to be hanged" (x). The motive in the search for a cop-killer is not justice but revenge. When a police officer has been murdered, Captain Delaney tells himself, "all cops become Sicilians." Corruption, ineptitude, even cowardice of the victim are forgotten; the community has been violated, and every member of the force has suffered accordingly.[18]

The ultimate development of the Tight Enclave is the police union, which formalizes and legitimizes the need for group security. Now, it is important to notice that, in the stories in which the union appears, the real professionals have reservations about it. Norah Mulcahaney is not a union member, and her feelings regarding the aims of the PBA are mixed, but when two thousand off-duty cops demonstrate at Yankee Stadium, pull down police barriers, and release hundreds of young hoodlums to prey upon the public, it is, in Norah's words, a night of shame.[19] Gabriel Wager is more openly bitter toward the unionization of the Denver Police Department. He does unauthorized overtime without pay, knowing it will irritate the union, which he enjoys doing anyway.[20] "If you're so goddamned professional," one of his fellow officers asks, "why in hell don't you belong to the union?" "The union doesn't make better cops," is Wager's reply. "It just makes more lawyers."[21]

Here is a contradiction between the sense of professionalism and the need for the security of the group. In the three books just cited, one by Lillian O'Donnell and two by Rex Burns, there are indications that the conflict between professionalism and unionism in the police force will not be easily resolved.

The convention of the Tight Enclave is an important component of the procedural formula, because it underscores one of the important differences between this type of detective fiction and the traditional formal-problem story and also the private-eye hard-boiled story. Sherlock Holmes, Hercule Poirot, and Nero Wolfe are essentially individualists. They have their Watson, their Hastings, and their Archie Goodwin only as assistants, not as equals or colleagues. The same is true of the private investigators of the Hammett-Chandler tradition, who are loners by both choice and disposition. "What," Nadya Aisenberg asks, "keeps the Hammett world from becoming sheer anarchy? The answer lies in the simple integrity of the lone detective."[22] Obviously, things have changed in the procedural tale. Down the mean streets of Raymond Chandler's world another man must go, not because he is not himself mean, or tarnished, or afraid, but because he is a cop and it is his job. Most importantly, he does not go alone. He is a member of a fellowship that will rush to his aid if he is physically threatened, cover for him if he gets into trouble with the public or the Department, and track down and convict his murderer if he is killed.

The Fickle Breaks

The element of chance is not allowed to play a determinant role in the classic detective story, because the formal-problem tale, with its heavy emphasis on ratiocination, must not depend for its solution on the way the breaks fall. Reliance on chance and accident was, moreover, considered to be unfair to the reader and hence forbidden by the "Rules of the Game." Thus we see S.S. Van Dine laying down the principle in Rule 5 of his "Twenty Rules": "The culprit must be determined by logical deductions—not by accident or coincidence or unmotivated confession"; and Ronald Knox in Commandment VI of his "Decalogue": "No accident must ever help the detective."[23] The hard-boiled story is set in a chancier world, but the private investigator of the Hammett-Chandler-Macdonald tradition tends to make his own breaks. "Hammett's reversal of the trap of naturalism," says Robert Edenbaum in his interpretation of the Flitcraft "parable" in *The Maltese Falcon*, "gives his heroes a kind of absolute power over their own destiny, a daemonic power...."[24]

There is no rule for the exclusion of chance in the police procedural, and the cops in these stories have little power over the fickle breaks, daemonic or otherwise. Virgil Tibbs has learned from his ten years in police work how the perverse breaks can go against the police: "For every good one that came along at least three others seemed to go the wrong way."[25] Policemen, according to these stories, are dogged by the unpredictable and the unexpected; they rely on their own dedication to thoroughness of detail and to following up every promising lead, but even so there is never any certainty in police work. There are indications that, if St. Michael is the patron saint of policemen, Lady Luck is at least the Good Fairy.

Sometimes the bad breaks are the result of pure rotten chance, as when Mitch Taylor sneaks a ham sandwich on a stakeout, gets ptomaine poisoning, and lets a gunman escape.[26] More often they have their origin in the overwhelming complexity of the police world, where important clues get lost in the unmanageable flood of available information, or where one policeman has access to something vital but fails to communicate it to the people working on the case because he does not recognize its significance. An example of the first type occurs in Hogstrand's *On the Prime Minister's Account*, in which the public, "The Great Detective," calls in such a rash of tips that the cop on the phone misses the really important one (51-2). There are numerous examples of the second one, as when Arthur Brown takes Steve Carella's place at a lineup in McBain's *The Con Man*. Carella misses seeing the murderer he is seeking, and of course Brown does not make the connection (xi).

Sometimes, of course, the breaks fall right side up and the police get lucky, but they are likely to be appalled at their dependence on pure dumb luck. "It's frightening to think that, but for sheer chance, we would have known nothing about it," says Superintendent Matt Anders in reference to a kidnapping which came to the attention of the police only as the result of the persistence of a suspicious civilian.[27] Often the good breaks come not as a result of the favors of Lady Luck but rather from the propensity of criminals for making mistakes. Consider, for example, the case of Roger Broome, who commits the perfect crime in McBain's *He Who Hesitates*, gets drunk four and a half years later in *Shotgun*, and makes a public confession. Not all cases are so dramatic; more often than not, a criminal will escape detection in one case only to get caught in the perpetration of a later felony.

Policemen learn to live with the breaks, morever. One device for coping with chance is the propagation of a myth. You make your own breaks, says Edward X. Delaney, knowing that this is not exactly true. The important thing is to know how to recognize good fortune when it comes, because luck wears a thousand disguises, including calamity.[28] Another way of dealing with the breaks is to develop a nose for the odds, as Christie Opara does in *The Bait*. This is "the unteachable part of police work: the intuitive chance-taking of being a good police officer" (ix).

Actually, no major case in the procedurals is solved by pure chance, though the solutions to some are delayed by bad breaks. This is another convention whose truth is generally assumed by the police, but the authors of the stories, keeping faith with the traditions of mystery fiction, will not leave too much to chance. McBain's handling of Roger Broome's perfect murder is a choice example: as it stands, the conclusion of *He Who Hesitates* is satisfying and logical, and the ironic tone is preserved. To have the case broken by a confession at the end of the story would be a letdown; to have it happen years later in the midst of another case preserves the myth of the convention without doing violence to narrative interest.

Later in this chapter we will take a look at certain myths that are almost always present as part of the atmosphere of the procedural story but must be denied in specific instances because of the dictates of narrative necessity. The convention of the Fickle Breaks is a good example. Policemen operate in an uncertain world from which the neat logic of the classic story is missing, and they lack the powers of the heroic private investigators to control their own destinies, because they must be Ordinary Mortals, but they are still characters in the mystery fiction tradition, and the resolutions of their stories are still controlled by the obligation of their authors to play fair with the readers.

The Tyranny of Time

One component of the formula remains to be considered, the Tyranny of Time. The assumption in this case is that time works against the police to the extent that if a case can not be solved quickly, it is not likely to be solved at all.

George Gideon states the principle succinctly: "If you don't find 'em quick you often don't find 'em at all."[29] Gideon is speaking of kidnapped children, but the premise applies as well to perpetrators, to stolen property and to useful clues. In the case of a homicide, which most of the stories involve, the formula is more specific: if the case is not solved within the first forty-eight hours, the probability of its ever being solved drops off rapidly toward zero. We are told, moreover, that the police usually know within twenty-four hours who did it. A special problem arises when the police are called in after the case is cold; this kind of thing often happens in fiction, because it gives the author an opportunity to develop the mystery while the corpse cools and the murderer covers his tracks. To the police, though, every hour that passes before they get on with the investigation will prolong their work by many hours, or days, or weeks. Trompie Kramer, in one of McClure's South African stories, remembers an old Bantu saying about delay: "It is better to fill your belly with the meat of the bush pig before seeking out the buck whose droppings are dry."[30]

For this reason the cops in the procedural stories envy the leisurely pace afforded detectives in other types of mystery fiction. Television detectives are given all the time in the world, says Gabriel Wager, to work on a single case.[31] On the other hand, as Swedish Detective Sergeant Gustavsson puts it, "You can't start playing at Sherlock Holmes every time one comes across a dead bum."[32]

Holmes' advantage, and that of the television detectives, is that they have the happy privilege of working on one case at a time. The procedural authors, though, know that this can not be the way things are in real life police work, and they consequently habitually burden their protagonists with heavier case loads than an understaffed force can handle, with the result that police never have enough time for anything. Perpetual overwork leads to all kinds of short-cuts, like permitting a murderer to cop an insanity plea and thus save the court's time, or the administration of "street justice," whereby the policeman on the scene settles most minor cases on the spot and never lets them get to the arrest stage.

Besides the pressure of overwork, there are all kinds of circumstances that make time the tyrant. In one of Knox's stories, Colin Thane is told that a current murder must be cleared up in a couple of days because the upcoming championship football match, to be played in Glasgow, will necessitate the re-assignment of every available policeman.[33] Politics may provide the pressure, as in Uhnak's *The Investigation,* where a quick solution to a homicide is needed in order to help the district attorney's bid for election as mayor (I,xiv). And of course certain types of crimes automatically demand fast work: if a stolen baby is not recovered quickly, the problem may be murder and not kidnapping.

Superiors are bad about putting police detectives under time-pressure, and the worst of these is William "Buddha" Ilford, commander of the Millside (Glasgow) Division. In *The Tallyman* he tells Thane that he must have a notorious loan-shark under indictment by the next term of the court, or "someone's head goes on the chopping block" (ii). In that story "Buddha" is himself under pressure from an indignant judge, but he is also capable of pushing his subordinates to justify his pride in his squad, as when he bets the chief of the Scottish Crime Squad in *Live Bait* that Thane will have a difficult case wrapped up within two weeks (i).

Then, as might be expected, there are pressures from outside the department. The hostile public is likely to be critical of anything that looks like time mis-spent and is quick to accuse the police of wasting the taxpayers' money and time. The pressure may take a more specific direction, however, when outsiders have a personal interest in a case. This kind of thing happens when the chief of detectives tells his subordinates he has been getting pressure from the chief of police, who is in turn being called by the friends of the victim.

Considering the high-speed technology and mobility available to criminals, it is not surprising that the factor of time-stress is getting worse. Sherlock Holmes could shut himself up with a pound of shag and spend a day thinking things through before he began a course of action, but the policeman of a century later must move, and fast. The leisurely response almost ruins an old-style cop in Gilbert's *The Night of the Twelfth*. Sergeant Callaghan takes his time about getting word to his superintendent, with the result that the trail is cold before the hunt is mounted. Later in the story his superiors agree that the only question they face is how stiff Callaghan's punishment must be in order to make him an example (i,ii). We should not waste sympathy on the Sergeant, who ought to have put his call through before making himself a nice cup of tea, but we can sympathize with all those hard-pushed policemen who must move so fast that they do not have time to think and whose professional lives are geared to the phrase, "not a second to lose."

The time-convention presents us with another of those curious ambiguities we have observed in connection with most of the other components of the procedural formula. The principle, on which there is general agreement in these stories, is that if you don't catch them quickly you don't catch them at all, and if a homicide is not solved within forty-eight hours the chances are that it will never be solved. The fact is that most of the crimes dealt with in the novels take much longer than forty-eight hours. Actually, a month would be closer to the average than two days. Many of the minor cases are cleared up very quickly (and a considerable number are never solved at all), but the major crimes—those that make up the narrative content—take considerably longer.

As a matter of practical necessity, most cases can not be wrapped up in forty-eight hours if the writer hopes to extend the suspense through a novel of 150-200 pages. Marric's *Gideon's Day*, which covers a time-span of fifteen hours, is an exception, and so is McBain's *Hail, Hail, the Gang's All Here!* which represents a twenty-four hour day. Usually, though, a full-length novel needs more time, and as in the earlier cases, narrative necessity takes precedence over convention.

In four of the five components of the procedural formula, then, we have a kind of double image, a paradox that asserts the pervasive convention as part of the folk-wisdom of police life, while the specific instance contradicts it. The single exception is the convention of the Tight Enclave, for which the action of the stories concurs in the overall assumption.

We might describe the phenomenon in terms of stereotype and

denial, the stereotype of the cop as an ordinary person without special gifts being contradicted by the present instance of the cop who is capable of brilliance and heroism. Or, we might borrow from the terminology used in teaching the structure of fiction, "enveloping action" and "immediate action," the enveloping action constituting everything that happened before this story started and everything that will happen after it ends, which constitute the frame of the convention, and the immediate action being the things that happen within the time-frame of the present story, which constitute the denial of the convention. The effect is that the stereotype or the "enveloping action" gives lip-service to a generally accepted principle (success in police work is largely dependent on luck). The denial of the stereotype, which is the "immediate action," contradicts the principle (the outcome of a given case is never the result of luck alone).

The reason for the contradiction, as we have seen, is the necessity for telling a good story: the folk-wisdom is that police work is a thankless job, but the writer of a series can not afford to let his or her main characters resign in favor of something more gratifying. The one exception is the convention of the Tight Enclave, which presents no narrative problems; the cops can stick together in the face of the rest of society without any damage to the story.

The real reason for the double image is not hard to see when we remember that the procedural policeman has a non-fictional counterpart; almost everybody knows what real policemen are like, and we readily accept such conventions as the Ordinary Mortals and the Thankless Profession. As we have said earlier, however, an author who would undertake to adhere strictly to reality, to write a suspenseful mystery involving ordinary mortals in a job they will leave at the first opportunity, has undertaken a task of surpassing difficulty for a single novel and practical impossibility for a series. The solution, which most of them manage successfully, is to give allegiance to the enveloping stereotype while denying it in the present story.

We should not miss the curious reversal that becomes involved in this process. The "reality" of the world of non-fiction becomes the myth of the story. In the next section of this chapter we will examine the place of myth in the procedural, keeping in mind that the formula itself is largely grounded in mythic components.

Myth

One of the special qualities of detective fiction has always been its ability to create a reality of its own. Formula accounts for some of this ability; as John Cawelti says, "...The formula creates its own world with which we become familiar with repetition."[34] The result is the creation of myth, to which readers give assent and with which they feel comfortable.

Especially in detective fiction (and possibly to only a slightly less degree in science fiction), myth serves to set limits of acceptance. Situations are accepted as part of the normal scheme of things that would be alarming or merely ridiculous without the overriding authority of myth. Undoubtedly one of the major differences between the person who loves detective fiction and reads it avidly, and the person who considers it merely artificial and sensational, is the degree to which each is willing to concur in these limits of acceptance.

Consider, for example, the remarkable career of John Putnam Thatcher, Emma Lathen's gifted amateur series detective. Thatcher is a banker of conservative habits, Vice-President of the eminently respectable Sloan Guaranty Trust. In each of the stories Thatcher finds it necessary to undertake some kind of operation to protect the interests of the Sloan—and, as surely as he does, somebody gets killed. Such a state of affairs would be infamous if we take the stories too seriously, or merely silly if we do not take them seriously enough. To the reader who has learned to live with and enjoy the myth, however, each of Thatcher's coincidental murder cases is accepted as the opportunity for a first-rate mystery.

Myth is a means of interpreting the world and organizing our experience of reality. "Since myths offer explanations maintained through ritual," says Nadya Aisenberg, "...they provide the concord which man seeks to make of his life."[35] Myth does not necessarily reveal the patterns behind the chaos of the world, nor does it necessarily simplify the world, as Jan Van Meter points out, but it does provide us with a comprehension of the "what" and "how" of ourselves and the world.[36] In this sense, myth states those basic (and often sub-conscious) assumptions that allow us to make sense of our relationships with our own ambiance.

In fiction, myth may or may not serve as a correlative of non-fictional reality. A little earlier we referred to the convention of the happily married policeman, which is generally accepted in the procedural stories. Very few of these cops are divorced; several enjoy marriages that are blissful, and most have marriages that are at least reasonably satisfactory. Statistics from the real world, though, show just the opposite: the divorce rate among policemen is considerably higher than that of the general population.[37] The circumstance is, apparently, that readers feel more comfortable with the image of the well-married fictional policeman, which becomes one of those "collective shared fantasies" of popular fiction.

Which reminds us that one of the fundamental qualities of any myth is its *usefulness*. When a myth ceases to have applicable value, it dies out, usually replaced by some other myth with other limits of acceptance. When the convention of the happily married policeman becomes unacceptable to readers and authors (regardless of the real state of affairs in the external world), we will see a change in the family patterns in the stories.

The mythic element in the classic formal-problem detective story is the theme of W.H. Auden's often-cited essay "The Guilty Vicarage." Auden sees parallels between the detective story and the classical Greek tragedy: the peaceful state before the murder is equated with the false innocence at the beginning of the tragedy; the solution of the crime by the detective with the location of guilt in the tragedy; and the arrest of the murderer and the resulting peaceful state of society with catharsis and restoration of innocence, as in the Aristotelian description of tragedy.[38] Later in the same essay he suggests a parallel between the detective story and the Eden myth, wherein the state of innocence (cosmos) is disrupted by the invasion of evil (chaos), final expiation is achieved and the community restored to the state of grace (403-4). The task of the detective (the deliverer from outside the stricken society) is to discover the guilt, to restore the innocence of the community, and finally to retire from the scene (406). Other critics, largely following Auden's lead, have found parallels between the design of the classic detective story and the Oedipus myth, where "murder pollutes the land" and where guilt must be atoned in order for society to be redeemed.

The mythic elements in the hard-boiled private investigator story have also been variously examined, probably most

successfully by George Grella in "Murder and the Mean Streets."
Grella makes two important comparisons. One is the parallel of the
private detective of the Hammett-Chandler school with the knight-
errant of chivalric legend. The task of the detective in these stories is
not only to seek the truth, says Grella, but to do battle against evil,[39]
which is not a temporary fall from grace (as in the formal-problem
story) but a ubiquitous fact (419). The other point of comparison in
this essay lies in the identification of the archetype of the tough
detective hero as Cooper's Leatherstocking, who, like the hard-
boiled dicks of fiction, is technically skilled, courageous, basically
anti-intellectual, and critical of all established institutions (414).
"The detective is finally alone," says Grella, "not only because the
romantic hero is doomed to solitude, but because he is too good for
the society he inhabits. Although not a perfect man, he is the best
man in his world" (418).

   In the discussion of the components of the procedural formula
we have already identified several mythic elements, those
presumptions of reality within the stories not necessarily confirmed
in the narrative experience. Several others are recognizable, though
they do not dominate the stories to the degree that they can be
considered formulaic. Two of these are cosmic myths, which are of
special interest in this context because they illustrate some of the
differences between the police procedural and the older traditions of
detective fiction.

   First, there is the myth of the Moral Absolutes, which represents
police work as engagement in the struggle of Good versus Evil,
Right versus Wrong. In the stories of Elizabeth Linington
(including those she writes as Dell Shannon) the struggle is
expressed in religious terms, God versus Satan, Truth versus Error,
Good versus Bad, with "no fuzzy edges." Elsewhere, the myth is
maintained without theological overtones but with emphasis on a
loyalty that has the practical value of building morale and
upholding standards. As far as Steve Carella is concerned, law
enforcement is the good guys against the bad guys, and he is one of
the good guys.[40] Patrick Petrella would agree: the police force is an
army, and criminals are the enemy.[41] A cop has to see things in
terms of black and white, of Yes and No, Edward X. Delaney tells
himself, because in police work there must be a rock standard and an
iron law.[42] There are others, though, who hold to the myth because it

is comfortable. These are the insensitive, unprofessional policemen with one-track minds who simplify all humanity into good people and bad people, with nobody left over.

There are dissenters, however, who reject the myth of Moral Absolutes and the battle of Good versus Evil, thinking rather in terms of blurred lines of distinction. Sometimes their attitudes are based on a kind of moral relativism, as in the case of Steve Carella's colleague on the 87th Squad, Meyer Meyer. Like Carella, Meyer thinks in terms of good guys and bad guys, but he is not always sure which are which.[43] Peter Van der Valk believes there are very few good men, and perhaps even fewer bad ones, but plenty of silly and stupid ones.[44] Sometimes it is not any moral bias but rather human sympathy that rejects the myth, as when George Gideon thinks about the crooks of London who also have patient wives, and children who go to school hungry.[45] In many cases the refusal to accept the Good versus Bad dichotomy is based on the very practical necessity for getting inside the criminal's mind, learning to understand how he thinks and works, establishing a community with him.

It may be that these two attitudes, myth and denial, represent the twofold heritage of the police procedural from the older traditions, the classic story with its affirmation of moral absolutes and the hard-boiled story with its inclination toward situational ethics and the individualistic sense of justice.

There is another cosmic myth in the procedural from which there is almost no dissent. This is the perception of the war that can never be won, the battle that must always be fought over, and here is the sharpest difference between the orientation of the police procedural and that of the classic formal-problem tale of detection. When the community is returned to the state of grace at the conclusion of the classic story, says Auden, "innocence is restored, and the law retires forever" (403). The detective who brings about the atonement is a total stranger from outside the community, who must not possibly be involved in the crime. This, says Auden, excludes the local police (406). As members of the community they share the general guilt, and they can not withdraw when the taint of a single crime is removed. Thus the never-ending war between police and criminals, says George Gideon, the inevitability of crime, which never stops.[46] Nor can there be any respite after the solution of a single case, because there is always another battle ready to be fought. At the end of a particularly difficult investigation, Steve Carella senses that everything is wrapped up and in place, "just like in a phony mystery novel." But the phone on his desk is ringing again, calling him to move on into the next case.[47] In a war where there are no final victories and where one battle is not complete until another one must be joined, zeal gives way to boredom, and we can empathize with the patrolman in one of Rex Burns' stories who has been assigned the unpromising task of digging up the grounds in search of a body that obviously is not there. "What the hell," says the cop, cheerfully tossing up dirt, "the pay's the same."[48]

This attitude engenders another myth which, like some of the components of the formula examined earlier, gains broad assent in the procedural story but is denied by the demands of the immediate story. "The dullsville security of Civil Service" Pete Friedman calls it,[49] and policemen generally call it a dull, deadly bore, apathetic routine, leg work, a waiting game. There are not many exchanges of gunfire and car-chases in police work, and even fewer cases involving rare untraceable poisons or ancient family secrets. This is the myth, but the immediate reality in a given story contradicts it. The frame is the Dullsville World, but *this* case is the exciting exception.

Another myth denied by narrative necessity is the Unsolved Case. The image of the Open File (the repository of unsolved crimes) is imminent in the police procedural, and statistics quoted in the stories are nothing short of alarming: 50% of Scotland Yard's cases have been unsolved over a four-year period; in Denmark, only 25% of cases are ever solved; in America, 70% of homicides go unsolved; and so on.[50] The myth naturally represents another break with other traditions of detective fiction, where nothing is ever unsolved. Actually, though, the myth is only a part of the atmosphere that produced the conventions of the Ordinary Mortals and the Fickle Breaks; in each immediate context it is honored more in the breach than in the observance, because writers of mystery fiction must keep faith with their audiences, and *this* case in *this* story is always solved, at least the ones that have held the reader's interest. In a few instances—a very few—cases are left hanging, but they are always minor.[51]

These apparent paradoxes in the formulaic and mythic

elements of the police procedural are symbolic of the commitments of fictional policemen, which are bound up in a whole set of ambiguities and even ambivalences. Publicly and officially, the policeman is enlisted in the struggle of Right against Wrong, for the defense of society. Privately, he may wonder if much of society is worth defending, or if it always represents the Right. He is constantly reminded, moreover, that even if he is on the side of good and virtue, the struggle can never be finally won. Unlike his predecessors in the older traditions of detective fiction, he can not be the genius from outside that restores the community to its original state of grace, partly because he is very much part of that community and partly because he knows that it was never in a state of grace to begin with.

Reality

At first glance the creation of "realism" in the police procedural should present very few problems. A writer who wants to produce this kind of story would familiarize himself or herself with police detectives and their work, with the methods of criminology and the laws of evidence, and then proceed to weave these things into a narrative. The problem is that (at least so the myth tells us) policemen are lacklustre characters, police work is largely dull and deadly routine, and the cases with which police deal are prosaic and lacking in excitement. Any author who insisted upon so literal a representation of reality would soon find himself with his audience limited to a few readers interested in the sociology and psychology of crime. Hillary Waugh, who has been more successful than most other mystery writers in the development of the sense of reality, explores the question in a highly perceptive essay and sums up: "My personal guess is that total reality can never exist in mystery fiction and my definite conclusion is that it certainly can not exist in the procedural."[52]

The question of the kind and amount of "realism" in the detective story has long been a subject for debate. The classic tale of the Poe-Conan Doyle formula has been criticized as artificial, stylized, far removed from the dirty world of "real" crime. The hard-boiled story of the Hammett-Chandler world was intended, at least in part, to restore reality to the detective story by moving it out of the well-appointed drawing-room and the fumed oak library and into the dark alley where it belonged, and by taking it out of the manicured hands of the transcendent genius and giving it back to the people who really knew how to handle it. The question remained, though, whether the tough private eye story had not substituted one kind of fantasy for another. Is Lew Archer's Hollywood any more "realistic" than Sherlock Holmes' London, or the intense, lone knight-errant more real than the urbane dabbler in incunabula? It might be more productive to ask how much and what kind of reality readers want, or how much the detective story can tolerate without being changed into something else.

The problem of reality in mystery fiction (and this would certainly apply to the police procedural) is not one of literal representation of objective reality, but of plausibility. In the case of any story, the problem of the writer is to induce the reader to accept *this* situation as real, to set the limits of acceptance just broad enough to make the story interesting without setting them so wide that the situation becomes fantastic or ridiculous.

As we have seen in the discussion of the convention of the Ordinary Mortals, one problem the procedural writer faces is the limitation almost automatically placed upon the nature of his detective protagonist. If he wants to hold his readers, particularly if he wants to hold them through a series of ten or so novels, our author must create police detectives who are memorable. "Immediately he's in trouble," says Hillary Waugh, "for the attractive superman hero is denied him by the nature of the genre" (177). We will accept a James Bond in the world of international intrigue or a Philip Marlowe in the mean streets of the private investigator, but the public perception of the image of the policeman constitutes a barrier to acceptance of the gifted, colorful personality in the police detective. Then there is the prosaic world of police work, which imposes a further limitation: "Procedurals are dull," Lillian O'Donnell argues, "and their heroes even duller." The procedural heroes tend to merge into their own backgrounds, says O'Donnell, and she challenges us to think back and try to recall a hero of one of these stories: "Pretty hard, isn't it?"[53]

Really, now, it isn't all that hard. In response to her challenge, one might immediately recall O'Donnell's own Norah Mulcahaney, one of the best realized and most memorable detectives in mystery fiction. Or Waugh's Fred Fellows and Frank Sessions, who, although not "attractive superman heroes," are endowed with such qualities and are given such depth as characters that they emerge from the narrative background as memorable people. Later in her article O'Donnell suggests a method for making a police detective seem real by adding some depth to him as a person during his off-duty hours, individualizing him as a human being and not just as a cop (18). Writers of procedural stories tend to give us more extended pictures of their detectives than do the authors of other types of mystery fiction, and one way of achieving this breadth is to endow the policeman with qualities of character that shape his existence as a person: Virgil Tibbs' integrity, Gabriel Wager's loneliness, Norah Mulcahaney's determination to make a success of her marriage. Sometimes it is done by affording the reader insights into those things that absorb a policeman's interests when he is outside his detective role: Luis Mendoza's assorted menagerie of cats and dogs, Peter Van der Valk's joy in good food and wine, Martin Beck's ship models. This kind of "roundness" is not only appropriate but essential to the characterization of the policeman, because his function in the story is that of a member of the community, not a lone individual from outside.

Then there is the problem of setting, which tends to be more complicated in the procedural than in other kinds of mysteries, because the location of the story, if the writer wants to be strictly "realistic," will almost automatically impose limits on the nature of the police routines. A private detective operating in the environs of Los Angeles may have a wide variety of options in his methods and approaches, but if he is member of the LAPD, the story must at least have the impression of Los Angeles police work. Some writers avoid this involvement by laying their stories in fictitious settings, like McBain's "imaginary city" (obviously New York but not *really* New York), McClure's Trekkersburg, and Procter's Granchester. If he chooses an identifiable city, though, he faces the question of a literal reality which involves strict adherence to the customs and usages of his setting. Lillian O'Donnell cites an extreme example: the Los Angeles Police Department is the only one in the country with a Hypnosis Squad. Therefore, she says, "if your story is laid in New York, don't have a hypnosis squad in it" (19). At which point we might raise the question of how many readers would know, or, more important, how many would *care*? Actually, O'Donnell overstates the case for absolute adherence because she is addressing her advice to aspiring writers of procedural stories, who may need to be reminded not to stretch the limits of acceptance too far.

Another opportunity denied to the police procedural by definition is that of the colorful, bizarre situation. In the normal course of events, real-life policemen handle very few cases involving Moabite ciphers, Cyprian bees, or Maltese falcons. Instead, they work on commonplace crimes like muggings, rapes and shotgun slayings. Most procedural writers observe the prescriptions of reality and center their stories around these prosaic situations, thereby depriving themselves of the advantages of such inherently picturesque weapons as the thorn dipped in curare and such piquant circumstances as the murder committed by the fireplace while the potential witnesses are absorbed in a hand played at seven no-trump doubled and re-doubled in the far corner of the room.

We need only look at the work of several successful writers to see that it is possible to set the limits of acceptance quite broad and still preserve a sense of the reality of police work. It would be hard to imagine a more potentially fantastic situation than Ed McBain's *The Heckler*, in which the series villain blows up and burns large areas of the metropolitan downtown during the commission of a crime, or a more exotic one than John Creasey's *Theft of Magna Carta*, in which a gang undertakes to steal a national historic treasure; yet both stories come off very well as procedural fiction. Likewise, it is eminently possible to set narrow limits of plausibility without losing the interest of the reader. For *The Investigation* Dorothy Uhnak chose a commonplace crime, the kidnapping of two children, and a recognizable setting, Queens, New York. There is no sensationalism in the situation or development of this novel, but it is one of the very few procedurals to make the best-seller list.

The two aims are not incompatible, but in order to achieve both a writer must have two qualities: the ability to devise and present an intriguing mystery, and a "feel" for police investigation. The police procedural belongs in the mystery genre, and people read them at least in part for the satisfaction of watching detectives detect, of participating in the solution of a problem. If the writer is skillful in the techniques of suspense, the audience will stay with him or her for the outcome, no matter how prosaic the crime or commonplace the setting. The other quality is a sense of police work, which involves narrative control of such elements as the use of police technology, teamwork and informants. It must also involve the feelings of policemen about their work, their reactions to the pressures of politics, and their attitudes toward their colleagues in law enforcement.

Writers of procedural stories use a device—not unknown to writers of other traditions of detective fiction—to establish the reality of the fiction through a denial by the characters themselves that they are participants in a mystery.[54] Police procedurals abound in references by policemen to the gifted amateur detectives and private eyes in books, on television, and in the movies, and to ordinary policemen like themselves in other people's fiction. Sometimes the references are scornful (as when Fred Fellows asks a bumbling private investigator, "Where did you learn the private eye business? Out of Mickey Spillane?"[55]), sometimes envious (as when Bert Kling takes one last covetous look at Dick Tracy's wrist radio in the Sunday comics before going out on a case),[56] and sometimes merely whimsical (as when Van der Valk reflects on the way a private detective, "the beautiful unspoiled darling of a detective story,"[57] would handle a case). Whatever the context, the effect of these allusions is a disassociation of the present *real* account from the contrived world of mystery fiction.

Two procedurals contain especially pointed examples of this conscious effort at disassociation. In Elizabeth Linington's *Greenmask!* (the first book in the Ivor Maddox series), Detective Rodriguez becomes addicted to mystery fiction, and this situation gives Maddox a number of opportunities to comment on the contrast between reality and fantasy. In one passage Rodriguez praises the nice symmetry of his current reading, Agatha Christie's *The ABC Murders,* in which the murders are spaced out in leisurely fashion, in contrast to the frantic pressure of their own current case. "Crime in real life has never really satisfied you," Maddox tells him, "it's too crude and simple" (xii). Later Rodriguez has become absorbed in a police procedural, Michael Gilbert's *Blood and Judgment*: "You've found it's fun to read about it," says Maddox, "because it's a lot tidier that way—hell of a lot more interesting than the crude real-life stuff" (xix)—an especially revealing remark in view of the fact that *Blood and Judgment* involves situations just as crude and untidy as

142   Police Procedural

those in *Greenmask!*

The other is Ed McBain's *The Empty Hours,* in one of those incidental commentaries in which the author speaks as the voice of the novel. "There are no mysteries in police work," says the commentator, no carefully preconceived schemes, no climactic progressions, or contrived suspense. These things are for the movies. What policemen object to in mystery fiction is the control that is absent from their own investigations. A criminal case is not "an algebraic problem whose constants are death and a victim, whose unknown is a murderer." There are only whys in police work, not mysteries, and the whys add up to hard work for the investigators (ix). None of which, we ought to observe, keeps *The Empty Hours* from being an excellent mystery story, with clues deftly handled and with Fair Play convention strictly observed.

In a sense, then, setting the limits of acceptance at just the right point presents a greater problem to the writer of procedural stories than to writers of the other schools. Authors of the classic tales could (and did) kill off their victims with a vial of poison dropped into the sherry by one of five or six suspects, all of whom had equally valid motives, but we know that policemen in real life deal with murders commited with meat cleavers or sawed-off shotguns or even the bare hands of the strangler, in cases where there may be no suspects or maybe hundreds of them, often with no motive or a trivial one. Likewise, authors of the hard-boiled tradition can allow their private investigators to re-arrange or conceal evidence in keeping with their own private codes of ethics, but we expect the morality of the individual policeman at the very least to conform to the code of the police sub-culture. At the same time, the procedural writer enjoys some latitude denied to writers of other genres: it may seem a little odd that every time a respectable banker enters the story a murder results, but for a police detective in a big city squad a new homicide every week is perfectly plausible.

Generally, though, it is not the basic situation of the story that determines its sense of reality but the approach used by the writer to develop what we have called the "feel" of police investigation. In a procedural we must expect a policeman to have ambiguous and even ambivalent feelings toward himself and the job he is doing. We must concede that a policeman may get more reliable information from an informant than he could get from his own psychologizing about the habits and inclinations of his suspects. We expect that he will get better data from the police lab than he could supply from his knowledge of 114 types of tobacco ash.

The problem, then, is not "realism" but *plausibility*, which is easier to achieve now than it was in the 1940s and 50s, because the formula is established and the myths are accommodated, and the sense of reality in the police procedural develops in the context of those conventions.

Chapter 9

European Style, and American

THE POLICE PROCEDURAL story, as we have pointed out earlier, is universally adaptable. The classic formal-problem tale has been characterized as "English", although it was invented by an American, because it seems to fit better in vicarages, isolated country mansions and smoky pubs. The hard-boiled private-eye story is often called the "American" type of mystery, partly because Americans are better at it and partly because it is at home in the gangster hideout and the neon-lit plastic worlds of California and Florida. The procedural, though, seems equally suitable in New York, Stockholm or a small town in Connecticut, for reasons that have their origin in the non-fictional world. Wherever there is society there will be threats to security, and there must be systematic means of protection, namely policemen.

One idea that should emerge from our examination of the police sub-culture, and the formula and the myth, is that cops are pretty much the same the world over. Their loyalties, their attitudes toward their calling, and their frustrations are fairly consistent, whether they are Dutch, Scottish or American. There are, at the same time, certain variations between the qualities and perceptions of European and American policemen, which we will examine in this chapter. American cops tend to be rougher on suspects, Europeans more humane. The cultural level of the Europeans is generally higher than that of the Americans. The Europeans tend more to the "mental" approach to detection, the Americans to the "physical." There are significant differences in conceptions of citizenship and civic responsibility between the two groups, as there are between their conceptions of the role of the policeman. European policemen are inclined to call upon civilian expertise when faced with a technical problem, Americans to rely on the police lab. Both groups express concerns about the breakdown of morality, though the Europeans tend to worry more specifically about what the new

144

permissiveness is doing to the reputation of the country.

With respect to the handling of suspects and "subjects" (the police term for any civilian directly involved in a case), we have an excellent opportunity for comparison of American and European methods in *The Maine Massacre* by Janwillem van de Wetering, in which two Amsterdam policemen, Sergeant DeGier and the un-named commisaris, find themselves working with the county police in rural Maine. DeGier is hardly off the plane when it becomes necessary for him to subdue a suspect who is holding a gun on the local sheriff. DeGier uses karate; he is trained in judo, which is a gentler method, but the suspect is a big man and DeGier is afraid he might lose his footing on the icy ground. The sheriff casually remarks that he customarily uses a foot-long flashlight to cool suspects; it knocks them senseless, and it doesn't hurt his hand (iii).

This is not intended to imply, of course, that European cops always handle dangerous suspects gently or that all Americans are automatically violent, but it is representative of an attitude, which can be best illustrated in the oft-repeated situation where the police are questioning a suspect late at night, when irritated impatience increases the aggressiveness of the police and fatigue heightens the vulnerability of the suspect. In *Strike Out Where Not Applicable*, Van der Valk sends a suspect back to his cell to get some sleep; tomorrow, with both of them fresher, their counsels may be more productive of the truth (217). Gunvald Larsson in *The Man on the Balcony* gives a mugger the same treatment at midnight, sending him off to get food and sleep, with the intention of starting over the next day (xvi). American cops, under the same circumstances, tend to exploit the immediate advantage. Chief Frank Ford, questioning a young woman late at night, will not even let her go to the toilet, threatens and badgers her until she breaks down.[1] Frank Hastings in *Power Plays* presses the same kind of advantage over a junkie who needs a fix, letting him stew in jail until morning with the promise of a methadone shot when he decides to co-operate (iii, iv).

The European approach follows the same pattern in the treatment of witnesses and other people who have information that may be valuable to the police. Jonas Morck is sharp with a witness-suspect in *Nothing But the Truth*, lets him make mistakes and trap himself, then apologizes for flaring up during interrogation (xvii). The Amsterdam cops browbeat a shady character named "The

Mouse" into giving information, then have a friendly drink with him.[2] In Stockholm, Lars Kollin reassures a witness who is also a possible suspect, after questioning, that he will probably not call back for another round of interrogation.[3] What these Europeans do *not* do, and what an American detective almost automatically does, is to threaten to take the witness-suspect down to headquarters for questioning. In securing evidence and confessions, American policemen in the stories tend to take advantage of weaknesses and to play the breaks, whereas Europeans tend to create breaks by means of distraction and psychological intimidation.

Not that European cops can't get rough when the occasion demands. Philip Hunter calls an arrogant industrial executive, orders him to be at headquarters in twenty minutes, and, when the man demurs, threatens to come and get him.[4] Van der Valk on one occasion orders his subordinate to choke a contemptuous witness who has lied to him.[5] As a rule, though, they do not resort to such tactics short of complete exasperation.

With respect to cultural level, at least that aspect represented by personal knowledge, the perceptions of Europeans are inclined to be more oriented toward the liberal arts, while those of the American counterparts tend to the practical and utilitarian. There is a passage in *The King of the Rainy Country* in which Van der Valk, waiting for a train in the pre-dawn hours, meditates on passion as motive for crime. His mind roams over the emotional differences between northern and southern Europeans, and over the nature of royalty and romance. The passage is rich in literary allusions and historical references, full of almost abstract speculations and well-informed reminiscences of the kind not ordinarily expected of anyone but a highly literate individual (92-3). There is a suggestion of some of the same degree of literacy in the recurrent dream of Martin Beck, in which Beck prevents the assassination of President Garfield: he knows the details of the assassination and the name of Garfield's murderer. For intellectual grasp far beyond mere literacy, we should cite the cases of Sergeant DeGier, who understands Eastern imagery well enough to explain it to a colleague and who has a good working knowledge of surrealism, and his superior the commisaris, whose wisdom verges on the ultimates of Zen Buddhism.[6]

American cops are not illiterate. Virgil Tibbs can cite an episode in the second act of *Tosca*. Luis Mendoza quotes Omar Khayyam, and Jason Grace identifies a quotation from Thoreau.[7] The knowledge of the Americans, though, usually has an empirical base. One of the most knowledgeable of policemen is Fred Fellows, whose subordinate in *Road Block* calls him a walking encyclopedia; we should not miss the point, however, that it is Fellows' amazing knowledge of the history of crime that excites this expression of admiration. In the same story Fellows identifies a '53 Chrysler at a glance; he knows all makes of cars for all years (xii, xxii). Even the literary acquaintance of American policemen sometimes has a background in practical experience: Cotton Hawes in *Ax* surprises the daughter of an actress by quoting from *Henry V*, then explains that he stage-managed the play in high school (ii).

In view of these differences in cultural orientation, we should not be surprised that American policemen are inclined to take a "physical" approach to the business of detection in comparison to the "mental" approach of the Europeans. Actually, that is an over-simplification. It is more accurate to say that, in their efforts to perceive patterns and meanings, Americans usually throw themselves into the middle of a situation, whereas Europeans back away from it and take the broad view. This inclination may explain why, in at least one case, we are almost one-third of the way into the story before the Swedish police get around to questioning the most likely suspect.[8] Once again, it is the thoughtful Van der Valk who states the principle. In spite of all the laws and regulations, he tells another Dutch cop, in spite of the standardization and mechanization of law enforcement, the police must be interested in character, otherwise they would never understand anything at all.[9] Jonas Morck thinks in much the same terms when he ponders the logic of investigation. The police deal in probabilities, Morck thinks, testing the most likely hypotheses, judging people on the basis of such hypotheses, rejecting the untenable hypotheses, bracing themselves against improbabilities.[10]

For interpretation of the American approach, we can accept the testimony of two of the most perceptive policemen in the literature, Fred Fellows and Edward X. Delaney. By theorizing, Fellows tells a subordinate, a policeman can anticipate a subject's next move and intercept him at it.[11] Delaney's explanation of the basis of detective work in *The First Deadly Sin* is grounded in common sense, a realization of the necessity of starting somewhere, commitment to the hard grind of routine, and sensitivity to the percentages (V,v). Notice that Fellows and Delaney are dealing with the same general

topics as Van der Valk and Morck, even sharing some of their
assumptions, but using a different mode of thought. The difference
lies at the verbal level, with the Americans talking in terms of speed,
energy, getting the jump on criminals, the Europeans in terms of
judgment and understanding.

The difference between the conceptions of citizenship and civic
responsibility in the two groups manifests itself with special clarity
in the tendency of European cops to lecture suspects and other
"subjects" on their duties as citizens. Just before he orders him
choked, Van der Valk rebukes the contemptuous young artist with
the assurance that, before he is through, Van der Valk is going to
teach him to answer for his actions.[12] Colin Thane in *Draw Batons!*
is in no position to get rough with a gambling-boss who is unwilling
to co-operate with the police, but he demands and gets co-operation
by means of a stern lecture on the impropriety of selfishness when a
murder case is under investigation (ii). European policemen seem to
expect a sense of civic responsibility from civilians. Thus the wise
old commisaris, when "The Mouse" snorts derisively at the mention
of "taxpayers' money" in *The Corpse on the Dike*, reminds him that
they are talking about "holy money" (viii). And thus Harry
Martineau distrusts the concept of "diminished responsibility"
(mental incompetence) because he does not like the idea of criminals
evading punishment by pretending to be "crackers."[13] American
policemen are not inclined to lecture "subjects" on the
responsibilities of citizenship. In *Eighty Million Eyes*, Bert Kling of
the 87th Squad turns down an opportunity for such a lecture when
he is questioning the manager of a diner about a suspect. The
manager asks Kling if the charge is serious, in which case he will co-
operate, but "For minor things, who needs to be a good citizen?" (ix).
Kling ignores the question, which would have been answered by a
European detective with a discourse on the obligations of civilians.

Their conceptions of the role of the policeman, as we have seen,
are much the same with respect to such things as laws and
regulations, the vulnerability of the police, and attitudes toward
society. The one important difference between Europeans and
Americans in this respect is in their concern about police brutality
and violence, which worries European police more than it does the
Americans. When the Amsterdam cops engage in a shoot-out with a
gang of thieves, the commisaris is more concerned about the

shootings than he is about the recovery of the stolen goods.[14] Jonas Morck is so anxious about a clash between the Danish police and a group of demonstrators in *The Whipping Boy* that he tries to intervene physically in order to prevent rough handling of the civilians (i). The theme of Blom's *The Moment of Truth* is the consequences of police violence. Part of the difference arises out of the tradition regarding the use of firearms by policemen: in European countries (especially Britain), policemen use guns only in emergency situations and then by special prior authorization. American detectives always carry guns, even off duty. On the other hand, policemen on both sides of the Atlantic habitually kick doors open whenever the situation demands, though the Europeans do so with somewhat more restraint and are more apologetic about this kind of violent ingress than are Americans. Gunvald Larsson hestitates a moment before kicking open a door, knowing that if he does so without valid reason he may be suspended or fired,[15] and when Harry Martineau finds it necessary to break one open he promises the tenant that he will send a man round to repair it the next day.[16]

Faced with a technical problem, Europeans are much more likely to rely on civilian expertise than are American police. The Stockholm cops, needing an analysis of a taped dying statement, enlist the help of a sound expert from the Swedish Broadcasting Corporation.[17] "Buddha" Ilford, needing x-rays of some documents in *Rally to Kill*, goes around to a hospital to get the job done (vi). A large number of other examples could be cited. American policemen, at least in big departments with specialized divisions, customarily call upon the police lab or some other special branch. The one notable exception is Delaney's use of a civilian team in *The First Deadly Sin*, necessitated in this case because even the NYPD has no resident experts on mountain climbing or medieval weapons (III,v).

As part of their generally conservative outlook on society, policemen all over the world deplore the decline of morality and social standards: parents are too permissive toward their children, schools do not require enough work of their students, sexual modesty has become a thing of the past, and so on. The sharpest difference between the attitudes of Americans and Europeans with regard to the breakdown of society is that the Europeans often place their concerns in a context of patriotic worry about the reputation of their country. Earlier we cited Knud Einarsen's disgust over downtown Copenhagen's becoming a "gigantic whorehouse." What especially bothers Einarsen, though, is that tourists coming out of the Central Station see the porn shops and junkie prostitutes as their first impression of the city (xxiii). Gunvald Larsson worries about what the indifference of parents toward their children's morals is doing to the reputation of Sweden.[18] In London, Chief Superintendent Hazlerigg is sure that Britain is in danger of being corrupted by the irresponsibility of the labor unions to the extent that Britain, the "Old Firm," will be going into liquidation.[19] American policemen are frequently concerned about the effects of the breakdown of morality on the reputations of their local communities, but there is no noticeable evidence of anxiety about the good name of the United States.

These differences should not surprise us, when we recall that policemen are the only kind of fictional detectives who are based upon the reading public's perception of the "real" world. People who have never seen a consulting detective or a private investigator are willing to accept the literary stereotype of the transcendent genius or the lone knight-errant, but they expect fictional policemen to behave like policemen. Moreover, a Swedish audience wants its policemen to *act* like Swedish policemen, as a New York audience will not accept New York cops in a story unless they project at least a suggestion of the New York reality. Such is not the case with the protagonists of the classic school, whom we do not expect to be realistic. An effete snob like Philo Vance seems as much in place in New York as Lord Peter Wimsey does in London, but the mercurial Piet Van der Valk, with his sophisticated musings on history and the arts, would be too much to accept on the San Francisco force. The literary formula has dictated that all police detectives everywhere have certain qualities in common, but the perception of reality in the procedural story has at the same time made appropriate allowance for the differences discussed in this chapter.

Chapter 10

The Woman Police Detective

HER POSITION IN THE DEPARTMENT is a dubious one. She is
every man's little sister, the squad pet who is protected by the older
brothers, but she is at the same time resented and scorned because,
as everybody knows, police work is a man's business. She is
regarded as a sort of necessary nuisance who can do the typing and
filing for the squad, and the men are usually glad to turn the
"matron duty" and "baby-sitting" jobs over to her. If she is
attractive the male cops will almost inevitably consider her a sex-
object, but she can take satisfaction in her ability to do certain
things a man can not be expected to handle. Our own problem, in
considering her role in the procedural stories, is to avoid thinking
about her "as a woman" and "as a detective," because, as the novels
themselves demonstrate, the two functions are not incompatible.

The first policewoman to be featured in a procedural series was
Christie Opara, the central character in three novels by Dorothy
Uhnak. When we meet her in *The Bait*, Christie is a detective second-
grade on the New York District Attorney's Special Investigations
Squad, the only woman on her team. Her name, as she will pointedly
remind anybody who mispronounces it, is "*O*per-uh," and she is
annoyed when it comes out "Opera" or "O'Para" (xii). Christie is
twenty-six years old in *The Bait*; her husband Mike would have been
thirty, but he was killed five years ago in performance of police duty,
a source of special sorrow to Christie because they would have been
the first husband-wife team in the NYPD (i). She is fortunate in her
home life, though, which she shares with her mother-in-law Nora,
another police widow who lost her husband sixteen years ago and
her son five years ago (vi), and her five-year-old son Mickey, with
whom she was pregnant when Mike was killed. Both of Christie's
parents are dead, her mother in an automobile collision and her
father in an accident on the job (xvi).

After three violents deaths so close to her, Nora tells Christie's boss, Christie feels the need to prove herself, to know she can meet it (xvi). If anybody needs to be told about Christie's motivations, it is her superior officer Casey Reardon, who heads the District Attorney's Special Investigations Squad, and who is the most formidable challenge to Christie's ability to cope. Reardon, one of the toughest, most thoroughly competent, and most demanding superiors in the literature, can never quite decide whether he resents Christie more, or lusts for her sexually, or admires her, or feels the need to protect her. Christie has her own mixture of feelings toward Reardon, including hate, sexual need, resentment, and above all a need to win his approval. He usually succeeds temporarily in browbeating her, but Christie can put him in his place, as she does when he grabs her and kisses her passionately during a stakeout to give an onlooker the impression that they are lovers; Christie calls him "Dad" loudly enough to be heard and asks him to re-assure Mother that she'll be fine (xvii). Sometimes, though, when he carries intimidation to almost unbearable extremes, Christie points out to Reardon that she responds better to kindness than to threats.[1]

Christie is not just a young woman motivated by a need to prove herself, however; she is also something of a pixie. She has a talent for mimicry, with which she delights to infuriate Reardon, who tells her she is "fresh." She is also a master of the devastating squelch. When the call girl Elena Vargas in *The Ledger* flaunts her sexuality at Christie, archly informing her that Reardon is good in bed, Christie pertly replies, "Yes, I know" (x).

The probationer and the pixie combine to produce the tomboy. Christie broke her wrist at age twelve playing football, and she has played boys' rules all her life. She reminds Reardon of the tomboy of his youth, who insisted on playing every game with the boys; they were careful not to hurt her, and especially careful not to let her know about their protectiveness.[2] The image is a metaphor of Christie's position on the squad; she is determined to carry her part of the load, and while her male colleagues go out of their way to protect her from harm, they habitually conceal their caution from her.

More than tomboy, though, more than a young woman needing to prove herself, Christie Opara is a capable police officer. An accomplished actor, she uses a combination of sympathy and guile to break down the arrogance of a housewife in *The Bait* who has been taking calls for a ring of bookies (ix). She can also handle herself in physical combat, as the hood Tonio LoMarco finds in *The Ledger* when he tries to kill her but winds up with stitches in his head (xix).

Her most appealing quality as a fictional character, though, is a talent for getting herself into scrapes, from which she habitually emerges unscathed. One of the best comic scenes in the literature is the one in *The Witness,* in which Christie, almost dead with fatigue, takes an amphetamine capsule to get her through a conference with the mayor of New York and Casey Reardon, becomes giddy and talkative to the extent that she almost ruins the meeting, with the result that Reardon whispers that if she doesn't shut up he will murder her. During her "high," though, Christie has hit upon an idea that resolves the one major problem in the case under investigation (xxxii).

Christie's complex and often contradictory personality is expertly handled in the three novels, as she is seen through her own eyes, through those of other people in the stories (notably Elena Vargas in *The Ledger*), and especially through the eyes of Casey Reardon, who can never quite decide what to make of her.

The only other woman to be featured in a series of police procedurals is Lillian O'Donnell's Norah Mulcahaney. Norah is a uniformed police officer in the first story, *The Phone Calls*, is promoted to detective third-grade in Homicide on the basis of her performance in that story, then makes detective second-grade and eventually sergeant as a result of hard work and merit.

Norah is a well-organized, goal-oriented person, conscientious and systematic in her approach to her professional work. In the fifth novel of the series, *Leisure Dying*, she secures permission to organize the Street Crimes Unit, which she heads with credit to herself and the other members of the squad, and in the next one, *No Business Being a Cop*, she works with a group of angry and frightened New York policewomen with such intelligence and integrity that a serious panic and rebellion are averted.

The family life of the policewoman is accentuated in this series, as it is in the Christie Opara stories. In the first three novels Norah lives with her father, the aggressively Irish Patrick Mulcahaney, whose goal for his daughter is to marry her to a fine lad and get her out of police work, which is no place for a woman. Motherless since age twelve, Norah gave up the idea of college when her father was incapacitated, and kept house for him and her two brothers. At the beginning of the fourth story, *The Baby Merchants,* Norah has married Joe Capretto, her immediate superior on the force, and although their marriage is a good one, Norah and Joe face some problems, one of which is the fact that after two years they still have no children, and the other that there are perils in a police marriage when the partners are of unequal rank and on the same squad; a real crisis develops in *Leisure Dying* when Norah inadvertently makes Joe look bad, tries to help but only makes matters worse (x).

Unlike Christie Opara, Norah Mulcahaney (she keeps her maiden name after marriage for professional reasons) grows and changes during the series. In *The Phone Calls* she startles her sergeant with her stubbornness and sharpness, and comes dangerously close to insubordination with the lieutenant (vi), but in *No Business Being a Cop* she has schooled herself in the ability to get along well with people, especially her fellow-officers (v). In the first novel Norah suffers several attacks of insecurity over her identity as a woman; later, she has not only recovered from a need to prove herself but has come to think of herself as a competent police officer with her training and the resources of the department to call upon.

Norah's aim is to be identified as a capable person, not as a woman. Her creed (which she on occasion finds herself violating) is that all people—men and women—should be recognized on the basis of merit alone. Thus, though she is firmly insistent on equal professional opportunities for policewomen, she is no women's-rights activist. She is prepared to be patronized by civilians who say things like "So you're really a policewoman! Now isn't that nice," but she will not let her partner hold the door for her or pay for her coffee.[3]

Because *No Business Being a Cop* deals with the professional status of policewomen, we must say a few additional words about that novel. The mystery in the story is built around the murders of four New York women cops, and a parallel narrative strand involves the efforts of policewomen to protect their jobs. When a budget cut necessitates the elimination of a number of police positions, the last-hired-first-fired policy cuts in half the number of women in the department, but later when it becomes financially possible to hire back some of those fired, the first group of sixty reinstated includes only one woman. The women bring a class-action suit based on discrimination, and the result is increased friction between them and the men, who also need their jobs (iii). These tensions generate a number of observations on the status of policewomen. Norah, in spite of her own success, realizes that women have not gained acceptance in the department to the extent that the public thinks they have, and she wonders if policewomen will ever be able to shake the stereotype of "matron duty," those women-jobs men don't want to do (i).

Two women get at least secondary billing in other novels in procedural series, Pamela York in Nelson DeMille's *The Smack Man,* and Eileen Burke in Ed McBain's *The Mugger* and *Fuzz.*

Possibly the worst assigment ever wished on a policewoman is that presented to Pamela York, who is given the job of working with the bull rhinoceros Sergeant Joe Keller, in whose opinion women serve only one purpose, which has nothing to do with police work. When Detective York reports to him, Keller calls her an obscene sexist name, and tries to discourage her with a torrent of dirty talk, whereupon Pamela blisters his ears with an outpouring of as good as Keller can give, and he reluctantly accepts her as partner (viii). They have sex just before the end of the story (because she feels she owes it to him), and shortly afterward she is killed in line of duty (xix).

Detective Eileen Burke is somewhat more fortunate, in that she works in the 87th Precinct, where the male cops adjust fairly well to policewomen. In *The Mugger* she is given one of those dangerous jobs only a woman can do, serving as a decoy to lure a murderer, and although Detective Hal Willis is assigned the protective task of following her at a distance while she walks the streets at night, Eileen is severely beaten at the crucial moment when she is attacked and Willis arrives on the scene just a minute too late to be much help (xii). She also participates in the monumentally fouled-up stakeout in *Fuzz,* in which she and Willis pose as lovers in a sleeping bag in the park; when the perpetrator appears on the scene and action is demanded, the zipper of the sleeping bag gets stuck. Eileen evens the score for the mishap with the mugger, when they are back in the squadroom and she archly hints that more went on in the sleeping bag than duty required, much to the discomfiture of the bashful

Willis (vii).

Policewomen make occasional appearances in other series, though we should make special mention of the reliable Sue Carstairs, whom Maddox eventually marries, in the Ivor Maddox series of Elizabeth Linington. Several women also have repeat parts in the series of Maj Sjowall and Per Wahloo, notably Asa Torell, a policeman's widow who joins the force and becomes a series character.

The main cause of the policewoman's dubious position in her profession is the male cop's ambivalent feelings toward her. There is first the Little Sister Syndrome, which causes him to feel both protective and resentful toward her. The protective attitude may be generalized, as when a policeman tells Roger West that it is bad enough when a man runs into trouble, but harm to a woman officer is unthinkable,[4] or it may have specific reference to her lack of physical strength, as when Norah Mulcahaney's male partner will not let her approach danger, telling her that in spite of her brains God has made her a woman and there is nothing she can do about her shortage of brawn.[5] The other side of the picture is the instinctive male resentment, which expresses itself on one hand in the outraged bellows of Joe Keller when he finds himself paired with Pamela York, and on the other in the response of a woman inspector to Harry Martineau's request for the loan of a team of women "colleagues." "Colleagues?" the inspector replies, "We've just been promoted!"[6]

She is as often as not regarded as a necessary evil. Her male counterparts gladly turn over to her the typing and filing, partly because they despise those jobs and partly because she can do them better than men can. She is also useful for "baby-sitting" (monitoring women subjects and small children) and "matron duty" (going places where men are not permitted, like the women's powder room). The police administration values her presence as a means of taking over desk work so the fit and healthy male cop can be released to the business of catching thieves and murderers. Then, of course, she can serve a valuable purpose as the squad's Token Woman, which is good public relations.

Occasionally, men can face reality to the extent that they will admit there are some things only women can do, besides office work and "baby-sitting." The point is well proved when Policewoman

Jean Cranston of the Glasgow force assists a male team in searching the apartment of a woman who has disappeared in *To Kill a Witch*. Officer Cranston notices that the woman's clothes, though expensive, have been altered to bring them up to date, and that, whereas her perfurme is of best quality, her lipstick and eye-shadow are low-cost. The inference, which a man could never reach, is that the subject was recently affluent but has now fallen on hard times (i). Then, of course, there is the obvious fact that a woman makes a more convincing bait for a rapist or a mugger than a man possibly could. Besides Eileen Burke, Christie Opara, Norah Mulcahaney, and Sonja Hansson in Stockholm serve at various times as female bait, often suffering physical harm or coming close to being killed.

As we might expect, the woman detective frequently becomes an outright sex object. Gabriel Wager is impressed by the appearance of a good-looking young woman in Records, whom he privately calls Police Person Fabrizio, and whom he thinks of in terms of legs and breasts.[7] Daniel Comer, Assistant District Attorney of Nassau County, a smoothie always on the make, immediately spots Norah Mulcahaney as a target and reflexively turns on the charm the moment they start working together.[8] To most women cops the techniques for handling horny males are almost instinctive, though there is at least one case in which a policewoman loses her life as a result of sexual involvement with a man on the squad.[9]

The reaction of the woman detective to these attitudes varies according to her personal qualities. She may assert her pride in being a woman, as Christie Opara does when Elena Vargas tells her she is talking like a woman; Christie reminds her that she is what she is, in addition to being a detective.[10] She may boldly stand up for herself vis-a-vis the male establishment, as Norah Mulcahaney does when she faces down a waiter who refuses to admit her to a bar because she is not accompanied by a man.[11] She may cheerfully accept a modest role, like the loyal Wanda Larsen in the Mendoza series. Or she may develop a strong professional spirit that will make her as good a cop as the most muscular man. This last is not easy, as Norah Mulcahaney realizes, because a woman must do twice the job just to stay even (xiii).

Chapter 11

The Black Police Detective

ALMOST INVARIABLY, the policemen in the procedural stories are committed to cases by being assigned to them. In a few instances, police detectives have become involved in mysteries outside their own precincts as a result of having been present at or near the scene of the crime and being invited to participate in the investigation. There is one case on record, however, in which a police officer became involved in a homicide as a result of having been picked up as a suspect, the reason being that he was a black man waiting for a train late at night in a town in South Carolina. Actually, the apprehension of this "suspect" was a fortunate accident for the white policemen in Wells, South Carolina, because the black man was Virgil Tibbs of the Pasadena Police Department, whose subsequent involvement provided the expertise that permitted the case to be solved.

The story is John Ball's *In the Heat of the Night*, the first in the series featuring Virgil Tibbs, who is the only black police detective to have the leading role in a procedural series. Tibbs, by the way, does not like the designation "black": he would prefer to be classed as a human being or a police officer, but if racial consideration is necessary, he would choose to be a Negro. He is acutely sensitive to the problem of being a Negro in America, but he believes that the answer to the race question lies in the acceptance of the principle of assessing all people as persons of worth instead of members of racial groups. Tibbs deplores violent militancy and believes that Stokely Carmichael set the Negro cause back by a generation.[1]

Like several other black policemen, Virgil Tibbs grew up in an environment of severe poverty and racial deprivation. Addressing a crowd of angry black people in *Johnny Get Your Gun*, he reminds them that he, like most of them, had lived in a shack where his mother cooked their food, when there was any, over a wood stove,

and where there was no indoor plumbing (xi). In a later story we are
told how Tibbs, bending over the body of a black youth who had
been senselessly murdered, dedicated himself to the punishment of
cold-blooded, wanton violence.² The determination to escape the
deprivation of his childhood joins with an intense sense of justice to
produce a first-class detective.

Several of the novels are closer to the Great Policeman tradition
than to the police procedural because Tibbs, as a superior detective,
customarily works better on his own than as a member of a team.
His ratiocinative powers in *Then Came Violence* are almost
incredible: after examining a corpse, clothed but with all
identification removed, Tibbs concludes that he was a member of a
large family, a younger son, probably not married, who lived with
his mother (a good woman who did the best she could in spite of
limited resources); that he probably did not commit suicide, was
unemployed, had a record, was not a drifter, had a regular home,
and will be missed (v). His intellectual level comes through strongly
in *Five Pieces of Jade*, when he decides to read up on the subject of
jade and is told by the librarian that she would not be surprised by
any direction his reading interests might take (vi). His physical
prowess is the result of six years of hard work under a master of
karate, in which he has earned a black belt. Tibbs' most effective
teamwork is done in company with his Nisei office-mate Bob
Nakamura, with whom he teams up when either needs the other's
help.

Two of the novels have especially strong racial implications.
The primary theme of *The Cool Cottontail,* which involves a murder
in a nudist park, is "differentness": the Nunns, proprietors of the
park, refer frequently to their own "differentness," which they and
Tibbs compare to his, and which establishes a strong bond of
understanding between them. The secondary theme is a strong
sexual attraction between Tibbs and the beautiful Linda Nunn,
which both of them manage to suppress but which makes Tibbs
almost hate himself for being a Negro. *Johnny Get Your Gun* deals
with a potentially explosive situation involving white children and
black youths, in which Tibbs must deal with the McGuires, a
racially biased family of low-class whites who have migrated to
Pasadena from the South, and also with a crowd of blacks
dangerously close to becoming a violent mob as the result of the

murder of one of their own. This story does not confront Tibbs with the emotional crisis of *The Cool Cottontail*: he handles the McGuires with cool professionalism, ignoring all racial slurs, and in the most memorable scene in the book he diverts the hostility of the black crowd without offending their own sense of self-respect.

The racial problems of James McClure's Sergeant Mickey Zondi, of the Trekkersburg CID, Republic of South Africa, are at once more complicated and simpler than those faced by Virgil Tibbs: more complicated because the atmosphere of oppression is greater in Trekkersburg than anything possible in Pasadena, and at the same time simpler because Zondi, who is a Bantu policeman, has no hope of improving his lot or that of his fellows. What Zondi lacks in social status, however, he makes up in indispensability, a quality amply recognized by his white boss, Lieutenant Trompie Kramer. Officially, Zondi is attached to the CID to handle black problems, but Kramer thinks of himself and Zondi as a team, on two occasions kills men to save Zondi's life, and resorts to all kinds of subterfuge to prevent Zondi's being invalided out of the squad because of a wound he had received in line of duty. The South African ambiance being what it is, Kramer must call Zondi "boy" and deal with him as an inferior in the presence of other whites, but in private he not only treats him as a cherished friend and colleague but endures Zondi's sly insults.

Sergeant Zondi, his wife Miriam, and three children live in a tiny two-room house with a floor of stamped earth, in the black section of Trekkersburg. He is proud of his wife, whom he thinks of as a true Zulu and a warrior's woman; he is also proud of his people, though pride of race is always conditioned by his duty as a policeman. There is an especially revealing scene in *The Gooseberry Fool* in which Zondi stands watching the removal of a "Black Spot," the eviction of hundreds of Zulu villagers from their homes, which are immediately bulldozed while the blacks are transported to a "homeland" hundreds of miles away. If Zondi has any feelings about the plight of his countrymen they are not revealed; his ony recorded reaction is to call himself a fool for having misunderstood the nature of the operation (iv).

Mickey Zondi grew up in a mission school, where the white nuns taught him that all men are brothers and a boy can grow up to be whatever he wants to become. It did not take him long to learn that none of this is true, but he bears no resentment against whites. He does, as a matter of fact, consider white men foolish, especially in their reliance upon status and hierarchies and their fanatical devotion to science, but his disgust is limited to snorting to Kramer, "You whites!" His attitude toward Kramer is a mixture of affection for a good superior officer and a courteous disrespect, both elements usually combined into an elaborate compliment in which is concealed a barb sharp enough for Kramer to feel. Zondi is a resourceful policeman who can deal with whites as effectively as with blacks. At the conclusion of *The Sunday Hangman* he achieves what must be a record for dexterity, preventing a murder by temporarily reversing the direction of gravity.

The only black policeman on the squad of McBain's 87th Precinct is Detective Second-Grade Arthur Brown. Brown is an impatient man, largely because of his name, which gives the comedians on the squad an opportunity for endless ribbing. He does not seek identity with his color, but looks for it within himself as a man and usually finds it there. Brown lives with his wife and daughter in a four-room flat in an ancient building located in a black ghetto close to the precinct station. He shares with Virgil Tibbs and Mickey Zondi the legacy of a poverty-stricken, rat-infested childhood, but his is even more bitter than theirs because of the memory of his sister who died at age seventeen as the result of an overdose of heroin administered in the cellar headquarters of a street gang. Brown is unusually sensitive to racist attitudes; he can spot hatred at a distance, and he can look at a man and know instantly whether color will be a barrier between them. He is, however, the only black procedural detective with a sense of humor: Brown considers himself hilarious, an opinion not shared by his wife Caroline, and he can not miss the opportunity for a gag, as when another detective hands him a pair of white gloves to be used in handling evidence and Brown goes into a "Mistuh Bones" minstrel routine.[3]

It is difficult to characterize the two detectives in Chester Himes' stories as black policemen, because their sadism blends into the Harlem background with much the same effect as the harshness of policemen of any color would relate to the ethnic majority. Their names—Grave Digger Jones and Coffin Ed Johnson—are more descriptive than fanciful. Local folklore has it that they will shoot a man for not standing in line, and their shouted orders, "Straighten up!" and "Count off!" are enough to restore order to any potential mob.

Stoner Martin, in Uhnak's Christie Opara stories, is a black policeman whose professionalism is a match for that of Virgil Tibbs. A first-grade detective, he is second in command to Casey Reardon on the district Attorney's Special Investigation Squad, and he is the only member of the team who can get away with jokes with the overbearing Reardon. Martin is the kind of man who can always be described as "neat"; even when disguised as a tramp or a workman, his bearing gives him a certain distinction. He is also a person with a well developed sense of human relations, as he demonstrates in *The Ledger*, when he advises Christie on how to face Reardon after she has committed a serious blunder: play it straight, he tells her, without falsehoods and without excuses (iii). In the stakeout that traps the psychotic murderer at the conclusion of *The Bait*, it is Martin's calm competence that holds the other police steady through the whole nerve-jangling episode.

Jason Grace, who has a minor role in Shannon's Mendoza stories, is a gentle person who is especially good at dealing with children and who can get more out of them than the other cops can: questioning a five-year-old in *Whim to Kill*, who had seen his mother abducted in an automobile, Grace gets the child to show him a crayon the same color as the vehicle (ii). He is a realist who gets tired of all those well-meaning people who keep saying there is no difference between people; he knows damn well there is.[4]

Another black detective who has no illusions regarding racial differences is Charlie Masters, in Rex Burns' *The Alvarez Journal*. Masters puts the pressure to turn informant on a black woman who has been arrested for pushing heroin, reminding her that she is black and that she will be at the mercy of a honky public defender and a honky judge. When she consents, Masters remarks to Gabriel Wager that the old racist crap works every time (vi).

Jason T. Jason makes a brief but memorable appearance in Lawrence Sanders' *The Second Deadly Sin*. A patolman who is called in on the case because he is the only person who has spotted two potential witnesses, Jason takes his plainclothes assignment seriously, spending eighteen hours per day on the streets in an outfit which, according to his wife, makes him look like "the raunchiest pimp in New York." Jason has always wanted to be a detective, though he had almost lost hope during three years in uniform (xvi).

The writers of police procedurals have successfully resisted the temptation to stereotype the black policeman. He can be as noble as Virgil Tibbs or Stoner Martin, or as aggressively hostile as Charlie Masters. He can have the gentle kindness of Jason Grace or the wily irreverence of Mickey Zondi. As we can expect, however, heritage and environment have imposed certain common experiences and qualities on him and his fellow black cops.

One thing he can expect is an abundance of snubs on the job, automatic assumptions by whites of his inferiority. Even when Arthur Brown identifies himself as a policeman, people still believe that he is a criminal impersonating an officer, and when Virgil Tibbs goes to places where he is unknown, people usually assume that he is looking for work. On occasion, when he is recognized as a policeman, people are reluctant to admit him to their homes. After a while, though, he gets used to Sammy Davis, Jr., jokes and fails to react to sly remarks about fondness for chitterlings and watermelon.

At the same time, his early experiences have left him with the awareness of a gulf between himself and white people. Mickey Zondi was treated well by the nuns in the mission school he attended, but he had to share the one textbook per subject with the other black children. Arthur Brown, who worked on the docks before joining the police force, wishes people would look at him and see a detective or a husband instead of seeing him only as a Negro. Virgil Tibbs remembers the humiliation forced upon him because of his race, and no circumstances can make him completely forget the canyon between himself and Caucasians.

The black policeman's sympathy for the plight of other black people, however, does not engender any permissiveness where law-enforcement is involved. He can be, and usually is, rough on black criminals and suspects. We have already mentioned Charlie Masters' handling of the black pusher, which seems almost lenient in comparison to the way Grave Digger Jones and Coffin Ed Johnson deal with a fight in a Harlem police station: they restore order by firing a volley of pistol shots into the ceiling. Mickey Zondi on occasion uses his pistol to intimidate his fellow Bantu, though he never finds it necessary to fire a shot. In *Snake*, when he needs

information from the reluctant Beebop Williams, black proprietor of
a record bar, Zondi points his pistol at a stack of recordings and
threatens to put a second hole through two hundred pop songs;
Beebop becomes co-operative (vi). The willingness of black
policemen to bully their fellow blacks seems to confirm the assertion
so many of them make, that they are law officers first, Negroes
second.

At the same time, though, they have a certain reserve that
makes them reluctant to use their clout on law-abiding people.
Arthur Brown is frequently assigned to wiretap jobs because he is
good at it, but he dislikes the necessity of invading people's privacy
and wishes they would all stop using the telephone. Virgil Tibbs
comes close to quoting Brown's sentiments verbatim: in spite of the
demands of his profession, he does not enjoy penetrating the
privacy of respectable citizens. Even Jason T. Jason, whose
formidable size tends to frighten people, tells his wife that it makes
him uncomfortable to lean on people.

We should not fail to mention that there are occasions when a
black policeman's race gives him an advantage over his colleagues.
Sometimes the very presence of a black man on the police force
serves as a reminder to upset and disturbed black people that law
enforcement is not a monopoly of whites. Virgil Tibbs has often
found himself handicapped because of his color, but he is glad to be a
Negro when he talks with the family of a black youth involved in a
homicide, because they will know, if only for a few moments, that
the law does not have an exclusively white face.[5] There are
occasions when a black policeman can gain access to information
that would otherwise be sealed within the black community. The
Zulu world is closed against Trompie Kramer and other whites, but
Mickey Zondi can penetrate it easily; he flirts outrageously with the
village women who are doing their laundry beside a stream,
listening carefully to their gossip, and a little later pays a courtesy
call upon the Zulu headman, gaining vital information from the old
man, who is tired of being yelled at and intimidated by white cops.[6]
Then there are times when a black detective can operate in areas
where a white man would not be safe. When Jason Grace learns that
two of his colleagues intend to pick up a suspect in Watts, he
suggests that they had better let him go because, as he puts it, he
blends better into the shrubbery in that district.[7]

As in the case of the woman detective, the response of the black policeman to discrimination and injustice varies in correspondence to personal disposition and local circumstances. One possibility, though he does not often use it, is to employ his clout as a police officer to avenge the slurs of white racists.

This is the course followed by Arthur Brown in the *Con Man*, when he enters a flea-bitten dump of a hotel to interview a suspect and is told by the desk clerk that "we don't take niggers." Brown identifies himself as a policeman and reminds the clerk how easy it would be for him to obtain a warrant for violation of the law against racial discrimination in rentals (viii). Another option open to the black cop is to seize opportunities to remind whites of the prevalence of racial injustice, as Arthur Brown does in *Jigsaw* when somebody asks him if he is a skier: "How many blacks have you ever seen on the ski slopes?" (iv). Mickey Zondi is not one to complain about the disadvantages of his color, but he can not resist the opportunity to score a point when Kramer asks his opinion regarding a case involving white people: in the opinion of some, Zondi replies, that is none of his business.[8]

The most frequent response of the black detective, however, is to develop his own sense of integrity and pride in his profession. For Virgil Tibbs, professional integrity is equated with an ethical consciousness that prevents his parking by a red curb in *The Cool Cottontail*: police powers entail police responsibilities (xi). Tibbs can't be bought, and he doesn't make deals. For Mickey Zondi, pursued by a Zulu mob and injured by flying stones, pride in his profession is the only thing that prevents his falling into submissive depression.[9] For Stoner Martin, professional commitment means the development of such capability that he can successfully handle the formidable assignment of second in command under Casey Reardon.

Chapter 12

The Jewish Police Detective

WHY ARE THERE SO FEW Jewish police detectives in the procedural stories? In New York City, which has an unusually large Jewish population and which is the setting of so many of the novels, we should certainly expect a higher ratio than one Jew per squad, and the same would hold true for McBain's "imaginary city," which has the same ethnic makeup as New York. Young Max Segal in Greenburg's *Love Kills* offers an explanation that has a ring of plausibility, since Max is himself a Jew and a policeman: "Jewish parents," he tells his girl friend, "don't know from cop sons." Irish parents do, and so do Italian parents, but not Jewish parents, who can see their sons as doctors, lawyers, CPAs, and businessmen, but not policemen. Jewish parents are funny, says Max: they are prejudiced against the idea of their sons getting their heads blown off or their insides blown out, feeling more comfortable with the idea of their sons raising families and giving them grandchildren. "All that stuff works better with lawyer sons than with cop sons" (li).

The Jewish police detective most fully realized in the procedural story is Meyer Meyer of the 87th Squad, whom Ed McBain features in his series second only to Steve Carella. Meyer's replicated name was the legacy of his father; Max Meyer, who enjoyed a considerable reputation as a comedian among his circle, regarded the naming of his son as a masterpiece of humor, with the result that Meyer has been compelled to develop a monumental bulwark of patience in order to live with all those fellow-men who think his name a great joke. Meyer experienced another condition that generated a protective degree of patience during childhood, however: an Orthodox Jew in a predominantly Gentile neighborhood, Meyer learned to endure the other kids' chant of "Meyer Meyer, Jew-on-fire!" even in the face of their fun-loving threats to burn him at the stake.[1] This frolicksome anti-Semitism ceased when Meyer was sixteen years old and a muscular five-feet-eleven,[2] but the ingrown habit of patience saw him through the eight years between the time he became a policeman and the time when he finally made detective third-grade. Like many another policeman in these stories, Meyer did not originally plan to be a cop. He earned a law degree and passed his bar exams, but was drafted before he could set up a practice. After discharge from the service he decided the law was not for him and became a policeman.

Although he and his family keep the traditional observances (they celebrate Passover, and Meyer's son has had his *bar mitzvah*), Meyer himself has not been inside a synagogue in twenty years. His dubious religious position is brought home to him several times, notably on the occasion of the murder of an elderly rabbi, which produces in Meyer a genuine identity crisis. He discusses the question with his wife Sarah, telling her he really never felt much like a Jew until he became involved with this manifestation of violent anti-Semitism. Sarah, who knows Meyer well enough to touch the right button to put things into proper perspective, asks, "Should I get your prayer shawl?" Meyer utters, "Wise guy," and the crisis at least temporarily passes.[3] It returns, though, in another story, when Meyer and Steve Carella interview Ludwig Etterman: Meyer lets Carella do all the talking and later confesses that he "feels funny" around Germans. When Carella points out that he should not hate people for what their forebears did, Meyer reminds Carella that he is not a Jew.[4]

Meyer Myer, we should note, is a detective with keen deductive powers, as he ably demonstrates in the case of the "ghosts" in a wealthy Victorian-style mansion, which he solves single-handed. Meyer patiently hears out the evidence regarding the spectral visitations, but he also makes some skillful observations and comes up with a solution that is both logical and materialistic.[5]

The other Jewish detective in the McBain series is Sam Grossman, who is not attached to the 87th Squad but is head of the police laboratory downtown, the best police lab in the country, in the opinion of the men of the Eight-Seven. Besides being a lab man Grossman is a trained detective, and on more than one occasion he comes up with a valuable suggestion beyond the scope of his lab work.

Besides Meyer Meyer, the only Jewish detective to play a major part in a procedural series is Pete Friedman, the colleague and personal friend of Frank Hastings in Collin Wilcox's stories. Friedman meant to be a rabbi, but while in the seminary he became interested in amateur theatricals, dropped out and went to Hollywood, where he had one bit part in a Western, finally gave up and became a policeman. His acting career, however, shaped his personality to a far greater degree than did his rabbinical training; Friedman is an expert *poseur* who can turn on his "Holmesian mood" (knowing especially how it irks Hastings), with ponderous nod and lowered lid, and he loves to assume the professorial role in the squadroom, surrounded by admiring subordinates. His outward appearance and habits are deceiving. Friedman's clothes are perpetually rumpled, he never stands when he can sit, and he keeps the most disorganized files in the detective division, but when he talks everybody listens. He is a lieutenant who knows he will never make captain, partly because he is not a good politician and partly because he is not only a Jew, but, as he puts it, a *smart* Jew, too smart for his own good in terms of departmental politics. His feuds with the various law enforcement offices are legendary, but he loves nothing better than an opportunity to upstage the FBI, which he can do with considerable skill. Friedman's arrogance is only external, however. He delights in putting Hastings in his place, as he does when he reminds him that he was earning an honest living while Hastings was playing professional football, but he also urges Hastings to give his friends a chance to help him when Hastings is about to get himself into a dangerous jam.[6]

Marty Ginsburg, in the Christie Opara stories, comes closer than any of the others to being a parody of the stereotype. When we first meet him in *The Bait* he is selling bagels in the squadroom (two for a quarter, three for fifty cents), as a gag, of course, because Marty is a great comedian (iv). In a later story we learn that when swimming with the family he takes a flying leap into the pool howling like an enraged seal, an act that never fails to break up the kids, except for his oldest son, who doesn't think his old man is funny any more.[7] Marty is no *schmuck*, though, but a good cop who grew up in Greenpoint but now loves the East Side streets, and who feels that his own children are missing a lot because they have never experienced the atmosphere of the old Manhattan that is rapidly vanishing.

Joe Katz, in the Vic Varallo stories by Lesley Egan, is not so colorful a character as those just mentioned, and his role in the series is minor. We get at least one insight into his religious feelings, with specific reference to confession, when a freshly booked criminal tearfully asks for a priest. Joe is disgusted at the idea of squaring things with God as if they never happened.[8]

We have already mentioned Max Segal, the protagonist in Greenburg's *Love Kills,* who comes through more strongly as a young cop than as a Jew. Max does, however, feel the effects of bigotry when his partner implies that Max got his shield not because of merit but because of the influence of Jewish friends close to the Commissioner (viii).

These men share certain traits, one of which is their tendency to stoic calm, to what is conventionally called "ageless wisdom." None of the others share Meyer Meyer's monumental patience, though Joe Katz is described as something of a philosopher. Pete Friedman occasionally falls back on his own sagacity, as he does when a psychopathic suspect pleads that time is his enemy. Time, Friedman tells him, is everybody's enemy.[9]

Customarily, they are proud of being Jews and take their heritage seriously. Meyer Meyer loves the smell of a delicatessen, remembering from his boyhood the evocative scent of kosher food, and Marty Ginsburg, happily haggling his way through the Delancey Street merchants, enjoys the good feel of digging out his childhood Yiddish to use as a medium for bargaining with some aged vendor. Even Pete Friedman, not ordinarily one to feel himself shackled by tradition, seems strangely vulnerable when faced by the necessity of extreme sacrifice in order to see that his eldest son gets the best education available. The demands of the Covenant also shake the normally patient Meyer Meyer when he confronts the young junkie Samuel Rosenstein; Meyer is outraged at the thought of a nice Jewish boy filling his veins with poison.[10]

Not, however, that they can't joke about it, and some of them are experts in Jewish humor. When Frank Hastings suggests that Pete Friedman may be smoking too many cigars, reminding him of Freud's cancer of the jaw, Friedman straight-facedly replies that all Jews have the death wish, which was why he became a policeman.[11] Meyer Meyer, who sometimes wonders what his father would think about his eating ham sandwiches and owning a Mercedes-Benz, is accused by his friends of being a closet *goy*; Meyer tells them he is really a closet Jew.[12] Marty Ginsburg, in the office of the Good Shepherd Protectorate in *The Ledger*, appears to be puzzled by the number of crucifixes on display and wonders aloud if they are strictly necessary, and with pretended innocence addresses the mother superior as "Holy Mother" (vii). None of them try to be standard Jewish comedian, but they can recognize the humor of their situation.

The one talent most of them share in abundance is the ability to dramatize. Meyer Meyer is a master of the running gag, who keeps the story of the cat-kidnapper going through most of *The Mugger*, patiently stringing it out until somebody in an unguarded moment asks for an explanation. Sam Grossman is another lover of the delayed climax; bending over his microscope with his back turned when Steve Carella enters the lab, he calls Carella by name and invites him to be seated, provoking Carella's natural wonder as to how Grossman knew who it was. Grossman keeps it going for several minutes, with hints of Sherlockian perspicacity, and finally admits somebody had told him Steve was on his way to the lab.[13] Pete Friedman is an accomplished bombshell-dropper. When he has some big information that is likely to startle Frank Hastings, he builds up to it with proddings like ,"Are you ready for this?" before springing the big one. The real addict to the art of the dramatic, though, is Marty Ginsburg, who can't merely *do* something but must build a plot around the simplest job. When he takes Christie Opara to his cousin the doctor to have a cast put on her arm (for purposes of cover), Marty quite unnecessarily constructs a web of mystery and intrigue around the business, with the result that Dr. Sidney Ginsburg finishes the job convinced that it involves the Secretary-General of the United Nations.[14]

The authors do not make as much point of discrimination against Jewish detectives as they do in the cases of women and blacks, though we can't help wondering whether it would have taken Meyer Meyer eight years to make detective third-grade if his name had been Brien O'Brien, or if Pete Friedman would feel himself permanently blocked from promotion if he were a smart Catholic instead of a smart Jew.

Chapter 13

The Hispanic Police Detective

POLICE WORK, as we have seen, involves a kind of inherent schizophrenia that makes itself felt in the vocation as a whole and in the functions of its individual members. The police force is the defender of society against the criminal world and at the same time a tight enclave closed against the rest of society. The individual policeman is paid to serve the public, but his responsibility is to his superior officer, and his loyalty is to his fellow cops. If he is a policeman whose ancestors lived in Puerto Rico or Mexico, if his name is something like Hernandez or Delgado, and if his parents still speak Spanish at home, his problems are multiplied. His fellow Hispanics will either expect him to consider himself "one of them" and overlook infractions committed by other Puerto Ricans or Chicanos, or else they will regard him as the worst of traitors, a Latino who has gone over to the enemy. To the Anglo majority he may be a tolerable liaison who knows how to handle "his kind," but they will almost inevitably consider him an inferior and will relegate him to the "brown race" if he is a Chicano in one of the Western states.

Lieutenant Luis Rodolfo Vincente Mendoza, LAPD, is the main character in the series by Dell Shannon. Mendoza does not suffer a sense of deprivation because of his Spanish heritage, partly because he belongs to the "Old Hispanic" segment of Southern California society and is thus not classed as Chicano, and partly because his supreme egotism will not admit of any inconvenience because of ancestry. One of the first things we learn about Mendoza when we meet him in *Case Pending* is that he never pretends to less intelligence than he has, and a few pages later we are told that he does not enjoy solving puzzles, because confrontation with something he does not know is an outrage to his vanity (ii). His ego gives him the advantage of objectivity: unlike most policemen, Mendoza does not mind breaking bad news to strangers, partly

171

because their reactions enable him to observe the genuineness of their emotional involvement (iii).

Mendoza is unique among procedural policemen in that he is independently wealthy. Orphaned at an early age, he grew up in the home of his grandfather, a shrewd old miser who made his family wear second-hand clothes while he bought up real estate in those areas where Los Angeles was expanding. When the old man died, Luis, a rookie patrolman, inherited a fortune but decided to stay on in police work; now he drives a Ferrari, and the newspapers call him "the Millionaire Cop." Mendoza is another of those policemen whose family life receives full treatment in the stories. Besides his wife Alison (whom he met while working on the first case in the series) and the twins, the household is composed of a remarkable menagerie of four cats and one sheepdog.

Mendoza is an intuitive detective who combines the customary slogging routine of police work with his own talent for hunches; he has the reputation of using a crystal ball in his intuitive leaps, but his only real eccentricity is that he thinks best with a handful of playing cards and keeps a deck in his desk as a stimulant to thought.

Like most other procedural policemen, Mendoza does not belong to any organized religious group but is a long-time agnostic. He also shares the basic conservatism of other policemen, especially in his attitude toward gun-control laws, which he considers unenforceable and also unconstitutional, since they serve only to disarm the honest citizen.

Sergeant Gabriel Villanueva Wager of the Denver Police Department is the protagonist in the series by Rex Burns. The Hispanos call Wager a "coyote," that is, a person of mixed Chicano and Anglo ancestry. Because of his dual heritage, Wager represents a cultural conflict that expresses itself in terms of ethnic expectations, with his Anglo colleagues anticipating that he will react like a "Mex" and the Chicano community expecting him to side with and protect "his own" people or be considered a traitor. Wager's response to the conflict has been the development of a coat of protective hardness: "his" people are the police, and the hell with those who expect or demand automatic ethnic loyalties. The sense of disassociation comes through with special strength in a scene in *The Alvarez Journal*, in which Wager and several other policemen go down to Juarez, tailing a suspect. The Anglo cops joke with him about "coming home," but Wager feels no identity with the noise and dirt and artificiality, only isolation and alienation (xii). At the same time, he knows he has been discriminated against because of his Chicano half, with Anglos of no greater ability being promoted over him.

Gabriel Wager is one of the few procedural cops whose marriage has ended in divorce. As with his ethnic heritage, though, he refuses to suffer any trauma: it was a bad marriage to a woman not really suited to be a policeman's wife, and he feels no sense of loss. A more meaningful aspect of his past was his eight-year hitch in the Marine Corps, which involved service in Korea.

Wager is a hard-working cop, though, courageous and resourceful. He takes pride in his job and would like to think that his own work is like his father's carpentry, carefully and conscientiously done, not sloppy or negligent. His kinship with the police sub-culture finds expression chiefly in a sense of regret over the passing of old landmarks and other despoliation of old Denver in the name of urban renewal.

He is the only Hispanic policeman willing to joke about his ethnic origins. Wager and his friend Detective Billington engage in elaborate parodies of racist rhetoric, Billington accusing him of "greaser" cynicism and Wager responding with accusations of the wrongs done to the land of Aztlan. When, in another story, a female witness compliments his being an old-fashioned gentleman, Wager straight-facedly informs her that it is part of his "Hispano heritage."[1]

The only English procedural detective of Hispanic descent is Michael Gilbert's detective Chief Inspector Patrick Petrella of Q Division, London Metropolitan Police. Petrella's father was a member of the political branch of the Spanish police, with the special assignment of protecting the life of General Franco, and his mother a woman from an English professional family. Young Patrick spent the first eight years of his life in Spain, was then at his mother's insistence transplanted to an English preparatory school; upon completion of that phase of his education he was enrolled in the American University in Beirut, spent some time in Cairo, returned to London, and joined the Metropolitan Police as a constable.[2] Petrella feels no discrimination as a result of his foreign descent, nor does he suffer any schizophrenic symptoms because of his mixed blood, his only ethnic manifestations being a pleasant disposition that envelops and contains, deep inside him, his "black Iberian demon."[3]

Gilbert portrays Petrella as solid copper; he is a family man, though we never learn his wife's name or anything about her appearance. Scenes in the stories take place in the Petrella home, but without description or atmosphere. Even as a young detective he is ambitious, honest and conscientious to the extent that one of his superiors suspects that he aspires to be assistant commissioner one day.[4] His scrupulous honesty is manifested in *Blood and Judgment* in his refusal to accept what he considers an unjust verdict and his going ahead on his own to re-investigate the case (ix), and in *Petrella at Q* in his refusal to accept a bribe that would never have been discovered (72).

Petrella has one other quality that distinguishes him from most other policemen: he likes to attend church, though it should be noted that his affiliation is Church of England (40).

Frankie Hernandez of McBain's 87th Precinct is a detective of Puerto Rican descent who serves as a liaison between the police and the Puerto Rican community. His fellow cops, who expect him to know every Hispanic person in the city, come to him for advice and information, and the Puerto Ricans in the precinct depend on him for protection from both criminal elements and the law. Like Gabriel Wager, though, Hernandez refuses to accept alignment with "his people" and enforces the law to the limit of his ability.

Hernandez' dedication is to The Cause, which is his determination to prove to the neighborhood, the cops, and eventually the world that Puerto Ricans are people worthy of dignity and deserving of respect. He refuses to be angry with the overbearing Andy Parker, the sadist of the squad who in *See Them Die* insists on calling him "Chico" and who refers to the criminal Pepe Miranda as "your pal" (iii). When Miranda holes up in a house, shooting anybody who approaches, Hernandez insists on going in to get him. That way, he says, the community will feel itself vindicated: whether he gets Miranda or Miranda gets him, a Puerto Rican wins (xi). Frankie loses his life in this attempt, and as his body is borne away the Puerto Rican shopkeepers close their doors as a mark of respect (xvii).

Hernandez' successor on the 87th Squad is Alexiandre

Delagado, who investigates the beating of Jose Huerta by four men in *Hail, Hail the Gang's All Here!* Delgado lacks the idealism of Hernandez, but he does understand the Puerto Rican psyche. At the end of the investigation, having discovered that Huerta was a pusher who was corrupting the neighborhood and that his beating was an act of communal punishment, Delgado agrees that justice has been done, and the case goes down as officially unsolved (186-92).

Cesar Rodriguez, in the Ivor Maddox series by Elizabeth Linington, is a detective whose chief function in *Greenmask!* is to get hooked on mystery fiction, following his addiction through Agatha Christie, Michael Gilbert and Ed McBain. Rodriguez does, however, deliver one significant observation on the inconsistency of Anglo-Saxons, who celebrate the glorious Spanish heritage of California and at the same time talk about the dirty Mexes (xvi).

Fernando Arenas, a Puerto Rican in O'Donnell's Norah Mulcahaney series, is described as a thin, dark-haired detective whose nervous intensity is such that he burns up calories no matter how much he eats, and who left his native San Juan to find a job with dignity in order to help his family back home. To Ferdi, with his background in the old-fashioned virtues of hard work, the Patrol Guide is a bible to be followed to the letter, and he feels uncomfortable with the growing rebellion against discipline among his fellow policemen.[5]

There is one woman Puerto Rican cop, Pilar Nieves, who is the fiancee of Ferdi Arenas. She is one of the four policewomen killed in line of duty in *No Business Being a Cop* (ii).

Whether as a direct result of their heritage or as a reaction against the determination of the ethnic majority to consider them "different," the Hispanic cops have developed two qualities that are common to most of them: an intensity of commitment in their personal and professional lives, and a self-sufficiency that creates in them a tendency to independence.

The intensity manifests itself in the case of Patrick Petrella when his son is kidnapped by Augie the Pole in *Petrella at Q*. When Petrella and his colleagues capture Augie and he pretends not to know where the boy is being held, Petrella's "Spanish half," as one of his fellow policemen calls it, takes over. He takes Augie off into another room and works him over until the Pole is eager to tell

Petrella all he wants to know. Petrella is normally an easy-going policeman with a pleasant disposition, but the autopsy performed on Augie after he is killed with a shotgun by another hood shows extensive cutting and burning (219-21).

The intensity makes itself felt in the perfectionism of Luis Mendoza, who, according to one of his subordinates, would get off his deathbed to straighten a crooked picture, and in the determination of Gabriel Wager, whose captain can't decide whether to be pleased at Wager's dedication or to worry about his being a prima donna. It is evident in Frankie Hernandez' commitment to The Cause and even in Cesar Rodriguez' addiction to mystery fiction. Ferdi Arenas shows it when he discovers that his murdered fiancee had been beaten by a former boyfriend two weeks before her death; only a firm direct order from his superior officer keeps him from carrying out direct and personal vengeance.[6] Except in the reference to Petrella's "Spanish half" there is no mention of hot Latin blood in reference to the personalities of any of these policemen, but the intensity of spirit is undeniably there.

The other quality is their self-sufficiency. Gabriel Wager knows policemen must work together, but he does not give a damn for teams and prefers to feel pride in being able to do a job better than any other cop; he does not need to identify with any group, having found in himself all the identity he will ever need. The Director of Public Prosecutions sees the same quality in Patrick Petrella, whom he calls an "independent-minded animal" with good reason: Petrella is determined to see justice done whether the Department supports his efforts or not.[7] The strain of self-sufficiency is especially strong in the supreme egotism of Luis Mendoza, who, in the opinion of one of his colleagues, is over-compensating for the times when he was just another "dirty little Mex kid" in a slum street.[8]

Chapter 14

John Creasy

A READER THUMBING his way through almost any encyclopedia of mystery writers may find himself mildly puzzled by a succession of references like these:

ASHE, Gordon: See CREASEY, John
DEANE, Norman: See CREASEY, John
FRAZER, Robert Caine: See CREASEY, John

and so on through some twenty or more pseudonyms, all of whom are John Creasy. If the encyclopedia supplies a complete bibliography for each writer, the number of pages required merely to list Creasy's published books will be greater than the number devoted to the critical essay on a major writer like Arthur Conan Doyle or Raymond Chandler.

It would be unfortunate, really, if John Creasey were remembered only as the man who wrote six hundred books under twenty-six or twenty-eight pen names (commentators seem unable to agree on the number) rather than as a popular writer who was able to maintain a reasonably good quality along with his prodigious output, and especially as the author of the George Gideon series under the pseudonym of J.J. Marric and the Roger West series under his own name. We mention these two series as of special importance in the development of the police procedural, the West series having started in 1942 as an example of the Great Policeman school and later converted to the procedural format, and the much more significant Gideon series, which opened with *Gideon's Day* in 1955 and became one of the most popular and influential series in the procedural literature. When the presses finally caught up with Creasy's prolific typewriter five years after his death, there were forty-three titles in the West series and twenty-one Gideon books.

There are no avowed masterpieces among them, but neither are there any failures.

It was part of John Creasey's credo to write police stories in which the fiction is based upon a vast store of incidental knowledge of police work, court procedures, and forensic science, a determination that was to set a worthy example for procedural writers who followed him; as the ackowledgments page of any of his novels will show, he drew extensively upon the expertise of people in industry and government to authenticate the technical details of the story. Another of his aims, according to his own statement, was to portray a policeman—and also a criminal—as a human being first. The thought may now strike us as a little sentimental, but Creasey also held to the idea of the possibility of a near-perfect world and tried to exemplify that possibility in each book he wrote.[1] His desire, finally, was to write thrillers "without bedroom scenes,"[2] a delicacy in which he succeeds so well that a potentially sensational scene in *Gideon's River* (ii) is over before the reader is aware that a rape has taken place.

Creasey's narrative technique involves a certain amount of formulaic writing, as does that of most series authors. In the West stories the mystery is customarily built around a single major crime, whereas the Gideon novels usually have a multiple-plot structure, with the story-lines "nested," so that the mystery introduced first is the one solved last, the next-to-first solved next-to-last, and so on. Frequently, especially in the Gideon series, he uses the "inverted" technique, permitting the reader to witness the commission of the crime, with the result that a heavy sense of irony is added to the account of police efforts to solve it. The endings of the stories deserve comment: it is not unusual for a West novel to conclude with the involvement of military units equipped with helicopters and incendiary bombs, whereas the endings of the Gideon stories are usually "softer." Finally, Creasey is a remarkably careful writer considering the speed of his composition, to the extent that we will forgive him a slip like the one in *Inspector West Cries Wolf*, where he apparently forgot that the story was taking place on a Sunday (xvi, xviii).

Roger West makes his appearance in *Inspector West Takes Charge* (1942). The novel is not a procedural: police methods get scant attention; there is almost no feel of the police sub-culture, and no teamwork. West has little contact with his fellow policemen, working instead with his friend Mark Lessing, a brilliant amateur straight out of the Golden Age. Two years later, in *Inspector West at Home*, Creasey purposely steers away from police methodology, with West in the role of the Trapped Policeman who is under suspicion of having taken a bribe and who works again with Lessing and a private enquiry agent in the effort to vindicate himself. Actually, West is in a position to call on the Yard for help fairly early in the story, but he conceals information from them and enlists the aid of crime reporters and other civilians.

The transition of the West series into the spirit of the police procedural was neither sudden nor consistent. *Parcels for Inspector West* (1956) is marginal as a procedural, with much of the story-interest carried along by the families of the victims and the point of view away from the police for whole chapters, and so is *Strike for Death* (1958), in which West alone bears most of the burden of narrative interest. In the later stories, however, like *A Splinter of Glass* (1972) and *Theft of Magna Carta* (1973), West works as a team-member with his fellow cops, and the normal police procedures impel the story. Curiously, in the last West story, *A Sharp Rise in Crime* (1978), Creasey returns to the pattern of *Inspector West at Home,* with West once again working as a loner to clear himself of suspicion.

Roger West, whose nickname is Handsome, is a strikingly good-looking man whose superior calls him the Yard's Glamour Boy, and he is a hot-headed policeman who sometimes cuts corners and is frequently at odds with his boss, Commander Coppell, who rakes him over the coals on an average of once per novel. He is also an excellent detective. Only about 20% of his cases remain unsolved, in comparison to 50% for Scotland Yard as a whole. He is regarded as the most successful senior officer at the Yard, a policeman who, according to his wife, always expects the impossible and, according to himself, gets it. West's method is more intuitive than logical, with considerable reliance on hunches, which he prefers to call intelligent deductions. He is a policeman with a strong sense of honesty that wins him the respect of hostile newspaper reporters and even an admission from Commander Coppell that he is "too good to be true."[3]

West's relationships with his fellow policemen, especially his subordinates, are good in the same degree as his relations with his superiors are bad. Most of the people at the Yard, including those he commands, call him "Handsome" and respect his personal qualities as well as his professional ability. They know his reputation for being tough, but they have seen his capacity for softness and for taking people's troubles too hard. He can throw his weight around, can push his men almost as hard as he pushes himself, but he has the reputation of thinking of those men as human beings and not as ciphers.

Throughout the West series Creasey adheres to the procedural convention of lengthy and detailed accounts of his progatonist's family life. Janet West is one of a number of police wives who want their husbands in some other line of work; in one of the early stories she says marriage to Roger is like being married to a machine and complains that, whatever else happens, he always puts his job first.[4] Later, she accuses him of volunteering for night work in order to be away from her.[5] West's two sons also give him and Janet some problems, especially Martin, who eventually emigrates to Australia. Typically, however, by the end of the series, most of the family difficulties have been resolved: Janet has become reconciled to Roger's job, and Martin is back in London.

It may be, as we are told in several stories, that George Gideon is the most famous detective in the world, but there can be little question that among mystery lovers his name is better known than almost any other procedural policeman. One reason for this prestige is that Creasey (writing as J.J. Marric) takes us inside the personality of Gideon to a far greater extent than he did with Roger West, and to a greater degree than most writers do.

One of Gideon's strongest motivations as a policeman is the breadth of his empathy with all kinds of people, good and bad. Shortly after we meet him in *Gideon's Day* we learn of his "oneness with London," a quality that makes him love the hard pavement the way rural people love the soil (ii). This affection for his native city produces in Gideon an intense empathy with the victims of crime; he identifies with the weak and the elderly, and he has a special secret horror of child-molestors. He can also understand and sympathize with the problems of criminals and their families, partly because he knows how the hard London life can breed crime among the poor, and partly because he tends to feel for people in trouble, especially the young, whom he frequently identifies with his own children.[6] Gideon's "oneness" with his community thus becomes a representation of the policeman's unity with the Guilty Society, which he must seek to purge of evil while at the same time being a member of it.

Part of Gideon's compulsion is a sense of guilt, deriving from the night when his child lay seriously ill and his wife Kate had begged him not to go on duty; Gideon had told her to pull herself together and had gone to work. The child died during the night, and Gideon never forgave himself. The resulting tensions between George and Kate Gideon finally heal, but the death of the child is mentioned in almost every one of the stories, usually in connection with Gideon's sympathy for parents whose children have been killed or abducted, or in the context of his pity for young people in trouble with the law.

Gideon's ability to empathize with criminals gives him a special edge as a detective. One hood, who has made a study of the way he works, can testify that Gideon can put himself in criminals' shoes and anticipate what they are planning.[7] Another advantage is his enormous energy, which, according to a fellow policeman, would put most coppers in their graves. As an administrator, though, Gideon shows up to best advantage in his ability to organize and to delegate responsibility, though he is sometimes irritated by the necessity of turning over jobs to other people instead of seeing them through. It is Gideon's approach to problem-solving that sets him off in sharpest contrast to Roger West: where West is fundamentally intuitive, Gideon is logical and methodological.

As commander of Scotland Yard, Gideon has consistently won the loyalty of his subordinates, most of whom call him "George" or "Gee-Gee." His reputation for fairness is demonstrated in one instance when a policeman has made a hash of an assignment and Gideon wants him to have another opportunity as quickly as possible in order to restore his self-esteem,[8] and even more strongly in the case of the unfortunate Detective Superintendent Micklewright, who had gotten drunk and beaten his wife: Gideon knows Micklewright must be charged with attempted murder, but his first concern is to sober him up and get a psychiatrist to examine him, and then to get him a lawyer.[9] Gideon follows another practice unfortunately far too rare even among fictional superior officers, the policy of spotting the good work of bright youngsters and seeing to it that they are recognized, with the double result that he gets the best efforts out of his rookies and also enlists their strong personal loyalties to himself. During the latter part of his career Gideon comes to realize that, whether he likes it or not, he has become a father figure at the Yard. His relationships with his superiors also distinguish him from Roger West: whereas West's life is a succession of rows with Commander Coppell, Gideon enjoys a warm and pleasant association with Police Commissioner Scott-Marle.

George Gideon shares the social-political conservatism of most policemen, but unlike most of them he experiences a strong strain of what we can justifiably call old-fashioned patriotism. The quality manifests itself most strongly in the political theme of *Gideon's Vote,* in which Scotland Yard finds itself caught between two extremist factions in a parliamentary election, one a ban-the-bomb-type "Fight for Peace" group and the other a neo-facist "Queen and Country" clique. Gideon, who considers himself a middle-of-the-road man politically, regards both groups as fanatics, and although he respects their sincerity, he knows that passions can grow into extremism that will tolerate and excuse political evil. A kind of benign fate watches over England, Gideon tells himself, moderating the potentially dangerous effects of fanaticism (xiv). His concern for the common weal shows itself repeatedly in his efforts to prevent crime. Investigating a series of food-thefts, Gideon's concern is that the loss of supply may affect the standard of living, and in the case of a threat to a power plant he worries about the damage to the national economy from a series of blackouts.[10]

We are not surprised, finally, that George Gideon shares John Creasey's hope for the possibility of a near-perfect world and that he deplores some of the developments in contemporary society. He refuses to see the flower-children culture as the real pattern of modern society, though he knows there is small use hoping that these tendencies will be short-lived. In his last appearance in the series, Gideon is worried about the future of a young hippie-type woman, wondering how she will face the future in a society with such drastically altered conventions, morals and beliefs.[11]

Britain, in the West and Gideon series, is the land of law and order, where the rights of the individual are to be respected and police intimidation discouraged. The atmosphere of civil security pervades all the stories, enveloping even the violence and desperation of the gangs and individuals with whom West and Gideon must deal. The police are severely restricted in their handling of suspects, to the intense disgust of Roger West, who considers it unfair that policemen must never hurt a rogue. Illegal searches are not tolerated, the way they are in some locales, as West is reminded by the Police Commissioner, who calls his attention to the fact that a citizen is legally justified in shooting an intruder in his own home, even if the intruder is a policeman.[12] When a criminal is apprehended, the Judges' Rules apply: he must be informed of his rights, no matter how ludicrous the police may consider the routine. The use of firearms by policemen is restricted to cases where the need for them is clearly demonstrated, and even then only after the filing of a formal application and approval by a magistrate or a justice of the peace. The legendary courtesy of the British policeman in dealing with all kinds of civilians receives repeated attention, as it does in the case of the nameless sergeant in *Gideon's Power* who calls upon a man whose daughter is missing: the sergeant keeps urging the distraught father to calm down, offers to go get his wife, and suggests he have a drink to steady his nerves, even though, as he shortly confides to his superintendent, he considers the man to be off his rocker (viii).

The force of tradition and custom lies heavy on the stories, much to the disgust of policemen, who feel some need for revision of systems that are outmoded. There is, for example, the existence of the City of London police, an autonomous and independent force in the middle of the district covered by the Metropolitan Police Force, which George Gideon considers an anachronism.[13] Then there is the jurisdictional tangle created by the overlap of territory between Scotland Yard and the provincial forces, causing Roger West to support the idea of a Federal Police Force with national jurisdiction, a reform viewed with no enthusiasm by either the Home Office or the county men.[14]

Chapter 15

Maurice Procter

IN ADDITION TO HIS ABILITY to write suspenseful police novels, Maurice Procter has at least two claims to importance in the development of the police procedural, as one of the early pioneers in the field and as a transitional figure between the Great Policeman school and the straight procedural approach. For those readers who want police fiction to be an accurate reflection of real-life police work, his credentials are impeccable: Procter served for nineteen years on the Halifax Borough Police in Yorkshire, the scene of his stories. We are not surprised, then, at the emergence in his writing of keen insights into the police mind, like the observation in *The Chief Inspector's Statement* that it is important to appear busy even when one has nothing to do, because there is "a tremendous amount of bull in the police service" (II,vi).

After his resignation from the force, Procter turned to the writing of fiction and in 1951 published *The Chief Inspector's Statement* (U.S. title, *The Pennycross Murders*), featuring Chief Inspector Philip Hunter, New Scotland Yard. This novel, as we will presently explain, is basically a Great Policeman story with strong inclinations to the procedural approach. Historically, the date is significant, because in 1951 only Lawrence Treat had produced any stories that can be labeled procedurals. Three years later Procter began the series for which he is best remembered, with *Hell Is a City* (U.S. title, *Somewhere in This City*), a genuine procedural novel in which the protagonist is Detective Inspector Harry Martineau of the "Granchester" Police Department. Once again, the date (1954) is important, because it sets the beginning of the Martineau series a year ahead of the introduction of Creasey's George Gideon. Procter turned back to Philip Hunter for only one more novel, *I Will Speak Daggers* (1956), which appeared in the U.S. as *The Ripper*. He continued the Martineau series through *Hideaway*, which appeared in 1968, five years before his death.

We can call *The Chief Inspector's Statement* a transition between the Great Policeman type, in which the important detection is done almost solely by a single superior policeman, and the procedural story, in which teamwork is the point of emphasis, because in the telling of the story Philip Hunter necessarily holds the spotlight as narrator, but the book is full of penetration into police attitudes and plausible accounts of police methodology. The "statement" is more than just a police report; Hunter gives a full account of his participation in the investigation in the village of Pennycross, including his falling in love with a local woman. The pace is much slower than that of most procedurals, with incidents widely separated. Suspense frequently lags, interrupted by long "atmospheric" passages and by development of the love story. The second Hunter story, *I Will Speak Daggers*, comes close to qualifying as a "pure" procedural by any definition, the point of view resting almost exclusively with the police and their work, and substantially no side-issues or "atmosphere." In this novel Procter switches to the third-person narrator, and, although Hunter is the protagonist, he shares the action with his subordinates.

Philip Hunter is a harsh policeman whose deep, growling voice at one point is compared to the hinges of an old door and at another to radio interference. He can be rough on subjects, as when he takes the husband of a murder victim to headquarters for questioning in *I Will Speak Daggers,* refuses to let him smoke, outlines the case against him, and defies him to disprove it (viii), and rough on his subordinates, as when he bawls out one of the local policemen for losing a "client," in this case a murderer who had jumped into the river and drowned in spite of the policeman's risking own life to save him (xiv). He is, however, a fair officer, sharing his turn on the long watches during the Pennycross affair, not asking his men for something he will not endure himself.[1]

Procter invented fictitious towns and cities as the settings of all his mysteries, but we are especially interested in "Granchester," the locale of the Martineau stories. Granchester, which might be either Manchester or Liverpool, is an inland port, is called the "Metropolis of the North," and is about three hours by train from London. The Granchester City Police, 1100 strong, is a proud force with its own forensic experts, and it believes it can do anything Scotland Yard can do.[2]

In his first appearance in *Hell Is a City*, Harry Martineau has just a hint of the aura of the Great Policeman: he likes to play the piano, he already has a reputation as the Great Inspector Martineau, and his courage in the face of danger borders on the flamboyant (I,vi; II,iv). In the later stories, though, he reminds us more of the procedural cops, sharing their self-doubts and their stoic attitudes.

Martineau's family life does not enter into the stories to the degree that Roger West's and George Gideon's do, largely because he and his wife Julia solve their major problem in the first novel. Julia, who is inclined to frigidity, does not share Harry's wish for children, and the resulting tensions cause him to drink too much and her to become defensive and withdrawn. The problem is resolved when Martineau overhears a piece of earthy folk-wisdom in a pub, goes home determined to put it into effect, and finds Julia ready to concur (VI,v).

Martineau's chief abilities as a detective are his readily evocative memory and a sensitivity to the criminal mind which on occasion conveys the impression of superior intuition. Like most other fictional policemen he hates desk work, preferring to be in the field with his men. Unlike Gideon, he is not good at delegating tasks, being best satisfied with those jobs he does himself. The exception is a job involving technology, which he admits he does not understand. Neither is he the kind of superior office who prefers to sit quietly in his office while his men are in danger; in almost every story Martineau engages in hand-to-hand combat with a thug who is armed and desperate.

Martineau's relationships with his subordinates are good, especially with his assistant Sergeant Devery, who works closely with him on most cases. There is a rapport between the two that allows for status without intimidation, as when Martineau on one occasion reminds Devery to address him as "sir," an injunction Devery pointedly ignores the next time he speaks but which he remembers the next time after that; Martineau takes no notice.[3] Martineau is good at recognizing the promise of young policemen and placing them in positions where their talents will be used to best advantage, as he does with Police Constable Ainslie in *A Body to Spare* and Police Constable Norton in *Exercise Hoodwink*. We have spoken earlier of Martineau's good working relationship with

Superintendent Vanbrugh of the county force, always a touchy business because of the traditional rivalry between city and county, but one which Martineau handles well because he knows how to practice the ritual that simultaneously tolerates and minimizes the hostility.[4]

Procter introduced into the Martineau series an innovation that has been followed by only one other procedural writer (Ed McBain), the use of a series villain.[5] Dixie Costello, the chief mobster in Granchester, is the head of an organization that is either responsible for most of the crimes in the city or gets involved by hijacking stolen goods or simply absorbing the smaller operations. Costello is a suave, cool operator who considers himself a businessman and uses his legitimate projects as a cover for his criminal activities. Martineau expends much of his energy trying to put him behind bars, no easy task in regard to a man whose power is such that lesser criminals are afraid to mention his name and who can shut up a potential witness with a casual remark. Dixie has a better intelligence system than the police, which even includes agents under cover in police headquarters. Martineau finally nails him in *Exercise Hoodwink* (xxiii), puts him away for two years, and, after his release, catches him in another infraction and has him behind bars again at the end of the last novel in the series.[6]

Because of his own front-line experience, Procter's stories are especially good in the use of police methods, with a reasonable balance between those that involve forensic technology and those based on common sense. In the technical category we find the use of ultra-violet and infra-red light to bring out bloodstains on clothing, treating "hot" money with eosin that will show up on the perpetrator's hands, and identification of dandruff, which can be typed like blood.[7] There is also heavy reliance on those methods developed by cumulative police experience, like passing on gossip from one suspect to another to set them at odds with each other and get them to talk, making a suspect talk by threatening to get him and his family into trouble, and having a suspect sit in a freshly polished chair from which his fingerprints can be lifted without his awareness.

Britain in the Procter novels, as in those of John Creasy, is the country dominated by the principle of non-violence, where the use of firearms by the police is severely restricted. The restraint makes things hard for the police, in the opinion of Harry Martineau, but he agrees that it is better so in the long run, with less killing all around. Even a fleeing criminal has certain rights: the police may not shoot at him unless it is certain that he is armed and dangerous, and when he is captured the Judges' Rules govern the manner in which he may be placed under arrest. British law also protects the general public from invasion of privacy, and the police may not tap telephones. The duty of the policeman is made clear by the definition which lists the prevention of crime before its investigation, on the assumption that it is the more important responsibility.[8] A smart policeman who knows the law, however, can find ways to construe those regulations that tend to protect criminals. On both of the occasions when Martineau arrests Dixie Costello he enters the premises without a warrant: on the first occasion he uses the exception that no warrant is necessary when there is danger to life, and in the second instance he cites the principle of Immediate Pursuit, both of which are technically applicable.

Procter's formula involves frequent use of the reversal technique, with switches of point of view back and forth between the criminal in flight and the police, and the caper approach, in which the reader is given insights the police do not have. The free interchange between fictional viewponts is sometimes used to plaster over the cracks in the continuity of suspense, most obviously in *Killer at Large*, where detailed descriptions of the fugitive's efforts at concealment are apparently used to maintain the suspense lacking in the main plot.

Chapter 16
Hillary Waugh

LIKE MOST OF THE OTHER writers we are discussing, Hillary Waugh had experience as a mystery writer before undertaking a police procedural. In the late 1940s and early '50s he had produced a series of three novels featuring Sheridan Wesley, a standard private-eye type who conducted his investigations in the company of his gorgeous blonde wife, the two of them exchanging sparkling repartee in the manner of Nick and Nora Charles. Waugh's approach to mystery writing changed, according to his own report, when he read a little paperback collection of true accounts of murders of young women, and he was struck by the opportunities offered in stories of murders that are not mere puzzles designed to entertain, in which death is grim and ugly, and in which the vicim is an object of the reader's sympathy instead of the traditional unmourned corpse.[1] With these intentions in mind, Waugh turned out an acknowledged masterpiece, *Last Seen Wearing—* (1952).

Last Seen Wearing— is one of the few procedural stores that will not only endure a second reading but will reveal further evidences of expert craftsmanship in a second and even a third. The quality of the novel that strikes most readers on first acquaintance is the sustained sense of reality. Instead of an automatically glamorous setting like New York, Waugh chose as the locale of his story a small college town, and instead of a sensational crime the disappearance of a woman freshman from the campus. Even when the missing-person case turns out to be a homicide midway through the story, we are struck by the ordinariness of the murder, the bludgeoning of a young woman who is pregnant. The people in the story (including especially the police) are not gifted, wealthy or eccentric; even the private investigator called in at the insistence of the victim's parents is a conventional real-life shamus. The realism of the story is further sharpened by an accounting that is almost journalistic in tone, with calendar dates as chapter headings, and with constant references to well-known places, other colleges and universities, and even telephone numbers. As for the police, they impress us as standard small-town policemen: Chief Frank Ford relies more heavily on cop-sense than on forensic science in his role as detective protagonist, and so does his less gifted assistant, Sergeant Cameron.

If Waugh's intention in the writing of *Last Seen Wearing*— was to turn out a realistic tale, his accomplishment was to produce a well-made novel. The structure follows a clean classic line, in which the mystery solved at the end is the same as the problem introduced at the beginning, with no spinoffs, no secondary plots, and no residual mystery. The framework of the narrative is the traditional seven-step development introduced by Poe and refined by the formal-problem writers of the Golden Age. One of the strongest evidences of Waugh's complete control of his material is the manner in which the problem is defined in the opening sections: Lowell Mitchell is suddenly and unaccountably missing from the campus, with no tenable reason for her disappearance or clue to her whereabouts; all possible explanations are eliminated with the meticulous care that is customary in the locked-room mystery. With the arrival of the police, a suggestion is offered (Lowell is pregnant) and rejected, and a further evidence of Waugh's careful craftsmanship is the later revelation that this initial solution is at least part of the truth. Throughout the subsequent development of the narrative the initial problem is repeatedly re-analyzed, viewed from different perspectives, and enlarged by the accumulation of additional evidence, but not substantially altered.

Anyone who has read Hillary Waugh's critical essays on mystery-writing should not be surprised at the tight unity of *Last Seen Wearing*—. In one article he compares the plotting of the story to the way in which a master musician dominates and controls his instrument, and he draws a parallel between the effect of a well-plotted story and the intellectual pleasure of a subtle chess combination. In a really good plot, says Waugh, there is nothing extraneous.[2] Elsewhere, he compares the discipline of the mystery story with that of the sonnet, and insists that a novel must have form, shape and direction.[3]

In building the suspense in the story, Waugh seems to have made things as difficult as possible for himself, by deliberately refusing those hackneyed standbys,the cliffhanger, the red herring, and the sensational development. Where a less skillful writer will bring us to the edge of the chair at the end of a chapter and then move the story off in another direction, Waugh purposely builds the big developments into their natural places in the unfolding narrative. There are false clues in the story but they are disposed of after a few pages and are not permitted to mislead the reader. Finally, there is no suspense by means of sensationalism: the only shot fired in the story goes straight up in the air for the purpose of stopping a snooper, who turns out to be, prosaically enough, not even a Peeping Tom but a reporter looking for an angle (71-8).

The examination and re-examination of theories and evidence, which would be tedious in less gifted hands, becomes a major vehicle for suspense in *Last Seen Wearing—*. Lowell Mitchell's diary is studied four times during the investigation: first by the college officials for a clue to her whereabouts (11-24), then by Chief Ford to get a line on her male friends (55), once again at the inquest to explain some cryptic references (110-11), and finally by Chief Ford to decipher Lowell's private code (132); whole passages from the diary are repeated, but each time with heightened suspense as fresh interpretations are applied and new revelations made.

The police methodology, as we have already implied, is not spectacular or "scientific," consisting rather in questionings of possible witnesses and suspects, following up clues and hunches, and the employment of a cleaning woman as a spy (149-52). The only use of modern technology is the employment of a vacuum-cleaner in the suspect's room to determine whether the victim had been there (179). The most dramatic development in the story—Ford's floating a block of ice down the river to demonstrate where the body should have come ashore—is based rather on common sense than on forensic science (115-17).

What Hillary Waugh demonstrated in *Last Seen Wearing—* is that a police procedural story can be suspenseful without resort to cliffhangers and red herrings, realistic without shoot-outs and gadgetry, compelling without sensationalism. He also showed that a single well-constructed story-line can hold a reader's interest more effectively than a half-dozen or so interwoven plots where suspense is rescued by one element when it begins to lag in another. It is not surprising that this novel is regarded by many as the finest police procedural ever written, or that Julian Symons, at the suggestion of Raymond Chandler, included it in his list of the hundred greatest crime novels of all time.[4]

Waugh did not develop *Last Seen Wearing—* into a series, but seven years later he began the Fred Fellows series, which shares much of the tone of the earlier novel. "Bristol," Massachusetts, is replaced by "Stockford," Connecticut, another fictitious small city, and Chief Frank Ford by Chief Fred Fellows. Fellows reminds us of Ford in some respects: both are folksy types, both rely on common sense, and both share a strong sympathy with people in trouble. Fellows, however, has a more decidedly professional attitude toward police work, and he is insightful and even brilliant where Ford is tenacious and determined.

Fred Fellows is almost deceptively homespun. He chews tobacco and he tells folksy stories, but he has one of the best logical minds in detective fiction. In the first novel in the series, *Sleep Long, My Love* (1959), Sergeant Wilks accuses him of exploring meanings, not for what they represent, but as manifestations of fourth-dimensional thought (xxiii). Fellows does not deny his tendency to theorize: theory makes it possible to anticipate criminals' next moves and intercept them (xxi). In several of the stories Fellows performs feats of ratiocination in the best tradition of the classic mystery, as he does in *Pure Poison* when he tracks down a peripatetic suspect by comparing his normal itinerary with a list of places where his friends are located (x). Waugh calls him an "imaginative thinker,"[5] which he most decidedly is: in *Prisoner's Plea* his quick insight comes up with a possible explanation of a motive in a case a number of other people have worked on, without anyone's having thought of that possibility (vi).

Fred Fellows' intellectual strength, however, lies in his ability to reason from theory to application, from general principle to specific instance. This deductive power is made evident in those platitudinous-sounding stories he loves to tell, each of which illustrates a fundamental truth germane to the case under consideration. There is, for example, the one about the hunter who escaped a trespassing fine by committing a murder (a person will commit a crime to hide a greater crime, but not a lesser one), and the one about the man who shot a BB gun into the ceiling until it fell upon him (wait long enough, and something will develop).[6] Fellows' role as twentieth century Aesop does on occasion annoy Sergeant Wilks, who usually misses the point of the stories, and who at one point asks him to hurry one up when they are talking long-distance.[7]

In addition to his capacity for disciplined logic, Fellows has a cosiderable store of applicable knowledge. Some of it comes from reading, like the trick of bringing out indentations on a note pad by exposing it to iodine fumes, which he got out of a criminology book.[8] Much of it, though, has been developed by his habit of organizing his own experience: when Sergeant Wilks expresses amazement at his knowledge of local distances, Fellows explains that working out time- and distance-problems is a hobby of his.[9] In *The Late Mrs. D.* (xxiv), his ability to analyze typefaces has a strong flavor of Sherlock Holmes' feat with newspaper type in *The Hound of the Baskervilles*.

Fellows' capacities are such, as a matter of fact, as to place him on occasion in the Great Policeman school of detection. In *The Late Mrs. D.* he has solved the case slightly more than half way through the story, and though he does not have sufficient proof at that point, his solution turns out to be the right one at the conclusion (xvii). Fellows has a reputation for being right, and as he tells Sergeant Wilks, he is not the executive type but must try everything himself.

Two other qualities of Fred Fellows that come through strongly in the stories are his sense of professionalism and his compassion and sympathy for people in trouble.

Fellows' strongest motivation as police chief is his sense of responsibility. When his son reminds him that he is not the whole department and that Sergeant Wilks can look after things in his absence, Fellows agrees but insists that there is one important difference: as chief he, not Wilks or anybody else, is ultimately reponsible.[10] His treatment of the news media is a reflection of his concern for the dignity of police work: he places limitations on the photographers at a murder scene, because pictures of dead bodies appearing in the tabloids are not going to be pictures of dead bodies discovered in his territory,[11] and when he catches a bunch of reporters playing gin rummy at headquarters, he reminds them that they are not in Kelly's Pool Hall.[12] As chief, he is conscientious in instilling a sense of professionalism into his men. He can chew out a patrolman for appearing on duty with an improperly polished uniform button, but he is just as careful to compliment another one for using proper procedures in challenging a suspicious character at a crime scene.

Fellows' compassion for people in trouble, especially for victims of injustice, is the theme of *Prisoner's Plea,* in which he spends his vacation investigating the case of a convict who appeals for his help in correcting an unjust conviction. The prisoner appeals to Fellows as a humane man who is interested in justice; Wilks takes a satirical view, calling him a bleeding heart with an overdeveloped capacity for compassion (ii). Fellows' professional activity does not offset his sense of pity. Unlike Luis Mendoza, he hates the job of carrying news of a murder to the next of kin, although, characteristically, he will not assign the job to anyone else.

Stockford, Connecticut, which Waugh invented as the locale of the Fellows stories, has a population of less then 8500 and an eighteen-man police force that works out of headquarters in the basement of the town hall. Its location is close enough to Stamford for the distance to be driven in twenty-five minutes during a snowstorm,[13] and it is an hour and a half drive from New York City. Stockford is not the sticks: it is prosperous enough to pay its teachers as much as they would make in New Haven[14] and at the same time traditional enough to hold to such values as fairness and justice, as Fellows informs a smart-aleck Pittsfield lawyer who calls Stockford a "hick town."[15]

The last Fellows novel (*The Con Game*) appeared in 1968, and in that same year Waugh published *"30" Manhattan East,* the first of three novels featuring Detective Frank Sessions of Manhattan Homicide.

Sessions reminds us a little of Fred Fellows in his professional integrity and his intelligent approach to the business of detection, but his personal qualities belong to a different context from that of Fellows or Chief Frank Ford. Divorced fourteen years before the series begins, Sessions admits to being a woman-chaser, and he carries on love affairs with an assortment of women throughout the three stories, even having sex with suspects in two of them. He is a loner who is easily bored, whose loves are clothes, women, food, liquor, and books, in that order. Like many another policeman in the procedural stories, he is getting out when his twenty years are up.[16]

Despite the fact that Manhattan Homicide handles hundreds of cases per year and that any detective team would necessarily be dealing with several at one time, Waugh declines the temptation of multiple plotting. Each Sessions story involves a single mystery and has the same tight unity as the other Waugh procedurals.

The novels in this series are rich in the treatment of police procedures and insights into police attitudes, but, after the fresh originality of *Last Seen Wearing—* and the Fred Fellows stories, Frank Sessions produces the impression of the conventional hard-bitten big city cop.

Along with Lawrence Treat, Hillary Waugh has been a pioneer in the tone and direction of the American procedural. With respect to narrative content and story-development, each devised approaches that have set the patterns for subsequent writers. In the handling of police work, Treat tends to emphasize criminalistics and laboratory work, while Waugh uses commonplace routines and the employment of logic. In the Treat stories, the spotlight is usually shared by several protagonists, but Waugh focuses attention on the one central personality. Influences are easier to recognize than to trace, but, as we have already seen, popular fiction does tend to fall into formulaic molds, and the pattern set by Lawrence Treat can be recognized in the 87th Precinct series of Ed McBain, while the one set by Hillary Waugh shows up most strongly in the Deadly Sin stories of Lawrence Sanders, whose Captain Edward X. Delaney bears more than a coincidental resemblance to Fred Fellows.

Chapter 17

Ed McBain

IT WAS A DRAB LITTLE PAPERBACK that appeared on the stands in 1956, the cover composed of pictures in muted grays of policemen in various poses (plus the traditional terrified blonde) against a yellow background, and across the top the title in blood red, *Cop Hater*. This, of course, was the first of the 87th Precinct series, written by Evan Hunter under the pseudonym Ed McBain. The second and third stories (*The Mugger* and *The Pusher*) appeared during that year, and there have been only two years during which a new 87th Precinct story did not come out, and in several years as many as three. In spite of the heavy production, however, the series has maintained a consistently high level of popularity and critical acclaim. Anthony Boucher called the 87th Squad, collectively, "the most successful new series detective created in the 1950s" and "the outstanding contribution of the 1950s to the detective story,"[1] and Julian Symons awards to McBain the title of "the most consistently skillful writer of police novels."[2]

There are two good reasons for the continued reputation of the 87th Precinct series. One is the bright originality of the writing, of which we will have more to say a little later, and the other is the fact that McBain has maintained control over his formula instead of letting the formula control him. He is the kind of innovator who periodically experiments with his approaches. In *Killer's Wedge*, for example, he balances two apparently discordant plots, one a classic-style locked-room story and the other a blatant thriller in which an emotionally disturbed woman threatens to blow up the precinct station and most of the detective squad with a bottle of nitroglycerin, and he deftly ties the two together with the theme stated in the title. *He Who Hesitates* is a *tour de force* in point of view, the story of a "perfect crime" seen only through the eyes of the murderer. *Fuzz* is a farce, in which the police can not do anything right. Some of McBain's fans feared he had run into a hangup in the

late 1970s with three straight stories built around the theme of the
psychopathic killer, particularly *Calypso*, which was essentially a
replay of the situation in *Doll*, and also of *So Long as You Both Shall
Live* with the sex-intimidation roles reversed. Characteristically,
though, McBain came up with something completely original in
Ghosts (1980), in which the story delivers what the title promises,
and in which Steve Carella has an experience he will not discuss
with anybody.

The locale of the 87th Precinct series deserves special attention,
partly because it is an "imaginary city" that simultaneously is and
is not New York, and partly because the City is a major character in
the stories. The disclaimer page of every 87th Precinct novel
solemnly assures us that "the city in these pages is imaginary. The
people, the places are all fictitious," but the reader has the feeling
that the environment is familiar, though the directions and place-
names seem not quite to fit. Anyone desiring a useable map of
McBain's City can, however, devise one by following three simple
steps. First, draw an outline map of New York City. Second, rotate
this map 90 degrees clockwise, so that north becomes east, east
becomes south, and so on around the compass. Then, label all the
political and geographical features with new names: Isola (the
borough of the City in which the 87th Precinct is located) is
Manhattan, Riverhead is the Bronx, Majesta is Queens, Calm's
Point is Brooklyn, and Bethtown is Staten Island; the River Harb is
the Hudson, and the River Dix is the East River. This map can be
labeled in some detail, McBain's "the Stem" corresponding to
Broadway and Ramsey University to New York University. The
author explains that his reason for devising the City instead of
using the real one is that a writer who strives for a sense of literal
reality in police stories must be constantly changing the details of
his fiction to conform to changes in the police setup in the real
setting, a necessity that tends unduly to restrict the imaginative
approach of a creative writer.[3] There is, however, another and more
cogent reason for inventing the City: it is a much more plausible
setting for McBain's slightly whimsical and sometimes fantastic
plots than an already familiar metropolis would be. The most
obvious example is the bizarre caper in *The Heckler*, in which a
super-criminal blows up and burns large areas of "Isola," an
occurrence the reader can quite readily accept in the imaginary City

but would find hard to swallow in the real Manhattan without shifting his credulity to the level demanded by a Robert Ludlum story.

The City is more than a locale; she also has a leading role in the series, her moods and whims determining to a strong degree the actions and affections of the other characters. The "she" is literal; the narrator, who often steps into the story with commentaries that have a lyric tone, makes it clear that "the city could be nothing but a woman,"[4] with whom he feels a love-hate relationship. She is a lovely creature, with her sparkling gems and her Saturday-night black lace,but she is also a bitch:

> Take a look at this city.
> How can you possibly hate her?
>   *   *   *
> She's noisy and vulgar; there are
> runs in her nylons,
> and her heels are round...[5]

and so on. The personification makes herself felt in almost every one of the stories.

There is, however, no "hero" in the series. To a greater degree than any other writer, Ed McBain has achieved the ideal of the police procedural, making a team instead of a single individual the protagonist. While it is true that Steve Carella figures more prominently than any of the others, the typical 87th Precinct story features the joint efforts of two or more cops, and in one case (*Hail, Hail, the Gang's All Here!*) the whole squad. In his essay in *The Great Detectives* (the one in which he explains how he tried to kill Carella off and was dissuaded by his outraged editor) McBain states his intention of making the squad the hero, a "splintered hero" and a "conglomerate protagonist."[6]

Consequently, it is impossible to offer a character sketch as we have done in cases of the other writers' protagonists, but we can get an impression of the makeup of the team by doing what McBain does in the stories, tagging some of them with a few of the qualities that make them memorable. There is, first, Lieutenant Peter Byrnes, the commander of the squad, who feels toward his men the way a father feels about his sons, protecting them from organizational injustice as much as possible but not hesitating to chew them out when necessary. There is, of course, Steve Carella, who loves his deaf-mute wife Teddy and his twin children above all things on earth, and who feels repeatedly guilty after an encounter with a sexy woman witness or victim. There is Meyer Meyer, whose monumental patience has apparently made him bald at his permanent age of thirty-seven, but who once beat up a character for calling him "Jewboy." There is Bert Kling, the naive rookie of the early stories, who learns suffering from the murder of his fiancee and who finally enters upon a promising marriage after what must be the most harrowing wedding night in history. There is Cotton Hawes, who was named after Cotton Mather but has been deterred from any Puritan inclinations by a white streak in his red hair that has an incredibly erotic effect on women. There is the sadistic slob Andy Parker, who is disliked by his fellow officers as much as by the assorted small-time criminals and near-criminals he continually harasses. There is the impatient Arthur Brown, the only black cop on the squad, who resignedly endures jokes about the appropriateness of his name, none of which he considers funny. There is Richard Genero, who really did not have enough brains to walk a beat but was promoted to detective by happening to be lucky enough to be just once in the right place on the right occasion. There is Hal Willis, whose five-eight height barely qualified him for police work, a judo expert who once dumped a four-hundred-pounder right on his can.

One evidence of McBain's skill as a storyteller is his refusal to let his minor characters become mere names. There are several cops in the Eight-Seven who show up only in scattered episodes here and there, but they are always given as much flesh as the narrative will permit. Detective Bob O'Brien deplores violence, but he has gained the reputation of being a hard-luck cop because every time he is sent out on a case, somebody gets shot. Alf Miscolo, who runs the clerical office at the precinct station, resents the way people are always bleeding on his towels and yelling at him for coffee. Dave Murchison, the desk sergeant, believes the new cycle of intense summer heat has been caused by the H-bomb explosions in the Pacific: people are messing around with stuff that should be left to God.

No man, says McBain in reference to his squad-as-hero concept, is indispensable.[7] There are, however, two other components of the framework that, if not indispensable, have become trademarks of the 87th Precinct saga. One is Homicide, and the other is the Deaf Man.

Regulations demand that, when a murder has been committed within a precinct, detectives from Homicide must participate in the investigation. Such a pair appears at the beginning of *Cop Hater*, and McBain apparently saw the possibilities for satire and comedy in conection with the intrusion of these outsiders. Their participation, which occurs in almost every one of the stories, has become more thoroughly conventionalized than any other element in the series. First, they always have alliterative names: it is most often Monoghan Monroe, but it may be Carpenter and Calhoun or Forbes and Phelps. Second, they are never any help, acting like job foremen and wearing dressy clothes not intended for work. Their usual intention is to sweep the dirt under the rug and get back to more comfortable surroundings as quickly as possible, and one of their most frequent ploys is to suggest that the case is really a suicide, as Monroe does in *Ghosts* (i) when the corpse died of multiple stab-wounds with his hands tied behind his back. Their most memorable quality, and the one with which McBain seems to have the most fun, is their habit of rhythmic antiphonal patter, that makes their conversations come across like a verse-speaking choir. Here, obviously, is no attempt at photographic "realism," and another illustration of the advantage of an "imaginary city" over a real one: it would be inconceivable that a pair of clowns like Monoghan and Monroe, or any of their counterparts, could stay on the payroll of the NYPD, but they seem right at home in the slightly erratic atmosphere of McBain's City.

The other trademark of the series is the recurrent and apparently indestructible villain, the Deaf Man, who has made three appearances to date[8] and who is no persistently troublesome hood like Procter's Dixie Costello but a satanic super-criminal whose ambition is not only to outwit the police but to make them look like cretins in the process. The Deaf Man (whose real name is never given) is a calculating operator who thinks in terms of percentages and permutations and who never leaves anything to chance. His mathematically perfect plans are defeated at the conclusion of each of his contests with the 87th Squad, but it is typical of the McBain style that his failures come about as the result of the vagaries of dumb luck rather than any intelligent or heroic activity by the police.

For the most part, though, most of the criminals in the series are neither monsters nor degenerates. Some of them, like Pepe Miranda, who killed Detective Frankie Hernandez, are products of an abrasive environment. Some are pitiable, like Angelica Gomez, a prostitute in *Killer's Wedge* who longs for her native Puerto Rico because people in the City have no manners (xi). A great many are creations of the same sportive imagination that invented Monoghan and Monroe, like the woman in the squad room detention cage who threatens to tear off her blouse and accuse the police of trying to rape her in *Let's Hear It for the Deaf Man*; she does, and nobody pays any attention (ii). Or the man caught fornicating in the park in *Long Time No See*, who is more worried about what his mother will say than about a jail sentence (iii).

The policemen, according to Ed McBain, are the constants in the stories; invention and imagination enter the novels in the guise of the various people the cops have to deal with.[9] The most vivid personalities are neither villains nor victims, but a parade of eccentrics who enter and leave the stories in the space of a page or two. Some of them are plain dingbats, like Sadie the Nut (age 78), who comes in every Wednesday morning to report another attempted rape.[10] A few are grotesques, like Dean Kramer, who has memorized the opening sentences of thousands of novels and plays quizmaster with everybody he meets.[11] Many of them are egocentrics like David Oblinsky, who wants to complain to the phone company for helping the police trace him though his unlisted number.[12] As with his minor policemen, McBain will not allow any one of them to be only a name, but must touch him or her with a vivid dash that makes them, collectively, the most memorable *dramatic personae* in the procedural genre.

As we have seen earlier, one of the basic narrative problems of the police procedural is the question of how to make the everyday methods of the police as exciting and suspenseful as the mental gymnastics of the super-sleuths of the classic tradition and the spectacular involvements of the private eyes of the hard-boiled school. Ed McBain has solved this problem by letting the procedures stand on their own as elements of suspense. The descriptions of the reconstruction of a burnt matchbook in *The Heckler* (ix) and the test of the length of time required for a capsule to dissolve in *Eighty Million Eyes* (x) are accomplished with meticulous step-by-step detail and delineation of technical expertise, with the result that the procedures are in themselves suspenseful enough without resort to artificial strategems.

A genius for making platitudes exciting is really the essence of the McBain style. In a singularly perceptive essay, James McClure pictures Ed McBain as a writer with enough courage to wade unashamedly through a field of "cop corn" "knee-high in cliches." The aesthetic of the 87th Precinct stories is based on the author's honesty, empathy and gentle humor, permitting him to grind the "cop corn" fine and to render the mundane palatable, with a leaning to "grass-roots kitsch." Finally, with an impressive demonstration of his own ability to fashion an apt figure, McClure suggests that McBain has become the "Norman Rockwell of the police procedural."[13]

His skill in dramatizing the commonplace becomes most obvious in those passages in almost every one of the novels in which McBain steps on stage and speaks directly as narrator to the reader. Many of them, as we have pointed out, are lyric treatments of the personified City, and several deal with such naturally poetic subjects as the feel of October, but there is one in *The Mugger* (iii) on the songs about Saturday night as the loneliest night in the week, one in *The Con Man* (iii) on life as a con game, one in *Bread* (ii) on a burglarized apartment as a violation of self. The speaker is in a sense the omnipresent character in the series, the author who, according to his own testimony, likes to put in his two cents' worth.[14]

McBain's honesty and courage as a writer are such, as a matter of fact, that he will occasionally pause along the way and give his reader a little lecture on narrative technique. It may be only a passing comment, as when he calls our attention to the fact that nineteen-year-old Margaret Androvich might be described by one of the more skillful novelists as "willowy"; in other words, she was *skinny*.[15] Or, in a more extended treatment, he explains how the novelist-as-God can arrange things so that two characters will converge at the same place and at the right moment and everything will turn out just fine for the big, happy ending; only, in the world of hard realities, things just don't always work out that way.[16] On three occasions, he even describes the way the scene under consideration would look projected on a screen.[17]

Although the theme of the 87th Precinct series is death and violation, violence and discovery (as in all police procedurals), the comic spirit hangs over the saga from start to finish and is never far removed from the action. It takes many forms, some of which we have already mentioned, like the antiphonal patter of the pair from Homicide, the crack-brained characters who wander into and out of the stories, and even the comments of the ever-present narrator. Its most useful function is to relieve the tensions when things get too grim; an excellent example appears in *Doll*, when, at that point when it appears that Steve Carella has been murdered and Bert Kling has been permanently discredited, Meyer Meyer involves himself in an extended exercise of persiflage by assuming the role of "The Bald Eagle" (viii). McBain's humor is not easy to characterize. It has been called "slapstick humor," "rather ghoulish humor," "deadpan comedy," and "gentle humor." It could also be described as worldly-wise, eccentric or idiosyncratic. It is basically the expression of the ever-present narrator, the kind of humor perpetrated (sometimes as a practical joke) by a person who has been everywhere and seen everything, who has gained experience through both laughter and suffering, and has achieved perspective. He knows people, empathizes with them and pities them, but he can recognize their foibles. We may sometimes have the impression that the narrator never takes his eyes off the readers', watching closely to see if we are buying the gag.

Irony, almost always situational and never subtle, is another favorite narrative device of McBain. Consider, for example, the case of Roger Broome, who in *He Who Hesitates* commits a perfect crime, is never suspected by the police, and gets away clean at the end of the story; almost five years later he has too much to drink and makes a public confession. Consider also the case of poor stupid Genero, who unwittingly saves the life of the Deaf Man at the conclusion of *Fuzz*; the Deaf Man, wounded in a shootout, is about to be burned alive by a couple of young sadists who delight in incinerating drunks, when they are captured by Genero, who just happens to blunder into them (xiii). Or consider all the hard work done by Bert Kling and Meyer Meyer in *Doll* to find out what Tina Sachs' problem was; just after they have cleared up the business, the police lab calls to tell them she was a drug addict (xii).

In keeping with the tradition of realism, McBain has his policemen handling several cases concurrently, which means that most of the stories have multiple plots. The record to date was established in *Hail, Hail, the Gang's All Here!* which has fourteen separate story-lines. It is to the author's credit that he keeps his plots clearly distinct, so that it is never necessary, when a character or situation is re-introduced, to turn back to an earlier chapter to find out what this is all about. Of the fourteen plots in *Hail, Hail, the Gang's All Here!* for example, seven are minor plots with one or two episodes and are solved relatively quickly. The seven given extended treatment are identified with names of policemen or localities so that they do not get in one another's way.

We do not expect allegory and myth in a series like the 87th Precinct saga, but the sense of depth is so strong in one of the stories as to make us doubt that it is merely coincidental. At the beginning of *The Heckler*, the story in which the Deaf Man first makes his appearance, there is one of those lyric passages describing the arrival of April in Grover Park that suggests the atmosphere of the Garden of Eden, an idyllic calm that is soon corrupted by the discovery of a murder victim, heralding the imminent appearance of the satanic Deaf Man. The quintessential evil of the Deaf Man is apparent in the scene in which he seduces a nameless waitress, using his daemonic sexual skills to reduce her to a state of witlessness, a violation of innocence that in this case is not moral innocence but naivete (x). After the blasting and burning of extensive downtown areas, which has all the associations of Chaos and Apocalypse, the Deaf Man is defeated by innocence (again anonymous) in the person of a cop who wants an ice cream pop and who becomes suspicious of a man driving an ice cream truck who can not supply a single pop in any flavor (xvi).

The only story in which McBain loses his usual careful control of his material is *Hail to the Chief* (1973), apparently intended to satirize the scandals attendant upon the second Nixon administration. The perpetrator is Randall M. Nesbit (don't miss the initials), president of a street gang, who is loaded with so many Nixon attributes that he loses credibility as a fictional character: he tries to make peace by killing off his enemies, he has dark brooding eyes and a bulbous nose, his speech is sprinkled with expressions like "game plan" and "smear tactic," and he has had six crises in his life. The distortion is even more conspicuous in the characterization of Midge, one of the gang's "chicks," obviously intended as the Martha Mitchell parallel and consequently so forced as to be out of character (iii). For the longest series in the history of the procedural, though, one fumble is not bad, and McBain's overall quality has been consistently superior.

Chapter 18

Bill Knox

IN 1957, THE YEAR after the beginning of McBain's 87th Precinct series, Bill Knox published *Deadline for a Dream* (which appeared in the U.S. as *In at the Kill* in 1961), the first of a series of procedural novels featuring detectives Colin Thane and Phil Moss of the Glasgow police. The series has continued with the appearance of a new story every year or two, usually alternating with the other books Knox writes under his own name and his several pseudonyms. The two most immediately apparent qualities of the Thane-Moss series are the fast pace of the stories, undoubtedly the result of Knox's experience as a journalist, and his ready knowledge of policemen and police methods, growing out of his work as a crime reporter.

Chief Inspector (later Detective Superintendent) Colin Thane, chief of detectives in Glasgow's Millside Division, is an eminently successful policeman, the youngest CID man in Scotland to have his own division. His approach to detection is at once intuitive and impetuous; he learned the rules and has tried to work by them, but he sometimes has little more than a hunch to go on, in which case he throws caution aside, charges in, and sweats out the results. Like many other policemen, Thane has learned that there are pages in the rule book that must be left behind at police college; his definition of discretion is a mixture of common sense with a hunch, plus a flavor of humanity. He is a man of both physical and moral courage. In *Children of the Mist* (viii), he faces down a criminal holding him and Moss at gun-point in a room filled with explosives, and in *Draw Batons!* (viii) he responds to the threat of a gambler to call a lawyer by pointing to the phone and inviting him to go right ahead. Thane's most notable quality as a superior officer, however, is his insistence upon strict professionalism on the part of his subordinates. In *Rally to Kill* he is sharp with a pair of undignified probationers, reminding them that they are policemen (v), and in *Pilot Error* he dresses down an unenthusiastic rural highland cop who takes his time about meeting Thane at the local airfield (iii).

Thane's professional severity, however, is never extended to his second in command and partner, Phil Moss, who looks as if he had slept in his clothes and whose embodiment of privation is such that an elderly woman once pressed money into his hands and told him to go buy a good meal. Under this ratty exterior, though, is a superior mind, which can tackle the most tedious research job and do an expert analysis; give him a real job of burrowing to do and let him set his own pace, and Phil Moss develops a power of persistence that is the envy of his fellow policemen, especially Colin Thane. His most obvious feature is a duodenal ulcer, from which he suffers until he decides (in *Pilot Error*) to have surgery; that ulcer has served as a barometer of his day-to-day outlook, although he tries to control it by swallowing a half-dozen pills per day. It also endows Moss with a reverberant belch which on one occasion becomes a weapon surely unique in the annals of law enforcement, serving to distract an armed suspect and permitting the police to jump him.[1]

Thane and Moss are a well-matched team, because their temperaments and abilities complement each other. Where Thane is intuitive and impulsive, Moss is methodical and persistent. Thane is usually lucky, but when things go wrong Moss can always step in with some fresh possibility to rescue the situation. Moss is the key to their relationship; although ten years Thane's senior he is inferior to him in rank, but he sarcastically ignores the difference to the accompaniment of considerable insolence and complaint. While Moss is recovering from surgery, Thane misses him as the one person with whom he could argue and discuss things.

The other main series character is Chief Superintendent William "Buddha" Ilford, commander of the Millside District, who acquired his nickname from a habit of sitting hunched in his chair scowling down into the vicinity of his navel. Ilford is almost the stereotype of the overbearing SOB superior officer, a large, tweedy bear who carries around his own personal thundercloud. Not unexpectedly, "Buddha" favors the use of guns by policemen, expressing the opinion that no cop should ever have to take a bullet in the belly "for the sake of tradition,"[2] and when a hood who has killed a policeman is himself later killed in a raid, Ilford refuses to worry: "I'm Old Testament material."[3] He does, none the less, exhibit toward his subordinates a playfully ghoulish sense of humor: when Thane and Moss are sent up into the highlands to investigate the killing of a prize bull, "Buddha" supplies them with a copy of *A Child's Guide to Farm Animals*.[4] Small wonder that, as Colin Thane sits talking with him, he notices a loose acoustic tile in the office ceiling above "Buddha's" head and hopes it will fall on him.

The Millside Division encompasses the most dismal section of Glasgow, with dockland, rat-infested slums along the Clyde, grim factories, and tenement buildings. It has the worst pockets of unemployment, the highest welfare roll, and the toughest "neds" (local slang for hoods), but it also includes a high-class residential neighborhood and thus serves as a setting for low-, middle- and upper-class crimes. The city is attempting to rehabilitate the area with the construction of high-rise, low-rent residential blocks, and the reaction of the police is much the same as the response of policemen to urban renewal in every city in the world: they consider the effort to be a "new inheritance of social disaster" and the structures themselves "architect-designed filing cabinets."[5] It should be noted that there is not much of a drug problem in Glasgow: Scots prefer whiskey and gambling.[6]

In *Pilot Error* we learn that the Glasgow City Police has been absorbed into a new super-division, the Strathclyde Police, which includes five previous police forces and is responsible for law enforcement for half the population of Scotland. Typically, the new organization and changed lines of command are resented by the cops (i).

Not without reason: a strain of pride in the Glasgow force runs through the series, reflected chiefly in the kind of technical expertise to which the Glaswegians have access. There is, for example, the Scottish Criminal Records Office, with an index of close to a quarter million criminal conviction records, 130,000 offense conviction records, an imposing Modus Operandi file, a Photo Index, and a fingerprint collection.[7] Then there is the well-equipped Scientific Bureau for laboratory work, that can make microscopic examinations and identifications of animal hairs, pin down a sample of mud to within a few yards, and check the alcohol content of blood.[8] The most important single resource of the Glasgow Police, however, is the availability of Andrew MacMaster, Regius Professor of Forensic Medicine, Glasgow University, a lordly old expert who can put even medical doctors in their place, because most of them studied under him. MacMaster is a series character, but he plays an especially important role in *Children of the Mist*, in which he demonstrates a knowledge of veterinary medicine that supplies the crucial clue for the solution of the crime under investigation (viii).

Britain in the Knox stories, as in those of Creasey and Procter, is a land where the rights of individual citizens are protected and the use of firearms by the police is severely curtailed. It is, we are told, almost impossible to bug a telephone line: Scottish courts frown upon the results, and defense lawyers scream about the invasion of privacy.[9] The unarmed policeman is still the basis of the Scottish system; the issuing of guns needs high-level approval, and authorization is limited. A change was in the making in the late 1970s, however; we have already noted Ilford's disdain for the principle of the defenseless policeman, and in *Live Bait* (1979) we learn that the old image of the British cop as someone who treated firearms as a last resort is fading, because the opposition is armed and so the police must be (v).

Knox's style is uncomplicated, the action moving along with few interruptions, and with no attempts at allegory or myth, other than the enveloping myths of procedural fiction. Motivation is almost exclusively in the hands of the police, and solutions of the mysteries are the result of police detective work, to the extent that the stories can be classed as "pure" procedurals. They are also rich in insights into the police mind and police routines, as witnessed by our frequent references to them in the earlier discussions of the police sub-culture and police methods.

Story by story, Knox follows a tighter formula than most writers, which can be summarized as follows:

1. Investigating a murder, the police find themselves in confrontation with an influential individual/family/company who undertake to intimidate them.
2. The theme centers around some industry or hobby: painting, electronics, bonded whiskey, an auto rally, a travel agency.
3. A criminal type becomes partially (or indirectly) involved through part of the story and is cleared before the end, though he/she may be convicted of a lesser offence.

4. The big climactic scene takes place at a site associated with the industry or hobby, where there is violence and a second murder.

There are signs that Knox is changing his patterns, partly as a result of changing conditions and partly as a result of a new intention. We have observed two of these, the breakdown of the old idea of the unarmed policeman and the disappearance of the Millside Division into the new monster Strathclyde Police. It would appear also that the old team of Thane and Moss is to be broken up. In *Live Bait* we are told that Moss, recovering from surgery, has been reassigned as "Buddha" Ilford's liaison officer (in which position, we can speculate, he is well quit of his ulcer) and that Thane has been assigned to the Scottish Crime Squad where, apparently, his new partner will be young Sergeant Francey Dunbar (vii).

Chapter 19

Nicolas Freeling

ANYBODY SEEKING TO CONSTRUCT a model of the "typical" policeman in procedural fiction would be well advised to stay away from Nicolas Freeling's Peter Simon Joseph Van der Valk of the Amsterdam police, the reason being that very few cops can quote Baudelaire, or would undertake to wear down a suspect by means of a series of social calls, or would refuse to call the lab boys to a murder site because police technology isn't his style.

Freeling introduced this remarkable maverick in *Love in Amsterdam* (1962) and killed him off ten years—and ten novels— later in *A Long Silence*, which is better known by its U.S. title, *Aupres de ma Blonde,* taking Van der Valk through a series of unconventional cases that sent him on journeys over the Continent and into Ireland, witnessed his advancement from Inspector to Principal Commissiaire, left him on one occasion presumably dead of a gunshot wound on a hillside in Spain and finally unquestionably dead of two bullets in the back on a rain-soaked street in The Hague. In at least half of the stories, particularly those in which he pursues suspects and clues across national frontiers, Van der Valk belongs unquestionably to the Great Policeman school, completely dominating narrative progress and resolution, but he works enough with other policemen and follows customary police routines to put the series into the procedural class.

The reason Van der Valk is an unusual policeman is that his creator is an unusual writer. According to Nicolas Freeling's testimony, Van der Valk was born out of his own boredom with the platitudes of contemporary crime writers, particularly the premise that crime writing is an inferior genre, not to be taken seriously. The solution, he told himself, was to present a crime story that introduced people the reader could care about, having problems with which readers could identify.[1] Every crime novel, then, must center around "a moral problem for which you do not know too easily or quickly what the solution will be."[2] Consequently, discovery and revelation in the Van der Valk stories center frequently upon the question of *why* rather than *who* or *how*. In several instances (*Gun Before Butter* and *Criminal Conversation* are representative examples), Van der Valk knows fairly early who the perpetrator is but will not rest his case until he has satisfied himself with regard to origins and causes, values and influences.

Freeling's style can best be described as *literate*, daring to permit Van der Valk to quote not only the French impressionists but Raymond Chandler's essay "The Simple Art of Murder." He may not be "the educated man's Ian Fleming,"[3] as one reviewer called him, but his courage as a writer carries him to a level considerably above that of the ordinary sex, sensation and shoot-outs.

The final testament to this courage was his willingness to terminate Van der Valk when that detective had served his purpose. The sense of outrage among Van der Valk's fans when the policeman was not only gunned down but undeniably buried with no promise of recovery or revival may not have been as extensive as that which followed Holmes' plunge into the Reichenbach Gorge, but it was every bit as devout. The decision to commit "protagonisticide,"[4] though, was based not on waning popularity but on Freeling's own assessment: the formula (admittedly far less hackneyed than those of many other crime writers) was worn out; Van der Valk was beginning to parody himself, and his author was unwilling to see him go into a downhill slide.[5]

Though lacking much formal education, Van der Valk is one of the best-read of policemen, whose mind, more than his conversation, feeds incessantly on literature and history. In Chapter 9 we referred to that scene in *The King of the Rainy Country* in which an early-morning interior monologue swarms with allusions to European history, ethnography, geography and the works of three authors of as many nationalities. Thinking in these terms is not unusual for Van der Valk: lying wounded on a hillside in Spain he imagines himself one of Napoleon's soldiers in the Spanish campaign, and when he is dying he remembers Stendhal's remark about dying in the street.[6] Reading history even becomes a method of investigation in *Tsing-Boum*, when, in order to gain the Vietnamese background of a murder, he feels he must read up on the siege of Dienbienphu. Van der Valk likes history because it is one of the best ways of putting life into proportion, by "distancing things."[7]

Many of the literary allusions from Van der Valk's well-stocked memory will sail clean past the typical mystery-reader, but Freeling has also endowed his protagonist with a wide acquaintance with detective fiction, providing for a generous reliance upon the "Shades of Dupin!" convention mentioned in Chapter 8, a device used by detective-story writers to make their accounts seem more real by representing other detectives in other people's stories as "fiction." Van der Valk is a great reader of George Simenon, and he constantly compares his methods with those of Maigret, imitates Maigret's habits of walking and drinking, even tries to think like him. Another favorite is Raymond Chandler, whose sharp turns of phrase Van der Valk loves to quote. There is, as a matter of fact, no story in the series without allusions to Maigret, Marlowe, Philo Vance, Sherlock Holmes, or one of a dozen other fictional detectives, sometimes mildly contemptuous, more often envious, and often satirical of Van der Valk himself, as when he thinks of himself as "Philip van der Marlowe."[8] The habit of dramatizing himself as a fictitious mystery character demands more than passing notice, however, because, as we will presently see, it finally led to Van der Valk's getting himself killed.

We might, on the basis of his rich store of history and literature, class Van der Valk as a "civilized" person, but other qualities push him in the direction of barbarity. His rough joviality, which comes through strongly as crude garrulity in his first appearance, often lapses into bad taste and peasant vulgarity, which is characterized on one occasion as a tendency to "lavatory humor."[9] The bad taste manifests itself in a crude frankness, as when he tells the lover of a murdered woman that the police would prefer his being the murderer, because that circumstance would save everybody a world of trouble.[10] The roughness can become brutal, as it does when a young suspect lies to him; Van der Valk orders his subordinate to choke the youngster until he decides to co-operate.[11]

It is not because of his literacy or his jovial crudeness, however, that we call Van der Valk a maverick, but because of his unorthodox and eccentric approach to police work. A suspect in one of the stories makes a shrewd assessment when he tells Van der Valk that he has an acquired professionalism and the usual police skills but not the real police mentality, and that he lacks the art of pleasing his superiors.[12] His brigadier puts the case more strongly: Van der Valk is clever and well educated, but a lunatic.[13] Both evaluations are superficial. Van der Valk's problem is that he is a thoughtful individualist who has developed his own approaches and resents bureaucratic interference, preferring to fit the approach to a problem to the nature of the problem. His impatience with "administrative bumf," as he calls it, is explicit in the title *Strike Out Where Not Applicable*, which represents to Van der Valk the essence of government by insistence upon pre-determined response. His "style" in police work is nonconformist to the extent that he does not want the technical staff at a murder scene, preferring to think things out for himself (75-6).

Van der Valk's unorthodox approach to police work is rooted in his attitude toward people and justice. The police must be interested in character, he says, otherwise they would never understand anything at all; hence his concern with the *why* of crime as well as the *who* and *how*. Occasionally his interest in the "why" gives him the answer to the "who," as it does in *Criminal Conversation*: in that novel Van der Valk, with almost nothing to go on except a confidential unsubstantiated complaint, annoys, intimidates, and fascinates Dr. Van der Post until the guilty doctor writes out a detailed confession. In another case, though, the "why" becomes the overriding determinant: this is what happens in *Gun Before Butter* (U.S. title, *Question of Loyalty*), when Van der Valk has discovered the guilt of a young woman but refuses to arrest her. The reason he gives her is an esoteric one (the victim lived a double life, and the half she killed was unknown to the authorities), but the real reason is grounded in sympathy and pity. Van der Valk does not subscribe to the myth of police work as part of the struggle of Good versus Evil: he has found, in his job, that there are very few good men and perhaps even fewer bad ones, and crime has little to do with absolutes like Right and Wrong.

No discussion of Van der Valk would be complete without mention of his family life, which is featured in most of the stories. He is not satisfied with his relations to his two sons; like most other policemen, he is overworked, and is often irritable and nervous at home, pushing the boys away when they nag him, giving them curt answers, and generally feeling himself not to be a good father. Van der Valk's marriage, on the other hand, belongs in the Sublimely

Happy category. Arlette, a French woman by birth, is an excellent cook, and her exquisite taste in clothes gives Van der Valk his "Arlette-trained eye," which comes in handy during investigations. Arlette is also a person of steadfast purpose: when Van der Valk is gunned down, she undertakes, with the help of some friends (including Freeling, who introduces himself into the story), a successful search for his murderer.

Van der Valk's death in *A Long Silence* is no mere murder: the book is an extended parable of Fiction and Reality. As a result of the wound he received at the end of *The King of the Rainy Country,* Van der Valk is semi-invalided out of active service and is given a desk job in The Hague as consultant to the Commission for Inquiry into Law Reform, with the result that his boredom is excruciating. It is here that his fascination with detective fiction comes into play. Fiddling around his desk for want of something to occupy his mind, Van der Valk begins to make abstruse notes on theoretical subjects and is thus primed for the opportune arrival of a young man who presents him with a mysterious account of a presumed crime that is none of Van der Valk's business but fascinates him as a chance for action. He takes the case as a recreation, calling it is "private-detective lark" and his "experiment," (71) comparing himself with Holmes, Marlowe, and Maigret, and writing out elaborate summaries and analyses in the Golden Age style. Van der Valk resolves not to cheat, "as fictional private detectives always did" (27), but to apply to his "lark" the tested procedures of the professional policeman. Here Reality intervenes: the criminals he is trailing recognize him as a cop and perceive the danger. Van der Valk is eliminated in the spirit of an old gangster movie. Fantasy has the last word, however: as the dark-colored automobile speeds away from the scene, a witness has the impression of Peter Lorre and Sydney Greenstreet in the back seat (87).

Holland in the Van der Valk stories is a prosaic country, and the Dutch an insular, small-minded people. They are especially sensitive in matters of propriety: things that would not be noticed in France or Germany cause a scandal in Holland, where all Germans are vulgar and all Frenchmen frivolous.[14] The standard is polite mediocrity: everything is organized, and nobody is allowed to improvise.[15] The Dutch have an automatic distrust of anything imaginative, unusual, or unconventional. They are materialistic, to the extent that most criminal work in Holland is a matter of economics. We must remember, of course, that land and people come to us through the blase eyes of Van der Valk, who does not suffer dullness gladly and who can also be disdainful of the foibles of the other countries into which his activities carry him.

Chapter 20

Maj Sjöwall and Per Wahlöö

NO PROCEDURAL SERIES has been the object of more thorough critical attention than the ten novels produced by the Swedish husband-wife team, Maj Sjowall and Per Wahloo, between 1965 and 1975. These stories are customarily called the Martin Beck series, but although Beck's career and personal involvements carry more of the narrative burden than any other single element, the dominant background is the place of police in society,the perplexities of life in Sweden, and by extension the discontents of society as a whole. On the assumption that the crime novel provides a good vehicle for the analysis of society, Sjowall and Wahloo turned out a series that may be eventually remembered more for its sharp social comment than for its mystery and detection.

The couple conceived of the series as a single long novel in ten volumes, a chronicle of the National Homicide Squad in Stockholm with specific emphasis on the effect of police life upon one man and with broader consideration of the interaction between police and society. Whether as part of the original intent or as a result of increasing confidence in their conception, the writers broadened the scope of social criticism as the series progressed. K. Arne Blom divides the series into three phases, in terms of outside literary influences and general purposes. The first phase, according to Blom, includes the three novels *Roseanna* (1965), *The Man Who Went Up in Smoke* (1966) and *The Man on the Balcony* (1967), in which Sjowall and Wahloo were influenced by the Maigret stories of Georges Simenon, especially in the tendency of Martin Beck to study the psychology of the criminals with whom he deals and to try to understand their actions in relation to society. In the next four (*The Laughing Policeman*, 1968; *The Fire Engine That Disappeared*, 1969; *Murder at the Savoy*, 1970; and *The Abominable Man*, 1971) the couple owed much to Ed McBain's 87th Precinct stories, with emphasis on the police team and each policeman's response to the criminal. The last three (*The Locked Room,* 1972; *Cop Killer,* 1974; and *The Terrorists,* 1975), says Blom, show no external influence, are more political, more meditative, and transcend the purposes of the traditional mystery.[1] Frank Ochiogrosso also sees a three-stage development in the series. In the early novels, says Ochiogrosso, criminals are clearly the aberrant types within society, the society itself is basically sound, and the police are cast in the role of guardians and protectors. Later, however, the background of social unrest asserts itself, to the accompaniment of the theme of deprivation of individualism and annihilation of selfhood. In the last stories, there are more and more "criminals" who are depicted as victims of a brutalization process, of which society and government are the agents and the police are the operative force.[2]

Although the pervasive social commentary has understandably attracted more critical attention than any other feature of the Sjowall-Wahloo books, their narrative style has also won considerable praise. Steinbrunner and Penzler use such expressions as "reportorial," "spare," "disciplined" and "full of sharply observed detail."[3] Talburt and Montgomery, noting the absence of multiple unrelated plots in the stories, add that "in these novels, plot and structure are relatively tighter than in many other examples of the police procedural...."[4] As tales of detection, they compare well with other procedurals in terms of mystery and suspense.

In the Sjowall-Wahloo stories, however, the social environment plays so strong a role that the contry itself may be considered a major character, as both victim and villain. Especially in the novels of the middle and last periods, Sweden is represented as a land suffering from a malaise that manifests itself in high rates of unemployment and suicide, and in a general loss of a sense of values. Martin Beck's best friend on the squad, Lennart Kollberg, wants to quit police work, and Beck feels that he should but will not encourage him to do so because he knows the chances of employment for a fifty-year-old former policeman will be small in competition with university graduates and well-trained professionals who are out of work. Stockholm, we are told, has one of the highest suicide rates in the world, but the fact is either hushed up by the authorities or concealed behind manipulated statistics. An extreme attitude, but a representative one, is expressed in *The Abominable Man* by the father of the murderer-policeman Ake Eriksson, who had something to believe in as a young worker, but who now as an old man feels that no one cares and society is all wrong: "If we'd known what society was coming to, we wouldn't have had any children at all" (xxv). The government, by general consensus, is not helping but is rather making matters worse. The most constant criticism, especially by the police, is directed at the policy of urban renewal that is devastating large areas, destroying the special character of old Stockholm and ruining its original value. Worse still, for the inhabitants of the cleared slum areas, rents in the restored buildings are so high that the former tenants can not afford to live in them. To make matters worse still, policies of taxation, like the value-added tax on food, are "hitting those who have already been knocked out."[5]

The consequences of the socio-economic ills of Sweden affect the police in two ways. As society becomes more resentful and more violent, the police become more authoritarian and more secretive, and the public has fallen into the habit of laughing at them. In this context the most noticeable stylistic change in the novels comes into being, with the increase of editorial comment by the authors on the antagonisms between the public and the police, who have become a centrally directed paramilitary force with "frightening technical resources."[6] Most of the troubles, according to the authors (and the policemen in the novels), stem from the nationalization of the police force in 1965, after which it developed into a state within a state and became increasingly alienated from the private citizen. Recruitment of qualified personnel has consequently come to be almost impossible: most beginning policemen are drawn from the twenty per cent of the population that does not attend a university or a trade school; hundreds of vacancies remain unfilled, with resultant overwork for policemen in service. The alienation of the police from the rest of society comes to be caught in a vicious cause-and-effect relationship, in which the police become instigators rather than protectors. In *The Locked Room* Martin Beck is grateful for a system that gives him unrestricted access to other people's private affairs (xxvi), but in the same novel Lennart Kollberg in disgust reminds a district attorney that all he needs to do is to bring charges against people in order to put them away, even if they are innocent (xix), and in *The Terrorists* Kollberg, now completely disillusioned and retired from the force, is of the opinion that "putting the police in the vanguard of violence is like putting the cart before the horse" (xxix).

In the assignment of narrative roles, Sjowall and Wahloo have organized their police force in much the same pattern as that of Ed McBain's 87th Precinct series. The leading part throughout is assigned to Martin Beck, whose personal, family and professional involvements are a record of the changing relationships of the police to an increasingly difficult social scene. The secondary roles are played by Beck's only friend on the squad, Lennart Kollberg, and by the aggressive and often sadistic Gunvald Larsson. Other regulars are policemen like Fredrik Melander and Einar Ronn, and, in the later novels, the pompous and incompetent Superintendent Stig Malm. The two patrolmen Kristiansson and Kvant (replaced by Kvastmo after Kvant is killed) serve the double purpose of comic relief and an illustration of the low level of the Swedish uniformed police. Finally, there is Stockholm—or Sweden—that dominates the atmosphere in much the same way as McBain's Imaginary City affects the emotions and actions of the 87th Squad.

Martin Beck's unfortunate marriage and miserable family life are featured in the early novels to a greater degree than in most procedural stories. The first time we meet him, in *Roseanna*, Beck sits in his gloomy kitchen in the early morning, fingering a chipped and cracked teacup that symbolizes his ruined married life (iii). Relationships with his wife continue to deteriorate to the extent that Beck pretends to work in order to avoid being with his family and sleeps on the sofa to be free of his nagging wife. They are separated in *Murder at the Savoy* and divorced in *The Abominable Man*. Beck suffers from bad health in the earlier novels: he can not eat in the morning and does not enjoy food at any time, and in almost every story he is catching cold; after the marriage is dissolved he recovers from his stomach troubles, but his susceptibility to colds continues. The only member of his family with whom he has a satisfactory relationship is his daughter Ingrid; Beck does not really like his son Rolf, with whom he never seems able to establish a meaningful association. The general gloom of Beck's home life has two important effects in the series: it is a reflection of the absence of wholesome personal relationships in society, but it also makes Martin Beck more sympathetic and compassionate toward people in trouble than he would otherwise have been.

At the beginning of the series, Beck already has the reputation of being one of the best policemen in Sweden. He is not ambitious for promotion, but he does eventually become chief of the National Homicide Squad. The Commissioner of Police regards him as a decent administrator with criminological acumen and a good understanding of people, though his good reputation is on occasion a disadvantage, especially in dealing with his incompetent superior Stig Malm, who resents Beck's prestige. His strongest professional orientation is against violence; Beck has himself never killed anybody, and when he is planning the operation he heads in *The Terrorists*, he specifically warns the head of the oppressive "Sepo" that there is to be no preventive detention of people with unpopular political views, no provocation, and no unnecessary force (viii).

Like many another procedural policeman, though, Martin Beck is plagued by self-doubts, especially in regard to what he suspects to be his loss of ability with increasing age. His commitment to responsibility engenders a sense of guilt in *The Abominable Man*, when the police have trapped a psychotic sniper on a rooftop and Beck, feeling guilty about the development of a crisis he might have prevented, insists upon going after the man himself and is dangerously wounded (xxvii-viii). The emotional trauma of that experience is translated by Beck's own modesty into a parody of heroism, symbolized by his recurrent dream, in which he gallops into the railroad station in time to prevent the assassination of President Garfield, taking Guiteau's bullet in his own chest, as he had received the bullet of the crazed homicidal policeman in real life. Toward the end of the series, as a matter of fact, it becomes apparent that Beck purposely and satirically represses his emotional responses. In *The Terrorists* he enjoys an extremely satisfying sexual relationship with Rhea Nielsen, but when she makes a passionate avowal of her love for him—a declaration quite unusual in this series for its sincere intensity—Beck's response is, "Yes. Shall we go and eat now?" (iv).

Martin Beck's best and only friend on the squad is Lennart Kollberg, who enjoys a supremely happy married life but finds himself liking police work less and less and plans to resign. Kollberg's reflection upon what he calls the policeman's occupational disease, which we discussed in Chapter 6, leads him to conceive of police work as alienation from normal wholesome contacts with the rest of society. Kollberg's discontent is not generalized, however, but stems from his own sense of guilt over having accidentally killed a fellow policeman, with the result that he never carries a firearm on duty. His letter of resignation from the force, finally submitted in *Cop Killer*, is an indictment of police violence as a provocation of violent crime. It is typical of the man's commitment, however, that, having started the letter, he puts it aside to go and check out a stolen car, returns to finish the letter, and sends it in (xxviii). Martin Beck sympathizes with the reasons for Kollberg's resignation, but misses him after he leaves the squad, and considers him one of the best policemen in the country.

The one person Kollberg detests is Gunvald Larsson, who is generally disliked because of his crude manner and unorthodox methods. Larsson is a sadistic cop who refrains from hitting suspects only if a commissioner or a superintendent is present and who loves to browbeat and humiliate patrolmen. The authors are too skillful, however, to assign Larsson the simple role of squad SOB, but endow him with a mixture of qualities. He mercilessly humiliates Patrolman Zachrisson, who has been assigned a lonely vigil on a freezing night, but relieves him long enough to get a cup of coffee.[7] He accepts the help of a civilian in an effort to get the mad sniper off the roof, but after the civilian has brought his quarry down with a masterful shot, Larsson tells him he is in trouble for carrying an unlicensed pistol.[8] Larsson unquestionably wins the sympathy of the reader, though, when he barks "Heil Hitler!" in response to an authoritarian command from Superintendent Malm, and again when he crushes the hand of the pompous visiting U.S. senator.[9]

Kristiansson and Kvant, the hapless patrolmen who figure in most of the novels, have been called the Keystone Klutzes by one reviewer,[10] and they are indeed a pair of clowns who never seem able to do anything right. They trample all over the evidence at the scene of a crime, they forget about an important phone call, and they put themselves in a position where they are made fools of in public by a drunk. After Kvant is killed by the sniper and is replaced by Kvastmo, the bumbling ineptitude continues. Their place in the series is more than mere comedy, however. In the context of social criticism they illustrate the brutish level of insensitivity of the lower echelons of the police. Kvant's conversation, which frequently centers around his wife's anatomical ailments, even makes Kristiansson sick, and his commitment to duty is based upon the principle of seeing as little as possible. Kristiansson is described by a defense lawyer in *The Terrorists* as lazy and unintelligent, and although the prosecution objects, no evidence is presented to contradict the characterization (iii).

Another symbol of the deterioration of the police is Division Commander Stig Malm, who is Martin Beck's immediate superior. Malm is a politician who thinks in terms of public relations instead of the fundamentals of police work, which he does not really understand. He has achieved his present position by "clever careerist maneuvering" and knows how to play up to the right people for his own benefit. Malm would like to be a tyrant, but his political instincts warn him that some of his present subordinates may one day be his superiors, and he hesitates to sit too heavily on them. The result is that he is universally despised by the police, who recognize him as being self-satisfied, coquettish and rigid. Arriving at the scene of a crime in *Cop Killer* he bends down majestically to pet a police dog (hoping the television cameras are on him) and gets bitten. The reaction of the handler is addressed not to Malm but to the animal: "Good dog" (xxvi).

We have earlier mentioned the Security Division of the National Police Board, derisively known as "Sepo" and generally scorned by the regular police. In the opinion of Martin Beck, Sepo is a supremely incompetent arm of law enforcement that can not break a case or even arrest a spy unless the culprit is delivered into their hands with a full array of evidence already supplied. The presence of Sepo in the series is another representation of the loss of purpose in the police establishment: over the years the role of Sepo has become progressively confused, with the result that the public conception of the agency is that it exists only to make life miserable for people with left-wing convictions.

The social criticism of Sjöwall and Wahlöö is seldom heavy-handed, but expresses itself more often as intrinsic ridicule. Pomposity among superiors, absence of sound planning, and thoughtless zeal are the targets of their sharpest satire in some of the best comic scenes in police fiction. Few readers are likely to forget the epic bungle in *The Locked Room*, in which the police storm the apartment of two criminals with resultant casualties including one policeman shot, one police dog shot, another policeman bitten, several policemen gassed, and the apartment a shambles—followed by the revelation that the apartment was not only unoccupied but not even locked (xviii). Then there is the episode in *The Terrorists* in which Gunvald Larsson makes up a list of policemen (including Kristiansson and Kvastmo) to be kept out of the way so they will not foul up a carefully planned operation. He labels it "C.S." for "Clod Squad," but it accidentally falls into the hands of the head of Sepo, who interprets "C.S." to mean "Commando Section" and throws Larsson's clods into the action as shock troops (xix).

Chapter 21

Collin Wilcox

POLICE WORK, according to the procedural tales, is not a line of activity that promotes much introspection among its practitioners. Ordinarily, the preoccupations of these policemen are focused upon the society of which they are the protectors, and more specifically upon their own families and friends. Consequently, the authors do not often admit us to much self-analysis on the part of their policemen, nor do they reveal much of emotional trauma or inner conflict. Of the writers already discussed, Rex Burns comes closest to the level of inner revelation with the self-searching of Gabriel Wager, and to a limited degree so do Nicolas Freeling with the occasional inner monologues assigned to Inspector Van der Valk, and Dorothy Uhnak with the personal anxieties of Christie Opara. For the most part, though, the emotions and actions of the police protagonists are externalized; Collin Wilcox made a really drastic break with tradition in using the first-person point of view in his series featuring Lieutenant Frank Hastings of San Francisco Homicide.

Because Hastings is the narrator throughout, we get more of his personal history than that of any other policeman in procedural fiction. We learn that he spent his first seventeen years in San Francisco, where, when he was fourteen, his father left him and his mother, taking the profits of a small business and running off with his secretary. Young Frank played varsity football for three years in high school, became an All-American candidate at Stanford, and after graduation signed with the Detroit Lions as a second-string fullback. Hastings was not, according to his own account, a successful pro player because he "lacked the killer instinct" (a limitation that carries over into his police career), but his athletic image did attract the attention of the daughter of a wealthy Detroit manufacturer, whom he married. The marriage ended in divorce after four years, partly because Carolyn, the "beautiful, tawny predator," had found another man, and partly because Hastings, dissatisfied with his job as tour-guide for important visitors to his father-in-law's plant, was drinking heavily. Leaving his two children in Detroit, Hastings returned to San Francisco, where, at the age of thirty-three he became the oldest rookie in the police academy. His alcoholism almost ended his job as a policeman and would have done so except for the intervention of an experienced policeman, whom Hastings had known since childhood and who visited his apartment one night to tell him that if he did not stop drinking his career was finished. Hastings poured his remaining liquor down the drain and never touched another drop.

This story, which emerges in fragmentary references in each of the novels, is the background of the series. The residual trauma, which has the effect, especially in the early novels, of prompting Hastings' search for his own identity, drives him into casual sex with two women, one a witness and the other a possible suspect. The tone of the early portion of the series is made explicit in the title of the first novel, *The Lonely Hunter* (1969): although he has firm friendships with his colleage Lieutenant Pete Friedman and with Captain Kreiger, who rescued him from alcoholism, Hastings is an emotional loner until he meets Ann Haywood in the third book, *Dead Aim*. Like him, Ann is suffering from the pain of a recent divorce, and their subsequent love-affair provides Hastings a shelter into which he can withdraw and counteract the defeat of his own ruined marriage.

Because of the pervasive influence of his old emotional injuries, Hastings reminds us more nearly of one of the wounded knights-errant of the private investigator tradition, like Macdonald's Lew Archer, than he does of the typical extraverts of the procedural school like Knox's Colin Thane. In *The Lonely Hunter* Cecile Franks tells Hastings that he has a "bruised quality" about him (xi), and in *Doctor, Lawyer...* Pete Friedman calls him a "basically uptight personality" (xix). Hastings, with his strong inclination to introspection and self-analysis, thinks of himself on one occasion as one who, early in the game, had been a "graceful winner" but had later "come up a loser—a failure."[1]

Chance frustrations bring the defeats of the past back to him, as they do when he tries to prepare himself a quick breakfast of two bananas and a glass of milk in the blender, forgets to replace the lid before switching on the motor, and ends up with a pureed mess all over the kitchen. For Hastings, even so absurd an episode evokes the desperate loneliness of the past, when only drink could ease the pain.[2]

We must not suppose, however, that Frank Hastings is so dominated by his old traumas that he is not an expert detective; he is, as a matter of fact, one of the most thoroughly professional policemen in the literature. He works hard to maintain an objective attitude, recognizing that, when a policeman begins to feel pity he is like a fighter who lets himself get angry; he can't do the job. He believes in a strict interpretation of police regulations, reminding himself that, after a shotgun has been used, all shells must be ejected, the chambers cleared, and the gun uncocked, and that, when knocking on a strange door, a policeman must have already decided which way to jump in case of trouble. Hastings is at his professional best in *Twospot*, the novel done in collaboration with Bill Pronzini, in which Hastings' commitment to the police establishment stands in contrast to Pronzini's private investigator "Bill," who now assumes the role of the lonely hunter. Even so, Hastings has enough basic cop-quality in this story to instruct a subordinate to get hold of some needed information even if he has to bend the rules in the process (xvii).

His honesty and courage are above challenge. In *The Watcher* a vengeful criminal tries to implicate him in suspicion of bribery, but nobody in the Department believes Hastings guilty, because his honesty has never been questioned (iii). In Chapter 8 we mentioned the occasion on which he risked his own life in order to capture a suspect who must be taken alive and then modestly disclaimed credit for his own heroism, an episode typical of the man's disdain for heroics.

Hastings is a humane person: Friedman tells him he is essentially a "heavy" who spends a lot of energy repressing the instinct to lean on people.[3] He has strong feelings about the use of firearms, telling his daughter that carrying a gun is an admission of failure: no really happy men carry guns.[4] As a rule, his humanitarian instincts govern his dealings with his fellow policemen: in one story he realizes that a deputy is about to get sick in the presence of a corpse; Hastings purposely makes the man so angry that his weakness is submerged under a wave of resentment.[5]

His instinctive kindness, however, does not deter his use of a policeman's clout when necessary. In *Power Plays* he holds a junkie suspect overnight, knowing that lack of drugs and sleep will make him co-operative, though we must not miss the fact that Hastings promises to get him a methadone shot in the morning (v).

In the chapter on Jewish detectives we discussed Pete Friedman, who has an important role in the series. We must also mention Hastings' assistant in most of the stories, the good-natured atypical cop Canelli, whom Friedman calls an Italian schlemiel.[6] Canelli is characterized by his large, wondering brown eyes, his bumbling approach to investigation, and his capacity for getting his feelings hurt. His written reports read like high school compositions into which a mixture of prose from pulp magazines has been stirred, and his oral reports are dragged out to the point where Hastings must ask him to get on to the essentials. Canelli's surpassing virtue as an investigator, though, is his fantastic luck. He is the kind of innocent bungler who will trip over a weapon the rest of the squad have been searching for all night, and the whole homicide detail could be looking for a suspect who would be at that moment tapping Canelli on the shoulder, asking for a match.[7] Wilcox began the series with the unprofessional racial bigot Markham as Hastings' assistant, but wisely substituted Canelli, whose guileless simplicity tends to relieve the atmosphere created by Hastings' personal trauma.

A few paragraphs back we mentioned the similarity of Frank Hastings to one of the protagonists of the private-detective school, especially Ross Macdonald's Lew Archer. The first three novels of the Hastings series show strong evidence of the influence of the Macdonald style (an influence acknowledged in the dedication of *Hiding Place* to Kenneth Millar), and indeed there are a number of passages in these stories that could have come out of a Lew Archer novel.[8] It is possible that Wilcox's efforts to approach the rhetorical peaks of Macdonald's prose caused him to write sentences like this one from *Dead Aim*: "The slow, lazily suggestive swing of her hips seemed somehow more slatternly than sensuous—more listless than lustful" (xi). Whatever the cause, Wilcox recovered from this kind of verbal pyrotechnics and settled into an easy style appropriate to the procedural format.

Use of the first-person-narrator point of view has the advantage of giving the reader some considerable insights into the protagonist of the story, insights that would be awkward if supplied by an omniscient author or an external observer, but it does tend to create a distortion in perspective that may be troublesome in the unfolding story of such naturally overt activity as police work. Wilcox successfully resolves the difficulty and preserves the narrative perspective through the use of Pete Friedman and Ann Haywood as observers and interpreters whose comments supplement and add dimension to Hastings' own reactions. There is an especially significant passage in *Long Way Down* in which Friedman forces Hastings to listen to his analysis of Hastings' personal problem, at once jarring the policeman into a realistic appraisal of his situation and supplying some necessary insights for the benefit of the reader (xx).

The Hastings series is particularly strong in the treatment of police procedures that seem entirely plausible in the context of the big-city investigations, a quality especially remarkable in light of Wilcox's own attitude toward the place of "reality" in the procedural tale. In an article in *The Writer*, he minimizes his efforts in research (confessing to a total of two hours spent at the San Francisco Homicide Bureau), emphasizing rather the importance of imagination in the writing of a police story. Police work in real life is tedious and dull, and the fact of the matter is that no editor would want to buy a story that accurately reflects the average homicide investigation. What readers want, says Wilcox, is diabolical murders instead of the humdrum killings most policemen actually deal with, and shoot-outs and hot pursuit in place of the investigation of real life, most of which is accomplished on the telephone. The key to good crime writing is not mystery but suspense: readers addicted to television crime shows are caught in the question of what happens next rather than the classic *who? how?* and *why?*[9]

Chapter 22
James McClure

IT IS ALMOST INEVITABLE that crucial tensions within a society, particularly those involving ethnic conflicts, will stimulate the production of fiction based on social themes, as witness the Southern Renaissance in the United States in the 1920s and '30s, and more recently the rich harvest of distinguished fiction in the Republic of South Africa. One South African writer who has built his stories around the anxieties generated by the closed society of his native country, including the policy of racial Apartheid and the continuing conflicts between the ruling Afrikaner class and the minority of English descent, is James McClure, author of a series featuring Lieutenant Trompie Kramer (an Afrikaner) and Sergeant Mickey Zondi (a Bantu) of the "Trekkersburg" Murder Squad.[1]

In the chapter on black police detectives we discussed Zondi, who is probably the more interesting and certainly the more picturesque half of the team. Before we can undertake a reasonable portrayal of Lieutenant Kramer, we will need to review the ambiance of South Africa as it emerges in the stories, because Kramer is distinctively the product of that environment.

The social structure of South Africa is based upon the notion of inherent racial superiority, the assumption as Donald C. Wall says, "that any white is superior to any non-white."[2] The assumption is institutionalized in the law that keeps most Bantu out of white residential areas overnight, in the Group Areas Act that classifies towns and suburbs as white or non-white, and in the regulations that label lavatories and lifts as "For Whites" and "For Non-Whites." It makes distinctions with respect to the sanctity of human life, as in the statement regarding the murdered woman in McClure's *The Steam Pig*, "... She was only a colored. It was not quite the same thing as killing a white" (xv). It is axiomatic that blacks are automatically suspected of crime, "Bantu intruder" being the usual preliminary solution to any murder. The assumption of racial superiority manifests itself in the folkways of the white minority, as it does in the case where a white woman stops speaking to a neighbor who has been discovered to be "colored" (of mixed racial descent),[3] and, at least for the purposes of appearance, it is accepted by the blacks; when Kramer and another white policeman get into a discussion of white ways of thinking, Zondi tactfully excuses himself.[4] The bitterest consequence of racial classification is the tragedy of the Francis family in *The Steam Pig*, who had lived as whites until it was accidentally discovered that the father is "colored." The entire family must appear before the Classification Board and move into a "native" neighborhood. The son, who has his heart set on becoming a pilot, is deprived of the opportunity because "job reservation" denies that profession to non-whites, and the daughter, who assumes a false identity and passes for white, eventually becomes a prostitute (xi).

The white presumption of the mental incapacity of Bantu is as a rule not challenged by the blacks. In *The Blood of an Englishman* Zondi buys an atlas as a gift for his children, who have done well at school. The saleswoman is reluctant to allow him to complete the purchase, because he obviously will not be able to understand a book of maps. Zondi pretends it is for his "boss," and the clerk's objections are withdrawn (xxii).

At the same time, a curious delicacy enters into the verbalization of contempt for blacks. In *Snake* we are told that "kaffir" (a disparaging term for Bantu) is now officially banned from police use and that a white policeman was forced to make a public apology for using it to one of his black subordinates (iv).

Besides the official commitment to a policy of Apartheid, the cultural climate of South Africa is dominated by the Protestant fundamentalist moral ethic. In 1975, we learn, the Republic became the largest distributor of Bibles in the world; the Dutch Reformed Synod, moreover, was at one point pressing the government to ban all Sunday papers and to make living in sin a criminal offense.[5] Morality is, as a matter of fact, imposed by mandate: no female may enter a bar; *Playboy* is banned, and the censor clips erotic pictures from foreign photographic magazines; dresses are painted over bikini-clad women on cinema posters; sunbathers around swimming pools must lie at least eighteen inches apart.

The heavy hands of Apartheid and puritanism come together

with special force in those regulations designed to prevent the arousal of violence and lust among the non-white population. Blacks are not permitted to see gangster films, and they are forbidden to look at pictures of naked white women, this latter restriction whimsically ignored by Zondi when he must examine the police photograph of a murder victim in the course of an investigation.[6]

In the McClure stories South Africa is a closed society that defends itself against the threats of alien ideologies. The term "liberal" is a mark of opprobrium: when Lieutenant Kramer asks young Probationer Johnny Pembrook, "Are you a liberal or something?" Pembrook is affronted.[7] It is automatically assumed that white liberals are in league with the black population; thus a Bantu servant is dismissed as a suspect in a murder because the victim was known to have leftist sympathies, and no liberal is going to be carved up by his own kitchen boy.[8] The fear of communism becomes inbred at an early age: when Kramer asks a small boy if he likes policemen, the child unhesitatingly replies, "Yes, I do. They keep communists away."[9] The most chilling manifestation of the national fear of deviationsim is the Detective Club in *The Caterpillar Cop,* with membership open to Afrikaner boys between the ages of twelve and sixteen, whose chief activity is the ferreting out of liberals and the harassment of the Bantu population (v). And, as might be expected in the Bible Veldt, Catholicism, the "Roman Danger," is suspect because of its leftist tendencies.

Fragmentation of society in South Africa is further heightened by tensions between the Afrikaners (whites of Dutch descent) and the English minority. This conflict is the theme of the second novel in the series, *The Caterpillar Cop,* in which Kramer is placed in an adversary position with Captain Jarvis, a spit-and-polish type who considers the ruling white majority "Afrikaans scum" (xv). Elsewhere in the story we learn that the two white classes associate with each other as little as possible. Afrikaner and English children do not mix socially, and pure Afrikaner youths do not take dancing lessons because that is an *English* custom (vii). Sensitivity to English criticism is especially keen among the police: Colonel DuPlessis, Kramer's superior, cautions Kramer not to embarrass a cabinet member, because "the English-speaking press has its spies everywhere" (vi).

The policy of Apartheid, as Wall points out, provides James McClure with "a richly complicated cultural matrix" within which to write his procedural stories.[10] In the same sense, the heavily moralistic atmosphere reflected in the puritan legal code gives a mystery writer a special advantage over the authors of stories set in Sweden or America or one of the other western societies, for the reason that in South Africa so many more things are shocking or criminal than they would be in a more permissive culture. Having sex with a person of another race would hardly provide opportunity for blackmail in Frank Hastings' San Francisco, but it does in Trompie Kramer's Trekkersburg.

Kramer, as we have said, is himself a product of the Afrikaner ambiance, sharing most of the moral and social biases of his cultural heritage. He refers to blacks as "wogs," considers *Playboy* magazine "permissive society muck," and labels English families "rubbish."[11] He resents criticism of South Africa in the newspapers of Britain, because they do not, in his opinion, understand South Africa's problems.[12] In contrast to Kramer's Afrikaner bent, however, is his personal regard for Mickey Zondi, whom he privately regards as the equal of any white policeman of the non-commissioned ranks, with whom he jokes and whose playful insolence he gruffly endures, and whom he calls "old son" when nobody is around to hear. Kramer must, of course, conceal his regard for Zondi in the presence of others: he calls him "boy" for the benefit of a watching colored man, and when a white woman walks in on Zondi stretched out on a couch at the scene of an investigation, Kramer quickly explains "My boy's sick."[13] Kramer's affection for Zondi, and his respect for his competence, is especially evident in *The Sunday Hangman*, where Kramer's problem is his fear that Zondi will be invalided because of a wound that causes him considerable pain; he resorts to all kinds of subterfuge to keep Zondi active as his team-mate and even pleads with the police surgeon not to chuck him on the scrap-pile (v).

Kramer is an ugly-looking cop whom a small boy describes as "an uncle-ish sort of man with very short hair and big front teeth like a rodent,"[14] and he often assumes a role of crudeness and intentional rudeness to match his unlovely appearance. He deliberately refuses to shake hands with a doctor he has just met, he sighs in the face of a witness hoping his breath is bad, and he calls a rural cop an "idler" for not having completed a plan in the investigation of a murder-site. His approach to police work is individualistic and egocentric, though his occasional scorn of official channels does not make him much different from other fictional policemen, nor does his distrust of new methods: Kramer wants distances on a sketch expressed in inches, because "all this metrication business" is a nuisance.[15]

His professional commitment, at the same time, is as strong as any to be found in procedural literature. In *The Caterpillar Cop* he sharply reprimands the police surgeon and another officer when he catches them ridiculing a drunk at the Central Charge Office, reminding them that such conduct is dangerous (viii). Kramer's dedication on occasion even takes precedence over his love-live, as it does when he mentally reviews a current case while still lying in bed with a school-teacher with whom he has just made love, and again when he walks out on lunch with his mistress because he has just caught onto the significance of a clue (xi, xii).

Kramer is unmarried (he likes the idea of a wife and children but does not wat to take on the responsibility in view of the danger of getting killed),[16] but his relationship with the Widow Fourie is the solid husband-wife combination familiar to readers of procedural fiction. She acts as confidante and interpreter, and she and her children provide the Great Good Place for Kramer's escape from the pressures of the police world. Even the Widow Fourie, however, is no match for Kramer's regard for Mickey Zondi: when she suggests that Kramer should let Zondi retire from the force, he walks out on her in spite of the fact that they are about to enjoy a love-scene together.[17]

McClure's prose style makes heavier demands upon the reader than do the narratives of most mystery writers. His approach is often oblique and exacting, as in the scene in *The Caterpillar Cop* in which Zondi is attacked by a native witch doctor and is narrowly rescued by Kramer. The point of view is limited to Zondi's failing consciousness, with the result that the narration becomes impressionistic and obscure, though exceptionally effective to the attentive reader (viii). McClure's opening scenes, always dramatic and usually bizarre, have come to be trademarks of his stories, notably the exotic dancer with her pet python and presumptive lover at the beginning of *Snake*, and the puzzled victim about to be hanged in the first chapter of *The Sunday Hangman*.

Chapter 23

Conclusion

ALTHOUGH THE POLICE PROCEDURAL story represents a new approach to detective fiction in terms of the nature of its detective-protatonists and the methods of detection they employ, and although it has evolved a formula and even a set of myths of its own, it has never constituted a *rebellion* against the older traditions of mystery fiction. In a discussion of the question of realism in the hard-boiled story as opposed to that in the classic detective tale, John Cawelti calls attention to the fact that the hard-boiled view of reality can be as arbitrary as that of the more philosophical or genteel perspectives *it set out to attack*" (emphasis supllied).[1] Cawelti's wording is important, because it reminds us that there was an aggressive purpose among the writers of the *Black Mask* school and their successors, a revolt against what they considered to be the artificialities of the classic Golden Age.

The early writers of police procedurals, on the other hand, never "set out to attack" anything. As we read the apologias of Lawrence Treat, John Creasey and Hillary Waugh, we find among them no sardonic counterpart of Raymond Chandler, no "Simple Art of Murder" flaying the absurdities of the older traditions. Instead, the explanations of the procedural writers are usually set in the context of discussions of the mystery craft in general, with the result that the most specific interpretations of the procedural as sub-genre came from critics like Anthony Boucher. Lawrence Treat, as a matter of fact, has denied any intentions of starting a new trend, suggesting rather that his purpose in *V as in Victim* and its successors was to make an accurate portrayal of policemen as they are, with particular emphasis on the workings of the police mind.[2] Hillary Waugh, the other American pioneer in the field, in the most extensive discussion of the procedural tale written by a practicing author, devotes his attention almost exclusively to the problems with which a writer of procedurals must deal, with no hint of attack

235

on any other type of mystery.[3]

Neither is there much suggestion of dogma in the pronouncements of the procedural writers. The closest approximation to a doctrinaire approach was the one made by Lillian O'Donnell in her article "Routines and Rules for the Police Procedural," but even her "rules" are prescriptions for the representation of non-fictional reality, in contrast to the canonization of literary conventions practiced by the rules-makers of the Golden Age. O'Donnell's only "rule," as a matter of fact, is, "Tell it the way it is," in which writers and readers can broadly concur.[4]

Actually, in development of mystery and suspense, the police procedural is closer to the traditional classic school of detective fiction than to that of the hard-boiled variety, the most notable deviations being those cited earlier, the reliance on informants and the possibility of unsolved cases. Although the procedural, as we have just pointed out, has not devised a set of "rules" for itself, it measures up reasonably well against the dicta of the purists of the 1920s, S.S. Van Dine's Twenty Rules and Ronald Knox's Ten Commandments. Procedural writers habitually violate Van Dine's Rule 3 (no love interest), Rule 4 (no detective-culprit), Rule 5 (solution by logical deduction), Rule 9 (only one detective), Rule 12 (only one culprit), and Rule 17 (no professional criminals), but generally obey the other fourteen. They violate Knox's whimsical Fifth Commandment (no Chinamen in the story), but so do a great many other writers, and the Sixth (no solution by accident) and Seventh (no detective-perpetrator).[5] The fact that procedural writers observe most of the dogmas of the rules-makers is evidence of their presence in the mainstream of mystery fiction, especially so when we remember that those "rules" were propounded in an era of tidy murders committed by one of a neat list of suspects and solved by a genius of prodigious powers of observation and deduction.

Procedural writers as a matter of course observe the Fair Play convention, which holds that nothing of importance be withheld by the writer and that the reader must have equal opportunity with the detective to solve the mystery. Writers of the classic school were frequently criticized for the devices they employed to skirt this rule, most of the cheating being a result of the superiority of the detective, who could see in a clue the same thing the reader saw but could perceive vastly more, who could look at the shape of a person's ears and mutter, "Aha! So that's the way it is!" while the bemused reader had not the foggiest notion of the way it is. This particular temptation is not nearly so strong in the procedural, where the detective, quite frankly, is just not all that much brighter than the reader. Virgil Tibbs, whose methods are frequently closer to those of Sherlock Holmes than to those of George Gideon, can perform awesome feats of ratiocination like the one in *Five Pieces of Jade* (ii), where he deduces the nature of the secret research in which an industry is engaged by merely riding in the company car and observing the physical features of the plant, but most procedural cops find themselves in the position of Roger West in *A Splinter of Glass* (vi), who believes the glass sliver found at the crime-scene is an important clue but can not estimate its significance until he gets the report from the lab. When he does, nothing is withheld; the reader knows as much as West knows.

The procedural, moreover, tends to follow not only the rules but the conventional devices of the classic formal-problem story. Of the ten conventions Howard Haycraft identifies as having been introduced by Poe in "The Murders in the Rue Morgue,"[6] most show up more or less frequently in the procedural. The staged ruse to force the culprit's hand is a favorite: in O'Donnell's *Don't Wear Your Wedding Ring* (xvi) the police leak a false story to the newspapers to produce the same kind of effect as Dupin's notice in the Paris papers. Concealment by means of the ultra-obvious, used by Poe in the instance of the witnesses who in each case identified the language of the murderer as the one language he or she did not understand, is another device frequently borrowed, most notably in Uhnak's *The Ledger,* in which the "ledger" the police are seeking sits right there before their eyes. Other Poe devices like the expansive explanation, deduction by putting one's self in another's position, and the time-honored least likely suspect are employed in the procedural with almost the same regularity as in the classic story. Several conventions not specifically "invented" by Poe but familiar to the reader of classic detection make frequent appearance. The grumpy medical examiner, called away from his dinner or his sleep to do a preliminary examination of a corpse, is as irritable and overbearing as he was in the Golden Age novels, and uses much the same language. We even run into an old friend, the Singular Anomaly

(Holmes' dog that did not bark in the night) when Fred Fellows in *Prisoner's Plea* is puzzled by "the one freak thing that happened in the neighborhood on the murder night" (xxvii).

A few of the bad habits of writers of the older tradition also carry over into the procedural, notably the unaccountable coincidence. In *Gun Before Butter* Van der Valk becomes acquainted with a young woman in a case, then runs into her again in a totally unrelated case; he asks himself why but can only answer, "I know these things happen" (207). Colin Thane suggests no explanation (and neither does his author) in *The Tallyman* when, at the bank for an interview, he sees a clerk whose beating he had witnessed on a Glasgow street the night before (iii).

To this point we have tried to show how, in the handling of the mystery, the police procedural stays rather close to the norm of the classic formal-problem story. In terms of setting and atmosphere, however, the procedural shares more of the ambiance of the hard-boiled novel of the Hammett-Chandler-Macdonald tradition. George Grella, in "Murder and the Mean Streets," speaks of the "general tawdriness [that] characterizes the urban locale of all hard-boiled fiction." In the context of the American agrarian bias, the city is a place of wickedness, says Grella, but the detective has no other place to go.[7] The same applies to the procedural, in which the tone is set by the urban jungle, the plundered city that has replaced the despoliated frontier. Not only in America but in Europe and South Africa, the setting is almost invariably the big city: even when the writers invent locales, like Procter's Granchester and McClure's Trekkersburg, the environment is urban, the only exception being Waugh's Stockford. There is a logical explanation for the choice, in that the urban setting provides more opportunities for all kinds of crime, upper-, middle-, and lower-class, than a small town would. At the same time it must be remembered that policemen in the procedural stories do not deal exclusively with crimes committed in back alleys or "mean streets" (any more than those of the hard-boiled private-eye variety). The main advantage of the urban environment is that it gives the writer infinite opportunity for developing themes involving the anxieties, tensions and frustrations we associate with the city, as well as an almost unlimited choice of characters and situations.

In narrative technique, however, as in the development of

mystery and suspense, the writers of the procedural adhere fairly closely to the classic formula. The tendency is especially apparent in structure, where the procedural tends to follow the seven-step framework introduced by Poe in the Dupin tales: the Problem, the Initial Solution, the Complication, the Period of Confusion, the Dawning Light, the Solution, and the Explanation. One reason for use of the conventional format is that the early procedural writers, who set the pattern, were already experienced in that structure. Before *V as in Victim* Lawrence Treat had written his series featuring the brilliant Carl Wayward, John Creasey had produced an impressive volume of mysteries before West and Gideon, and Hillary Waugh had done the series featuring Sheridan Wesley and Philip Macadam, both of whom are private investigators but whose stories are structured according to the classic format rather than the convoluted plots of Chandler or Macdonald. Which brings us to the other reason: the structure associated with the private-eye narrative, with its spin-off plots and residual mystery, its pursuits of long-dead crimes and persistence of the private investigator after he has been pulled off a case, is not adaptable to the procedural. Philip Marlowe might follow up a side-issue out of curiosity, as he does in *The Big Sleep* and elsewhere, and Lew Archer may go back to investigate a fifty-year-old murder in order to solve a current mystery, as he habitually does, but such obsessive probings would not be plausible in a procedural. Policemen have enough to do on the immediate case-load without dredging up past—or even present— associations, no matter how mysteriously appealing.

In plotting the novel, a procedural writer must decide between the single story-line and the multiple; the multiple plot is the more plausible, actually, because policemen in real life normally work on more than one case at a time, but it is a risky approach that can produce a confused narrative unless handled with extreme care. Consequently many writers opt for the single plot even though their big-city cops are naturally handling the usual heavy case-load, as Hillary Waugh does in the Frank Sessions stories and John Creasey in the Roger West series (though Creasey does use the multiple story-line in the Gideon stories under the name of J.J. Marric). Ed McBain is generally successful in dealing with several stories at once (notably in *Hail, Hail, the Gang's All Here!* which has fourteen independent narrative strands) because he individualizes his plots by identifying them with people and places. One could wish that Elizabeth Linington might handle her multitudinous plots as well, especially in the Luis Mendoza series, written under the Dell Shannon pseudonym; sometimes, in the Mendoza stories, the reader finds it necessary to turn back fifteen or twenty pages in order to sort out a case from the four or five that have been introduced since the last treatment of the present one. Most writers who use multiple plots, as we have observed earlier, habitually "nest" the stories, the first introduced being the last solved, the second being the next-to-last solved, and so on, a technique Creasey developed for the Gideon series. The typical thriller structure, with sensational, episodic development, sometimes shows up in the procedural, notably in Greenburg's *Love Kills* and Ball's *Then Came Violence*.

The narrative point of view in the procedural is normally the unlimited one of the omniscient author, which has the advantage in the mystery of permitting the writer to tell the reader only what he wants him to know and also allows a commentator like McBain to insert his observations on his City and its inhabitants, or social critics like Sjowall and Wahloo to pass judgments on the problems of life in Sweden. Some writers prefer the limited central-intelligence viewpoint, like Nicolas Freeling, Bill Knox and Rex Burns, who habitually confine revelation and exposition to the consciousness of their main characters, a device also useful in preserving the Fair Play convention, because the reader knows what the detective knows, and no less. A rarely employed point of view is that of the outside observer; Freeling used this approach in *Love in Amsterdam*, the first novel in the Van der Valk series, where the story is seen through the eyes of the chief suspect, but he converted to the protagonist-central intelligence for the remainder of the series; McBain lets the reader see the story through the eyes of the murderer in *He Who Hesitates*, an experiment that works well for readers already familiar with the people and places developed earlier in the series, because the readers can enjoy the fine irony of the murderer's reactions to the 87th Precinct and its policemen. The first-person narrator is rare: Wilcox lets Frank Hastings tell the story throughout his series, with the result that we are admitted more fully to Hastings' personal trauma than is normal; Uhnak also puts the story of *The Investigation* into the mouth of Joe Peters for the purpose of insight into Peters' reactions to the departmental political maneuverings of the Queens County police organization. The alternating point of view appears in those "reversal" stories where the reader is admitted in turn to the consciousness of the criminal and that of the police, a favorite device of Maurice Procter, and of John Creasey in the Gideon stories. One point of view never used in the procedural is that of the Watson; there are, as we have seen, a number of policemen in these stories who can on occasion rise to the deductive heights of Sherlock Holmes, but to have their stories told by a wonder-stricken foil would violate the myth implied in the formulaic component of the Ordinary Mortals.

The language of the police procedural is characteristically direct, colloquial, unaffected. At least two of our writers (Michael Gilbert and Nicolas Freeling) have a talent for the well-turned phrase that is often striking, but even their prose is never consciously "literary." The one author who has produced a genuine innovation in narrative style is Dan Greenburg, who tells the story of *Love Kills* entirely in present tense. In general, though, there is no identifiable "procedural style" in the sense of the "hard-boiled style" of the *Black Mask* school.

The portrayal of character is too broad a subject to be attempted here, but two procedural writers are especially skillful in the use of multiple reactions as a means of achieving depth in the delineation of people in the stories. Thus Ed McBain will frequently describe in some detail the reactions of several people to the same situation, with the result that the reader gains a basis for comparing and contrasting them with each other. There is an especially good example in *Doll*, when it is reported that Steve Carella has been killed: Meyer Meyer goes into the park, sits alone on a bench, and quietly weeps for his friend; Cotton Hawes, the self-sufficient member of the squad, goes to a raucous Western movie, but is unable to concentrate on it; Andy Parker (who hates Carella) goes to a prostitute, gets drunk, verbally abuses her, and finally buries his head in a pillow; Bert Kling, who blames himself for Carella's death, is overcome with self-reproach (v,vi). Dorothy Uhnak uses the same device with the emphasis inverted in *The Ledger*, in which Christie Opara's complicated and often paradoxical personality is repeatedly reviewed and analyzed by the other people in the story, and by Christie herself, with a resultant "roundness" of character that will not let her be pigeonholed as tomboy, scatterbrain or sorrowful widow.

It is not unusual, of course, for a detective story in any tradition to develop a theme beyond the expected one of mystery and resolution, and such development is not uncommon in the procedural. We recall the theme of pathological emotions in Poul Orum's *Nothing But the Truth,* that of human "differentness" in John Ball's *The Cool Cottontail,* police violence in K. Arne Blom's *The Moment of Truth,* police corruption in Rex Burns' *The Farnsworth Score,* and the status of women in Lillian O'Donnell's *No Business Being a Cop.* Sometimes a theme runs throughout the series, like the social comment in the stories of Maj Sjowall and Per Wahloo, and in those of James McClure. In *For Love of Imabelle* Chester Himes achieves a poetic integration of theme and narrative through the use of a chorus-like commentary, first in the anonymous Harlem voices that express the fear and bewilderment of the onlookers, and then in the lines of old songs that run through the consciousness of the fleeing Jackson.

One of the more hazardous undertakings of the critic-historian is the effort to predict future developments in his genre; so many variables and intangibles affect the tastes of the reading public that even the most conservative prophecy is likely to be far from the mark after a decade or two. Consequently, this discussion will not conclude with any prediction on Whither the Procedural? but rather with a brief look at two writers whose work has demonstrated that the procedural tale is a much more flexible medium than could have been envisioned in the early efforts of Lawrence Treat, Hillary Waugh, Maurice Procter, and the writers of *Dragnet.* Although both of these writers operate within the procedural framework, Lawrence Sanders has built *The First Deadly Sin* around the theme that is philosophical and even theological in scope, and Janwillem van de Wetering has incorporated elements of surrealism, imagism, and even Zen Buddhism into his procedural series.

The features of *The First Deadly Sin* that become apparent on first reading are its length and complexity, the latter quality so pervasive that the busines of detection is often submerged in the intricate exploration of the themes of shared guilt and the dangers of the sin of pride, which is almost Hawthornian in its intensity. It is not surprising that reviewers almost unanimously disparaged the book as "a bloated, adipose novel inside which is a perfectly good but slender suspense story crying out to get out" and "a thriller with delusions of grandeur."[8] If we seek only mystery, *The First Deadly Sin* is indeed too long and aberrant, but if we concede the possibility of exploration of a great theme that is appropriate to the suspense in the story, length and complexity are no problem. Evidently the reading public was willing to accept the concession; *The First Deadly Sin* stayed on the best-seller lists for months.

As we pointed out in Chapter 6, the affinity between policemen and criminals is conventional in the procedural, but Sanders develops the sense of shared guilt to a depth that is unique in the genre. The criminal in the story is Daniel Blank, a computer expert whose hobby is mountain-climbing and whose passion to experience a reality beyond the normal limits of logic leads him to commit a series of murders that have no motive except his wish to please the witch-like Celia Montfort, to whose domination he has voluntarily submitted (IV,ii). Blank's quest for ultimate wisdom arises out of two personal qualities: he has no formal religious commitment ("Is there God?" he asks himself) and his obsession with orderliness, which causes him to organize his computer department around a set of almost meaningless ceremonies (I,iv). Both of these qualities are shared by his pursuer. Captain Edward X. Delaney was reared as a Catholic but gave up his religious commitment when in 1945 he witnessed the horrors of a concentration camp in Germany (II,ii). He also shares Blank's passion for orderliness: his wife at one point asks Delaney if he did not become a cop "to make the world neat and tidy" (II,i) and at another if he considers himself "Nemesis for the entire world" (II,iii), and Delaney gladly confesses that he became a policeman because "there is, or should be, logic to life" (II,ii). Criminal and policeman share the obsession, though their commitments are contrasted in terms of purpose when a psychiatrist explains to Delaney that what the murderer wants is to impose *his* own kind of order on a world in chaos (VII,i), and in degree when Delaney secretly searches Blank's apartment and decides that in comparison with the murderer's tidiness, he is himself a lubber (VII,iv).

Late in the story Delaney tells himself that he has never felt such affinity for a criminal and that if he could understand Blank, he might better understand himself (VII,iv), and when Blank is finally trapped and dying atop the shaft of stone called the Devil's Needle, he feels a compassion that almost makes him weep (VIII,vi). Besides these explicit references to the affinity between the two, Sanders employs parallel images to confirm the relationship. One is the use of the term "penetration" by Delaney in his unpublished paper on the "Dostoevskian relationship" between policeman and criminal, where he proposes that the detective must enter into the psyche of the criminal to bring him to justice (VII,iii), the word "penetration" echoed by Blank as he experiences the ecstasy of driving the point of his ice ax into the brains of his victims (VI,iii). The other is a shared perception: as Blank freezes to death on the Devil's Needle, he feels snowflakes on his face and wonders if he may be weeping; at the same moment Delaney looking up from below experiences the same sensation and asks himself, "Tears?" (VIII,vi).

There are two reasons for the intensity of Delaney's empathy: he feels guilt over having needlessly driven Blank to his death, but he also envies the murderer's achievement of ultimate knowledge in his dissolution; Blank, he tells himself, now knows it all or is moving toward the final attainment (VIII,v). The quest for ultimate knowledge has driven both men throughout the story, with the result that both have committed the sin of pride, the theme implicit in the title. The gravity of the sin is that of Prometheus in classical mythology and of Adam and Eve in the Judaeo-Christian tradition.

Delaney's pride expresses itself in his desire to set the world right, to be "God's surrogate on earth," which he recognizes as a sin (III,i). Blank's is evident in the fifty mirrors on his living-room wall, in which he enjoys the multiple reflections of his superb naked body (I,ii) and in his willingness to become a "saint of evil" at the urging of Celia Montfort (I,v).

A novel of the complexity of *The First Deadly Sin* naturally lends itself to allegorical interpretations, especially in the concluding pages of the story, in which the death of Daniel Blank atop the Devil's Needle becomes an expiatory act with several explicit parallels to the Christ-story: the date of Blank's death is January 6, Epiphany; the snow that covers his body is described as a stainless white shroud; as the helicopter lowers the frozen body to the earth, the arms are outstretched and the head thrown back in a cruciform pose, and the rays of the setting sun produce a nimbus about the flesh, prompting Delaney to murmur, "God help us all" (VIII,vi). As William Nelson has shown, "The relevant archetype for the novel is the story of the scapegoat and the idea of vicarious atonement which is the purpose of the scapegoat figure."[9] *The First Deadly Sin* is not alone among procedural novels in its examination of human frailty, but it is decidedly unique in its approach to the consequences of guilt on a level that assumes theological and mythic dimensions.

The Second Deadly Sin, which deals with the murder of a famous artist, is much closer to the tradition of the conventional procedural. The sin of covetousness is amply treated in the greed of the artist's family and his professional associates, but it is handled in terms of motive and is not allowed to overshadow the normal business of investigation and detection.

Another writer whose work demonstrates the possibilities for versatility in the police procedural is Janwillem van de Wetering, who in *Outsider in Amsterdam* (1975) began the series featuring three members of the Amsterdam "murder brigade": the commisaris, close to retirement and physically frail, who remains anonymous until his sister calls him "Jan" in the seventh novel; Adjutant Henk Grijpstra, a capable cop of the conventional type, who might be found in almost any procedural series; and Sergeant Rinus DeGier, the perceptive youngest member of the trio, who has the reputation for efficiency and go-getting.

A reader accustomed to the atmosphere of the conventional police story may be moderately puzzled by his first experience with van de Wetering. The tone is inclined to be somewhat more relaxed than in other procedurals, the policemen more considerate, the criminals and other characters more amiable, and the reader will be inclined to agree with the police when they say that this is "a funny case" or "a silly case."

The cast of characters in *The Corpse on the Dike* is illustrative: the victim, a lonely eccentric who keeps his garden neat but lets his house go filthy; a fence called "The Cat," who dresses in gaudy costumes; a giant nymphomaniac psychopath; a lesbian; and a squeaky, nasty informant called "The Mouse." So, frequently, are the dealings of the police with the criminals in the stories, the most dramatic example being the resolution of *The Japanese Corpse*, where the commisaris and DeGier have infiltrated the stronghold of a gang of Japanese smugglers. A company of commandos are prepared to converge on the scene in helicopters, but they arrive to find criminals and policemen completely incapable of violence, the whole cast having been rendered sodden by a particularly potent gin served by the Dutch cops, and the commisaris and the gangster chief weeping soppily in each other's arms. Not all the stories end on so affable a note; there is violence, as in the nightmare conclusion of *Death of a Hawker,* where the murderer chases the police around a vacant lot trying to run them down with a bulldozer, but the atmosphere throughout is almost invariably off-beat and often suggestive of the unreal or the irrational.

Actually, van de Wetering's novels have three levels of meaning, which correspond to the levels of awareness of his police protagonists.

The first is that of the standard police story, which is the level of awareness of Adjutant Grijpstra. Grijpstra is the typical fictional policeman, a competent cop who is good at observation and analysis, but who confesses, "I don't think. Offices think."[10] When the police become involved with a "Hindist Society" in *Outsider in Amsterdam* (i),Grijpstra is confused by the eastern imagery, which the well-read DeGier explains to him. Significantly, he shares with other procedural policemen the representative family problems, an unsatisfying wife and a disappointing son. Dreams, as we will shortly see, play an important part in the delineation of the three policemen: Grijpstra's represent the normal wish-fulfillment of the unsatisfied male, peopled with naked women.

The second level is that of reality-beyond-reality, the level of awareness of Sergeant DeGier. The prosaic Grijpstra does not understand the sergeant and calls him "an incurable romantic," much too bland a characterization for DeGier, who believes in "a miraculous surrealist world," a world of inexplicable beauty that echoes in the half-conscious dreams to which he is subject. "Life is a dream," he says in *Tumbleweed* (v), and later asks, "Who is alive?" (xviii). DeGier has learned the trick of controlling his dreams, so that he can lapse into a state of semi-consiousness in which he is free, not only of routine and responsibility but of mundane existence; he can even direct his recurrent nightmare, which involves at various times a warship, a gang of hoods from the era of Al Capone, and the Queen of the Netherlands, but which always

ends well for DeGier. Dream-like symbolism occasionally floats
reassuringly into his consciousness, as it does when he is walking
beside the sea and sees a white horse in a meadow emblazoned by a
shaft of sunlight as if it were afire; DeGier has the impression that
the horse feels itself part of the inexpressible, and he sighs.[11]
DeGier's sensitivity is such that he is repelled by ugliness and
violence. Grijpstra usually searches corpses, because DeGier has a
tendency to faint in the presence of death. He feels revulsion in the
company of "Elizabeth," a trans-sexual ex-policeman now living as
a woman in *Death of a Hawker* (v); the commisaris likes "Elizabeth"
and respects him. In terms of levels of awareness, the commisaris is
above revulsion, Grijpstra beneath it.

The highest level, wisdom-beyond-wisdom, is that of the aged
commisaris, who has learned through suffering resulting from his
imprisonment and torture by the Germans during the occupation of
Holland and also from his painful rheumatism that has almost
crippled him. The wisdom of the commisaris rises above logic:
"Don't be too sensible," he tells a young policeman. "If you do you'll
never get further than the surface."[12] It also rises above DeGier's
surrealism, a term the commisaris considers nonsensical.[13] He has
acquired the ability to detach himself from external reality, to the
extent that he can feel himself close to the "terrible secret" of life, in
a state of awareness where he is neither awake nor asleep.[14] His
dreams, in contrast to the commonplace wish-fulfillment of
Grijpstra and the controlled dream of DeGier, are seraphic; sitting
alone in his garden with his pet turtle, whose supreme indifference
he admires and envies, the commisaris has a vision of female
winged creatures of supernatural beauty, who observe him and
seem amused.[15] The detached wisdom of the commisaris can be
better understood in the light of van de Wetering's two
autobiographical books, *The Empty Mirror* (the account of his study
in a Zen Buddhist monastery in Japan) and *A Glimpse of
Nothingness* (the story of his experience in a Zen community in
Maine), because the commisaris' awareness sometimes verges on
Oriental mysticism: "I've often been tempted to think that right
equals nothing," he says in *The Maine Massacre*. "Perhaps
'nothing' is the ultimate wisdom" (xi).

In *The Corpse on the Dike* the three levels merge in the solution
of a crime. Grijpstra, sitting in his office idly tapping on his drum

while reading a report, suddenly realizes that the murder was a
mistake. The same solution pops into the mind of DeGier as he lies
on his bed between waking and sleeping. The commisaris sits
watching his turtle, becomes detached and experiences a moment of
almost complete liberation, whereupon he knows the answer also
(xi).

One of van de Wetering's achievements is his ability to handle
imagery on a symbolic plane, a device he frequently uses to
establish correlatives of the emotional states of his characters.
Sometimes the association is only suggested, as in DeGier's sense of
revelation at the sight of the transfigured horse. Occasionally it is
almost allegorical, as in the scene in *Outsider in Amsterdam* where
Grijpstra steps into a room in which the wife of a murdered man is
sewing, and sees her surrounded by a white fluffy cloud that seems
to fill the room. What has happened is that the woman has removed
the eiderdown from a cover to repair it, and the open door has
created a draft that sends the tiny feathers swirling. Grijpstra is
frightened by the eerie picture and reaches for his gun (xi).

In most of the novels whole clusters of associated images
accomplish the integration of character and theme. More often than
not the clusters are composed of animal-images that are identified
with the people in the story. In *The Blond Baboon* they are off-beat
and bizarre: DeGier's cat Tabriz, that delights in breaking a jar of
marmalade so DeGier cuts his feet; Paul, a terrier belonging to the
murder victim, poisoned but recovering; "the baboon," in this case
the suspect Vleuten, so called because of his flat nose, powerful
body, and long arms; the commisaris' turtle, serenely oblivious to
the mess left by a hurricane; Tobias, a twenty-pound cat with "two
faces" (black on one side, yellow on the other) belonging to the dog-
poisoner; a picture of a rat ridden by a small boy in Vleuten's
apartment; a cow skull mounted on human bones, rigged by Vleuten
to jump from his closet; a dog in a restaurant noisily licking his
"private parts." Each of these animals complements some human
predicament in the story; Vleuten purposely rigged the cow skull
and skeleton to objectify a nightmare, in order to exorcise his fears
(xi). People are often identified as animals, like "the baboon" in this
story, "The Cat" and "The Mouse" in *The Corpse on the Dike*, and
"the fox" in *The Maine Massacre*.

There is a scene in *The Maine Massacre* (viii) that deserves special comment as an illustration of van de Wetering's ability to represent a condition symbolically. The commisaris and DeGier, who have come on a visit to a remote community in northern Maine, find themselves engaged in the investigation of a series of murders apparently involving a local gang of young people. DeGier goes to the general store to make a few purchases, finds himself confronted by a seemingly hostile merchant and several members of the gang, one of whom locks the door. Instead of attacking DeGier, however, they begin a rhythmic chant that is obviously intended to upset him. The unreality of the situation does not disturb the Sergeant, who believes in "a miraculous surrealist world" and who takes his flute from his pocket and supplies the melody of their chanting. The face-off between DeGier and his captors moves into a contest of rhythm and melody that assumes the special quality of ritual. What is happening, as the perceptive reader will shortly discover, is a playing-out of the true situation of the mystery; the locked door is really unlocked, DeGier is not physically held captive, the "gang" is bent more on annoyance than on violence. DeGier passes the test and is accepted, especially by the young woman member of the gang whose voice had merged with the notes of DeGier's flute, and to whom he shortly makes love.

It is very unlikely that Lawrence Sanders and Janwillem van de Wetering will attract any imitators or that either will start a new "school" of mystery writers. Not many people in the detective fiction field would have the ambition to tackle a philosophical-theological theme of the magnitude of that in *The First Deadly Sin,* and certainly few would be possessed of van de Wetering's remarkable background or would have the courage to endue their procedural stories with themes involving levels of awareness or appearance versus reality. Nevertheless, both of these men are pioneers in the sense that they have shown that the procedural, rather than being a prosaic tale limited to commonplace situations and surroundings, is an instrument of almost unlimited flexibility. Other writers will undoubtedly find additional means of extending its possibilities.

The optimism is justifiable, if for no other reason than the refusal of the procedural to stereotype itself. The range of possibilities for variation within its format is practically unlimited, because there is no "typical" procedural structure, no "normal" tone, not even a characteristic procedural language.

At the same time, the general direction of the police procedural will continue to be controlled by that combination of myth and reality discussed earlier. The myth, which also makes itself felt in the traditions of the classic and the hard-boiled mystery, assigns the fictional policeman to the role of member of the Guilty Community, so that he can never become the genius-from-outside or the knight-errant who purges society of its sins and then withdraws from the scene. The reality, moreover, also determines the police character in fiction because, unlike the classic sleuth who was born from the pages of Poe and Conan Doyle and the private eye from the pages of Hammett and Chandler, the fictional cop is one figure everybody knows from real life.

The effect of the discipline imposed on the procedural becomes most apparent in the conclusions of the stories. At that point where the transcendent classic sleuth gathers the suspects in the library, hooks his thumbs and forefingers into the pockets of his pearl-gray waistcoat and begins a twenty-page exegesis of the case that is flawless in its logical construction, and at that point at which the private detective hears the final footsteps receding down the dark, lonely corridor and debates whether he might not run up to his girl's apartment for a nightcap, at that same late hour the fictional policeman is up in the stuffy squadroom beating out his report (in triplicate or quadruplicate as required by regulations) with two fingers on the squad's ancient typewriter, hoping to finish in time to get a few hours' sleep before his next shift begins.

Appendix

The following are check-lists of police procedurals by the authors discussed in this book. As noted earlier, some individual items may not be strictly classified as procedurals, but they are listed if they are included in procedural series. For books first published in a foreign language, the English title is given, but the date is that of the original publication.

John Ball

Sergeant Virgil Tibbs, Pasadena Police Department

1965 *In the Heat of the Night*
1966 *The Cool Cottontail*
1969 *Johnny Get Your Gun*
1972 *Five Pieces of Jade*
1976 *The Eyes of Buddha*
1980 *Then Came Violence*

Chief Jack Tallon, "Whitewater" (Washington) Police Department

1977 *Police Chief*

K. Arne Blom

Violent Crime Section, Lund (Sweden)

1977 *The Moment of Truth*

Rex Burns

Sargeant Gabriel Wagner, Denver Police Department

1975 *The Alavarez Journal*
1977 *The Farnsworth Score*
1978 *Speak for the Dead*
1979 *The Angle of Attack*

John Creasey

Chief Superintendent Roger West, Scotland Yard

1942 *Inspector West Takes Charge*
1943 *Inspector West Leaves Town* (U.S. title, *Go Away to Murder*)
1944 *Inspector West at Home*
1945 *Inspector West Regrets*
1946 *Holiday for Inspector West*
1948 *Battle for Inspector West*
1948 *Triumph for Inspector West* (U.S. title *The Case Against Paul Raeburn*)
1949 *Inspector West Kicks Off* (U.S. title *Sport for Inspector West*)
1950 *Inspector West Alone*
1950 *Inspector West Cries Wolf* (U.S. title, *The Creepers*)
1951 *A Case for Inspector West* (U.S. title, *The Figure in the Dusk*)
1951 *Puzzle for Inspector West* (U.S. title, *The Dissemblers*)
1952 *Inspector West at Bay* (U.S. title, *The Blind Spot*)
1953 *A Gun for Inspector West* (U.S. title, *Give a Man a Gun*)
1953 *Send Inspector West* (U.S. title, *Send Superindent West*)
1954 *A Beauty for Inspector West* (U.S. title, *The Beauty Queen Killer*)
1955 *Inspector West Makes Haste* (U.S. title, *The Gelignite Gang*)
1955 *Two for Inspector West* (U.S. title, *Murder: One, Two, Three*)
1956 *Parcels for Inspector West* (U.S. title, *Death of a Postman*)
1956 *A Prince for Inspector West* (U.S. title, *Death of an Assassin*)
1957 *Accident for Inspector West* (U.S. title, *Hit and Run*)
1957 *Find Inspector West* (U.S. title, *The Trouble at Saxby's*)
1958 *Murder, London-New York*
1958 *Strike for Death* (U.S. title, *The Killing Strike*)
1959 *Death of a Racehorse*
1960 *The Case of the Innocent Victims*
1960 *Murder on the Line*
1961 *Death in Cold Print*
1961 *The Scene of the Crime*
1962 *Policeman's Dread*
1963 *Hang the Little Man*
1964 *Look Three Ways at Murder*
1965 *Murder, London-Australia*
1966 *Murder, London-South Africa*
1967 *The Executioners*
1968 *So Young to Burn*
1969 *Murder, London-Miami*
1970 *A Part for a Policeman*
1971 *Alibi*
1972 *A Splinter of Glass*
1973 *The Theft of Magna Carta*
1974 *The Extortioners*
1978 *A Sharp Rise in Crime*

Frank De Felitta

Chief Superintendent Martin Bauer, Munich Police Department

1973 *Oktoberfest*

Nelson De Mille

Sergeant Joe Keller, New York Police Department

1975 *The Cannibal*
1975 *Night of the Phoenix*
1975 *The Smack Man*

Lesley Egan (Elizabeth Linington)

Detective Vic Varallo, Glendale Police Department

1961 *A Case for Appeal*
1962 *The Borrowed Alibi*
1963 *Run to Evil*
1965 *Detective's Due*
1968 *The Nameless Ones*
1969 *The Wine of Violence*
1971 *Malicious Mischief*
1976 *Scenes of Crime*
1978 *A Dream Apart*
1979 *The Hunters and the Hunted*

Nicolas Freeling

Commisaire Peter Simon Joseph Van der Valk, Amsterdam and The Hague

1962 *Love in Amsterdam*
1963 *Because of the Cats*
1963 *Gun Before Butter* (U.S. title, *Question of Loyalty*)
1964 *Double-Barrel*
1965 *Criminal Conversation*
1966 *The King of the Rainy Country*
1967 *Strike Out Where Not Applicable*
1969 *Tsing-Boum* (U.S. title, *Tsing-Boom!*)
1971 *Over the High Side* (U.S. title, *The Lovely Ladies*)
1972 *A Long Silence* (U.S. title, *Aupres de ma Blonde*)

Michael Gilbert

Detective Inspector Patrick Petrella, London Metropolitan Police

1959 *Blood and Judgment*
1977 *Petrella at Q*

Detective Chief Inspector William Mercer, London Metropolitan Police

1972 *The Body of a Girl*

Dan Greenburg

Detective Max Segal, New York Police Department

1978 *Love Kills*

Reginald Hill

Detective Superintendent Andrew Dalziel, Yorkshire CID

1970 *A Clubbable Woman*
1971 *An Advancement of Learning*
1973 *Ruling Passion*
1975 *An April Shroud*
1978 *A Pinch of Snuff*

Chester Himes

Detectives Grave Digger Jones and Coffin Ed Johnson, New York Police Department

1957 *For Love of Imabelle*
1959 *The Crazy Kill*
1959 *The Real Cool Killers*
1960 *All Shot Up*
1960 *The Big Gold Dream*
1965 *Cotton Comes to Harlem*
1966 *The Heat's On*
1969 *Blind Man with a Pistol*

Olle Hogstrand

Chief Inspector Lars Kollin, Homicide Squad, Stockholm

1971 *On the Prime Minister's Account*
1974 *The Gambler*
1975 *The Debt*

Hamilton Jobson

Detective Chief Superintendent Matt Anders, "Forebridge" CID

1968 *Therefore I Killed Him*
1975 *The Evidence You Will Hear*
1977 *Waiting for Thursday*

Bill Knox

Detective Superintendent Colin Thane and Detective Inspector Phil Moss, Strathclyde (Scotland) Police

1957 *Deadline for a Dream* (U.S. title, *In at the Kill)*
1959 *Death Department*
1960 *Leave It to the Hangman*
1962 *Little Drops of Blood*
1962 *Sanctuary Isle* (U.S. title, *The Grey Sentinels)*
1963 *The Man in the Bottle* (U.S. title, *The Killing Game)*
1965 *The Taste of Proof*
1966 *The Deep Fall* (U.S. title, *The Ghost Car)*
1967 *Justice on the Rocks*
1969 *The Tallyman*
1970 *Children of the Mist* (U.S. title, *Who Shot the Bull?)*
1971 *To Kill a Witch*
1973 *Draw Batons!*
1975 *Rally to Kill*
1977 *Pilot Error*
1979 *Live Bait*

Elizabeth Linington

Sergeant Ivor Maddox, Los Angeles Police Department

1964 *Greenmask!*
1964 *No Evil Angel*
1966 *Date With Death*
1967 *Something Wrong*
1968 *Policeman's Lot*
1971 *Practice to Deceive*
1973 *Crime by Chance*

1977 *Perchance of Death*
1979 *No Villain Need Be*
1980 *Consequence of Crime*

J.J. Marric (John Creasey)

Commander George Gideon, Scotland Yard

1955 *Gideon's Day*
1956 *Gideon's Week*
1957 *Gideon's Night*
1958 *Gideon's Month*
1959 *Gideon's Staff*
1960 *Gideon's Risk*
1961 *Gideon's Fire*
1962 *Gideon's March*
1963 *Gideon's Ride*
1964 *Gideon's Vote*
1964 *Gideon's Lot*
1965 *Gideon's Badge*
1967 *Gideon's Wrath*
1968 *Gideon's River*
1969 *Gideon's Power*
1970 *Gideon's Sport*
1971 *Gideon's Art*
1972 *Gideon's Men*
1973 *Gideon's Press*
1974 *Gideon's Fog*
1976 *Gideon's Drive*

Ed McBain (Evan Hunter)

87th Detective Squad, "Imaginary City"

1956 *Cop Hater*
1956 *The Mugger*
1956 *The Pusher*
1957 *The Con Man*
1958 *Killer's Choice*
1958 *Killer's Payoff*
1958 *Lady Killer*
1959 *Killer's Wedge*
1959 *'Til Death*
1959 *King's Ransom*
1960 *Give the Boys a Great Big Hand*
1960 *The Heckler*
1960 *See Them Die*

1961 *Lady, Lady, I Did It!*
1962 *The Empty Hours*
1962 *Like Love*
1963 *Ten Plus One*
1964 *Ax*
1965 *He Who Hesitates*
1965 *Doll*
1966 *Eighty Million Eyes*
1968 *Fuzz*
1969 *Shotgun*
1970 *Jigsaw*
1971 *Hail, Hail, the Gang's All Here!*
1972 *Sadie When She Died*
1973 *Let's Hear It for the Deaf Man*
1973 *Hail to the Chief*
1974 *Bread*
1975 *Blood Relatives*
1976 *So Long as You Both Shall Live*
1977 *Long Time No See*
1979 *Calypso*
1980 *Ghosts*

James McClure

Lieutenant Trompie Kramer and Sergeant Mickey Zondi, "Trekkersburg" (Republic of South Africa) Murder Squad

1971 *The Steam Pig*
1972 *The Caterpillar Cop*
1974 *The Gooseberry Fool*
1975 *Snake*
1977 *The Sunday Hangman*
1980 *The Blood of an Englishman*

Lillian O'Donnell

Sergeant Norah Mulcahaney, New York Police Department

1972 *The Phone Calls*
1973 *Don't Wear Your Wedding Ring*
1974 *Dial 577 R-A-P-E*
1975 *The Baby Merchants*
1976 *Leisure Dying*
1979 *No Business Being a Cop*

Poul Orum

Detective Inspectors Jonas Morck and Knud Einarsen, Flying Squad (Denmark)

1975 *The Whipping Boy* (U.S. title, *Scapegoat*)
1976 *Nothing but the Truth*

Maurice Procter

Chief Inspector Philip Hunter, Scotland Yard

1951 *The Chief Inspector's Statement* (U.S. title, *The Pennycross Murders)*
1956 *I Will Speak Daggers* (U.S. title, *The Ripper)*

Chief Inspector Harry Martineau, "Granchester" (Yorkshire) CID

1954 *Hell Is a City* (U.S. title, *Somewhere in This City)*
1957 *The Midnight Plumber*
1958 *Man in Ambush*
1959 *Killer at Large*
1960 *Devil's Due*
1961 *The Devil Was Handsome*
1962 *A Body to Spare*
1963 *Moonlight Flitting* (U.S. title, *The Graveyard Rolls)*
1964 *Two Men in Twenty*
1965 *Death Has a Shadow* (U.S. title, *Homicide Blonde)*
1966 *His Weight in Gold*
1967 *Rogue Running*
1967 *Exercise Hoodwink*
1968 *Hideaway*

Detective Bill Knight, "Airechester" (Yorkshire) CID

1956 *The Pub Crawler*

Lawrence Sanders

Captain Edward X. Delaney, New York Police Department

1973 *The First Deadly Sin*
1977 *The Second Deadly Sin*

Dell Shannon (Elizabeth Linington)

Lieutenant Luis Mendoza, Los Angeles Police Department

1960 *Case Pending*
1961 *The Ace of Spades*
1962 *Extra Kill*
1962 *Knave of Hearts*
1963 *Death of a Busybody*
1963 *Double Bluff*
1964 *Mark of Murder*
1964 *Root of All Evil*
1965 *The Death-Bringers*
1965 *Death by Inches*
1966 *Coffin Corner*
1966 *With a Vengeance*
1967 *Chance to Kill*
1967 *Rain With Violence*
1968 *Kill With Kindness*
1969 *Schooled to Kill*
1969 *Crime on Their Hands*
1970 *Unexpected Death*
1971 *Whim to Kill*
1971 *The Ringer*
1972 *Murder with Love*
1972 *With Intent to Kill*
1973 *No Holiday for Crime*
1973 *Spring of Violence*
1974 *Crime File*
1975 *Deuces Wild*
1976 *Streets of Death*
1977 *Appearances of Death*
1978 *Cold Trail*
1979 *Felony at Random*

Maj Sjowall and Per Wahloo

Chief Inspector Martin Beck, National Homicide Squad, Stockholm

1965 *Roseanna*
1966 *The Man Who Went Up in Smoke*
1967 *The Man on the Balcony*
1968 *The Laughing Policeman*
1969 *The Fire Engine That Disappeared*
1970 *Murder at the Savoy*
1971 *The Abominable Man*

1972 *The Locked Room*
1974 *Cop Killer*
1975 *The Terrorists*

Lawrence Treat

Detectives Mitch Taylor and Jub Freeman, Lieutenant Bill Decker, New York and unidentified city

1945 *V as in Victim*
1946 *H as in Hunted*
1947 *Q as in Quicksand*
1947 *T as in Trapped*
1948 *F as in Flight*
1948 *Over the Edge*
1951 *Big Shot*
1956 *Weep for a Wanton*
1960 *Lady, Drop Dead*

Dorothy Uhnak

Detective First-Grade Christie Opara, District Attorney's Special Investigations Squad, New York City

1968 *The Bait*
1969 *The Witness*
1970 *The Ledger*

Detective Second-Grade Joe Peters, District Attorney's Investigating Squad, Queens County, New York

1977 *The Investigation*

Janwillem van de Wetering

The commisaris, Adjutant Henk Grijpstra, Sergeant Rinus DeGier, Amsterdam Municipal Police

1975 *Outsider in Amsterdam*
1976 *Tumbleweed*
1976 *The Corpse on the Dike*
1977 *Death of a Hawker*
1977 *The Japanese Corpse*
1978 *The Blond Baboon*
1979 *The Maine Massacre*

Hillary Waugh

Chief Frank Ford, "Bristol" (Massachusetts) Police Department

1952 *Last Seen Wearing—*

Chief Fred Fellows, "Stockford" (Connecticut) Police Department

1959 *Sleep Long, My Love*
1960 *Road Block*
1961 *That Night It Rained*
1962 *The Late Mrs. D.*
1962 *Born Victim*
1963 *Death and Circumstances*
1963 *Prisoner's Plea*
1964 *The Missing Man*
1965 *End of a Party*
1966 *Pure Poison*
1968 *The Con Game*

Detective Second-Grade Frank Sessions, New York Police Department

1968 *"30" Manhattan East*
1969 *The Young Prey*
1970 *Finish Me Off*

Collin Wilcox

Lieutenant Frank Hastings, San Francisco Police Department

1969 *The Lonely Hunter*
1970 *The Disappearance*
1971 *Dead Aim*
1973 *Hiding Place*
1974 *Long Way Down*
1975 *Aftershock*
1977 *Doctor, Lawyer...*
1978 *The Watcher*
1978 (with Bill Pronzini) Twospot
1979 *Power Plays*

Notes

Chapter 1

[1]"Murder and the Mean Streets: The Hard-Boiled Detective Novel," in *Detective Fiction: Crime and Compromise*, ed. Dick Allen and David Chacko (New York: Harcourt Brace Jovanovich, 1974), p. 414.

[2]"The Police Procedural," in *The Mystery Story*, ed. John Ball (Del Mar, Ca.: Univ. of California—San Diego, 1976), p. 177.

Chapter 2

[1]"Polis! Polis!" in *Murder Ink,* ed. Dilys Winn (New York: Workman, 1977), p. 335.

[2]Introduction to Ed McBain, *The 87th Precinct* (New York: Simon & Schuster, 1959), p. vii.

[3]Introduction to Lawrence Treat, *P as in Police* (New York: Davis, 1963), p. 7.

[4]Preface to *Mystery Writer's Handbook* (Cleveland: Writer's Digest, 1976), p. 3.

[5]Because most of the novels cited have gone through several editions, references are to chapter numbers or (as here) sections and chapters. For a novel without numbered chapters, references are to pages in the first U.S. edition.

[6]Introduction to *The 87th Precinct*, p. viii.

[7]*Dragnet*, Golden Age Record 5003 (n.d.), Side 2.

[8]*Mortal Consequences* (New York: Harper & Row, 1972), p. 204.

[9]"Fred Fellows," in *The Great Detectives*, ed. Otto Penzler (Boston: Little, Brown, 1978), p. 107.

[10]Ed McBain, "The 87th Precinct," in *The Great Detectives,* pp. 89-92.

[11]Chris Steinbrunner and Otto Penzler, *Encyclopedia of Mystery and Detection* (New York: McGraw-Hill, 1976), p. 401; Timothy Foote, "Once More with Freeling," *Time*, 31 July 1972, p. 59; Freeling, *Strike Out Where Not Applicable*, p. 214; Freeling, *Gun Before Butter*, p. 33.

[12]Martha Duffy, "Martin Beck Passes, *Time*, 11 August 1975, p. 58.

[13]*Murder for Pleasure*, Enlarged Edition (New York: Bilbo and Tannen, 1974), p. 169.

Chapter 3

[1]Introduction to *The 87th Precinct,* p. vii.

[2]*The Gentle Art of Murder* (Bowling Green, Ohio: The Popular Press, 1980), p. 139.

[3]*Royal Bloodline* (Bowling Green: The Popular Press, 1974), p. 18.

[4]In *Detective Fiction: Crime and Compromise*, p. 401.

[5]Nadya Aisenberg, *A Common Spring* (Bowling Green: The Popular Press, 1980), p. 23.

[6]Earl Bargainnier argues that Alleyn is a transitional figure between the classic Golden Age detective and the procedural policeman ("Roderick Alleyn: Ngaio

Marsh's Oxonion Superintendent," *The Armchair Detective,* 11 [January 1978], 68).

[7]*Dreamers Who Live Their Dreams* (Bowling Green: The Popular Press, 1976), p. 60.

[8]*Dreamers Who Live Their Dreams, p. 60.*

[9]"Murder and the Mean Streets," p. 419.

[10]Ross Macdonald, *The Blue Hammer,* ch. xxi.

[11]Raymond Chandler, *The Little Sister,* ch. xxix.

[12]"Murder and the Mean Streets," p. 414.

[13]Raymond Chandler, "The Simple Art of Murder," in *The Art of the Mystery Story,* New Ed., ed. Howard Haycraft (New York: Bilbo and Tannen, 1976), p. 237.

Chapter 4

[1]"The Jury Box," *Ellery Queen's Mystery Magazine,* Feb. 1976, pp. 120-1.

[2]Larry French has suggested that *Pandora's Box* and Chastain's *911* be placed in the category of the "new" or "revised" police procedural ("Thomas Chastain and the New Police Procedural," *The Mystery Fancier,* 2, No. 4 [July 1978], 17-18).

[3]Ed McBain, *Like Love,* ch. ix.

[4]J.J. Marric, *Gideon's Press,* ch. xvi.

[5]"Oh, England! Full of Sin," in *The Art of the Mystery Story,* pp. 348-9.

Chapter 5

[1]John Creasey, *Theft of Magna Carta,* ch. iii.

[2]Janwillem van de Wetering, *The Corpse on the Dike,* ch,. xvii.

[3]Bill Knox, *Children of the Mist,* ch. viii.

[4]McBain, *Blood Relatives,* ch. iii.

[5]Hillary Waugh, *The Young Prey,* ch. xxv.

[6]"Modus Operandi," in *Stay of Execution and Other Stories,* p. 96.

[7]*Eighty Million Eyes,* ch. vii.

[8]*Rogue Running,* ch. xv.

[9]Olle Hogstrand, *The Debt,* p. 204.

[10]McBain, *Blood Relatives,* ch. iv.

[11]Waugh, *Road Block,* ch. xx.

[12]Knox, *Live Bait,* ch. vi.

[13]Creasey, *A Sharp Rise in Crime,* chs. x-xi.

[14]Knox, *Live Bait,* ch. ii.

[15]*Rogue Running,* ch. xv.

[16]McBain, *Doll,* ch. ii.

[17]Knox, *Draw Batons!* chs. ii, iv.

Chapter 6

[1]Lawrence Sanders, *The Second Deadly Sin,* ch. xi.

[2]Hamilton Jobson, *Waiting for Thursday,* III, i.

[3]Collin Wilcox, *Long Way Down,* ch. vii.

[4]Wilcox, *The Lonely Hunter,* ch. ii.

[5]Creasey, *Strike for Death,* ch. iii.

[6]A representative example is in *Hail to the Chief,* ch. i.

[7]Dan Greenburg, *Love Kills,* ch. ii.

[8]McBain, *Ghosts,* ch. iv; *The Mugger,* ch. xix.

[9]Maj Sjowall and Per Wahloo, *Cop Killer*, ch. xii.

[10]Lillian O'Donnell, *The Baby Merchants*, ch. i.

[11]Sanders, *The First Deadly Sin*, VII, iv.

[12]Sanders, *The First Deadly Sin*, VII, v.

[13]Knox, *Live Bait*, ch. ii.

[14]Sanders, *The Second Deadly Sin*, ch. ii.

[15]Sjowall and Wahloo, *The Fire Engine That Disappeared*, ch. xviii.

[16]Lawrence Treat,*Big Shot*, ch. i.

[17]McBain, *Hail, Hail, the Gang's All Here!* p. 80.

[18]Maurice Procter, *The Chief Inspector's Statement*, II, iii.

[19]Nicolas Freeling, *Over the High Side*, p. 219; *Tsing-Boum*, ch. xxv.

[20]Sjowall and Wahloo, *Cop Killer*, ch. xv.

[21]Treat, *Lady, Drop Dead*, ch. xii.

[22]Rex Burns, *Speak for the Dead*, ch. xi.

[23]Knox, *Live Bait*, ch. i.

[24] Michael Gilbert, *Petrella at Q.*, p. 182.

[25]McBain, *Long Time No See*, ch. viii.

[26]Procter, *Rogue Running*, ch. x.

[27]A definition of the Judges' Rules can be found in P.D. James' Introduction to her *Crime Times Three* (New York: Scribners, 1979), p. viii.

[28]Knox, *Children of the Mist*, ch. vii.

[29]Sjowall and Wahloo, *The Fire Engine that Disappeared*, ch. i; *The Terrorists*, ch. xxiii.

[30]van de Wetering, *Death of a Hawker*, ch. vii.

[31]Poul Orum, *Nothing but the Truth*, ch. ix.

[32]Freeling, *Over the High Side*, p. 14.

[33]Waugh, *Finish Me Off*, p. 67.

[34]Procter, *Hell Is a City*, III, vii.

[35]Creasey, *Strike for Death*, ch. iv.

[36]Wilcox, *Doctor, Lawyer...* ch. iv.

[37]Wilcox, *Doctor, Lawyer...* ch. xviii.

[38]van de Wetering, *Death of a Hawker*, ch. ix.

[39]Freeling, *Strike Out Where Not Applicable*, p. 20.

[40]Sjowall and Wahloo, *Murder at the Savoy*, ch. xviii.

[41]Dell Shannon, *Spring of Violence*, ch. i.

[42]Burns, *Angle of Attack*, chs. iv, xiv.

[43]Sjowall and Wahloo, *The Laughing Policeman*, ch. xv.

[44]Wilcox, *The Watcher*, ch. ix.

[45]Freeling, *Because of the Cats*, ch. viii.

[46]Creasey, *Theft of Magna Carta*, ch. viii.

[47]Orum, *Nothing But the Truth*, ch. xxiii.

[48]Sanders, *The First Deadly Sin*,, III, i.

[49]Creasey, *A Sharp Rise in Crime*, ch. xii.

[50]Sjowall and Wahloo, *The Abominable Man*, ch. xxv.

[51]Gilbert, *The Body of a Girl*, ch. i.

[52]Sjowall and Wahloo, *Murder at the Savoy*, ch. xiv.

[53]Wilcox, *The Lonely Hunter*, ch. xi.

[54]Freeling, *Over the High Side*, p. 219.

[55]Orum, *The Whipping Boy*, ch. xxii.

[56]Gilbert, *Close Quarters*, ch. iii.

⁵⁷McBain, *Give the Boys a Great Big Hand,* ch. xvii.
⁵⁸James McClure, *The Steam Pig,* ch. iv.
⁵⁹Wilcox, *Long Way Down,* ch. i.
⁶⁰Marric, *Gideon's Night,* ch. ii.
⁶¹van de Wetering, *The Corpse on the Dike,* ch. xviii.
⁶²McBain, *Long Time No See,* ch. iii.
⁶³Sjowall and Wahloo, *The Man on the Balcony,* ch. xvi.
⁶⁴Freeling, *Strike Out Where Not Applicable,* p. 19.
⁶⁵Creasey, *Strike for Death,* chs. vi, xix.
⁶⁶Procter, *The Pub Crawler,* ch. vi.

Chapter 7

¹Procter, *The Chief Inspector's Statement,* I, i.
²Ball, *Police Chief,* ch. iv.
³Creasey, *Inspector West Cries Wolf* ch. xi.
⁴Sanders, *The First Deadly Sin,* V,vi.
⁵Freeling, *A Long Silence,* p. 30.
⁶Dorothy Uhnak, *The Bait,* ch. iv.
⁷Uhnak, *The Investigation,* I,v.
⁸Sanders, *The First Deadly Sin,* VIII,iii.
⁹Freeling, *Double-Barrel,* II,v.
¹⁰K. Arne Blom, *The Moment of Truth,* p. 17.
¹¹Gilbert, *Petrella at Q,* p. 135.
¹²Knox, *Draw Batons!* ch. iv.
¹³Ball, *The Cool Cottontail,* ch. vi.
¹⁴Procter, *Rogue Running,* ch. v.
¹⁵McBain, *Shotgun,* ch. i.
¹⁶Ball, *The Cool Cottontail,* ch. viii.
¹⁷O'Donnell, *Dial 577 R-A-P-E,* ch. viii.
¹⁸Marric, *Gideon's Risk,* ch. xiv.
¹⁹Sjowall and Wahloo, *The Laughing Policeman,* ch. xix.
²⁰O'Donnell, *No Business Being a Cop,* ch. viii.
²¹Creasey, *A Splinter of Glass,* ch. xi.
²²Procter, *The Chief Inspector's Statement,* I,i.
²³Sjowall and Wahloo, *The Fire Engine That Disappeared,* chs. v, xviii.
²⁴McBain, *Give the Boys a Great Big Hand,* ch. ii.
²⁵Procter, *A Body to Spare,* ch. xxii.
²⁶Procter, *Hell Is a City,* I,i.
²⁷Sanders, *The First Deadly Sin,* VIII,v.
²⁸Procter, *Hell Is a City,* I,i.
²⁹Knox, *Children of the Mist,* ch. vi.
³⁰Uhnak, *The Ledger,* ch. xiv.
³¹McClure, *The Gooseberry Fool,* ch. xii.
³²Bill Pronzini and Collin Wilcox, *Twospot,* ch. xix.
³³Shannon, *Deuces Wild,* ch. vi.
³⁴McClure, *The Gooseberry Fool,* ch. xii.
³⁵Sjowall and Wahloo, *The Terrorists,* ch. viii.
³⁶"The 87th Precinct," in *The Great Detectives,* p. 93.
³⁷McBain, *Killer's Payoff,* ch. viii.

[38]McBain, *So Long as You Both Shall Live,* ch. vii.
[39]Gilbert, Petrella at Q, p. 198.
[40]Procter, *Moonlight Flitting,* ch. ii.
[41]Marric, *Gideon's Day,* ch. xvi.
[42]Ball, *Then Came Violence,* ch. xx.
[43]Sanders, *The First Deadly Sin,* VII,iii.
[44]Sanders, *The Second Deadly Sin,* ch. iv.
[45]Hogstrand, *On the Prime Minister's Account,* p. 141; *The Debt,* p. 81.
[46]Sanders, *The First Deadly Sin,* VII,v.

Chapter 8

[1]"The concept of Formula in the Study of Literature," in *Popular Culture and the Expanding Consciousness,* ed. Ray B. Browne (New York: John Wiley and Sons, 1973), p. 113.

[2]*Adventure, Mystery, and Romance* (Chicago: Univ. of Chicago Press, 1976), p. 20. Subsequent references are included in the text.

[3]Sjowall and Wahloo, *The Fire Engine That Disappeared,* ch. v.

[4]Freeling, *The King of the Rainy Country,* pp. 36-7.

[5]Creasey, *A Splinter of Glass,* ch. iii.

[6]Waugh, *Sleep Long, My Love,* ch. xv.

[7]"Interview: Lawrence Treat," *Ellery Queen's Mystery Magazine,* July 1976, p. 116.

[8]Procter, *Rogue Running* ch. xvii.

[9]Ball, *Police Chief,* ch. iii.

[10]Burns, *The Farnsworth Score,* ch. ix.

[11]Treat, *V as in Victim,* V,i.

[12]Treat, *V as in Victim,* V,i.

[13]Jobson, *Waiting for Thursday,* III,i.

[14]McBain, *Lady, Lady, I Did It!,* ch. xv.

[15]Sanders, *The Second Deadly Sin,* ch. ii.

[16]Sanders, *The First Deadly Sin,* II,ii.

[17]O'Donnell, *No Business Being a Cop,* ch. x.

[18]Sanders, *The First Deadly Sin,* VIII, iv.

[19]O'Donnell, *No Business Being a Cop,* ch. v.

[20]Burns, *Speak for the Dead,* ch. ii.

[21]Burns, *Angle of Attack,* ch. iv.

[22]*A Common Spring,* pp. 45-46.

[23]In *The Art of the Mystery Story,* pp. 190, 195.

[24]"The Poetics of the Private Eye: The Novels of Dashiell Hammett," in *The Mystery Writer's Art,* ed. Francis M. Nevins, Jr. (Bowling Green: The Popular Press, 1970), p. 104.

[25]Ball, *Johnny Get Your Gun,* ch. ix.

[26]Treat, *Lady, Drop Dead,* ch. i.

[27]Jobson, *Waiting for Thursday,* V,iv.

[28]Sanders, *The First Deadly Sin,* V,v.

[29]Marric, *Gideon's Night,* ch. ii.

[30]McClure, *The Steam Pig,* ch. viii.

[31]Burns, *Speak for the Dead,* ch. vi.

[32]Sjowall and Wahloo, *The Locked Room*, ch. vii.

[33]Knox, *Draw Batons!*, ch. i.

[34]*Adventure, Mystery, and Romance*, p. 10.

[35]*A Common Spring*, p. 238.

[36]"Sophocles and the Rest of the Boys in the Pulps," in *Dimensions of Detective Fiction*, ed. Larry Landrum et al (Bowling Green: The Popular Press, 1976), p. 13.

[37]Frank D. McSherry, Jr., "Letters," *The Armchair Detective*, (11 July 1978), 310.

[38]In *Detective Fiction: Crime and Compromise*, p. 401. Subsequent references are included in the text.

[39]In *Detective Fiction: Crime and Compromise*, p. 423. Subsequent references are included in the text.

[40]McBain, *Fuzz*, ch. v.

[41]Gilbert, *Blood and Judgment*, ch. ix.

[42]Sanders, *The Second Deadly Sin*, ch. vi.

[43]McBain, *Calypso*, ch. vi.

[44]Freeling, *A Long Silence*, p. 68.

[45]Marric, *Gideon's Week*, ch. i.

[46]Marric, *Gideon's Night*, ch. i.

[47]McBain, *Calypso*, ch. xiii.

[48]Burns, *Speak for the Dead*, ch. iii.

[49]Wilcox, *Long Way Down*, ch. i.

[50]Creasey, *Alibi*, ch. iii; Orum, *Nothing But the Truth*, ch. vii; Waugh, *Sleep Long, My Love*, ch. xxiii.

[51]An exception would be the Huerta beating in McBain's *Hail, Hail the Gang's All Here!*, which is one of the major cases in the novel and is purposely left unsolved for the reason explained in Chapter 13.

[52]"The Police Procedural," pp. 171-2. Subsequent references are included in the text.

[53]"Routines and Rules for the Police Procedural," *The Writer*, 91, No. 1 (January 1978), 17. Subsequent references are included in the text.

[54]George N. Dove, " 'Shades of Dupin!': Fictional Detectives on Detective Fiction," *The Armchair Detective*, 8 (November 1974), 12-14.

[55]Waugh, *Prisoner's Plea*, ch. xviii.

[56]McBain *'Til Death*, ch. ii.

[57]Freeling, *The King of the Rainy Country*, p. 164.

Chapter 9

[1]Waugh, *Last Seen Wearing—*, pp. 159-69.

[2]van de Wetering, *The Corpse on the Dike*, ch. viii.

[3]Hogstrand, *On the Prime Minister's Account*, p. 171.

[4]Procter, *I Will Speak Daggers*, ch. ix.

[5]Freeling, *Strike Out Where Not Applicable*, p. 211.

[6]van de Wetering, *Outsider in Amsterdam*, chs. i, iv; *The Maine Massacre*, ch. xi.

[7]Ball, *Five Pieces of Jade*, ch. iii; Shannon, *The Death-Bringers*, ch. ii; Shannon, *Whim to Kill*, ch. ii.

[8]Sjowall and Wahloo, *Cop Killer*, ch. x.

[9]Freeling, *Strike Out Where Not Applicable*, p. 226.

[10]Orum, *The Whipping Boy*, ch. xxii.

[11]Waugh, *Sleep Long, My Love,* ch. xxi.
[12]Freeling, *Strike Out Where Not Applicable,* 212.
[13]Procter, *Killer at Large,* ch. x.
[14]van de Wetering, *The Corpse on the Dike,* ch. viii.
[15]Sjowall and Wahloo, *The Laughing Policeman,* ch. xxiii.
[16]Procter, *Rogue Running,* ch. xxvi.
[17]Sjowall and Wahloo, *The Laughing Policeman,* ch. xxiii.
[18]Sjowall and Wahloo, *The Fire Engine that Disappeared,* ch. xii.
[19]Gilbert, *Fear to Tread,* ch. xiii.

Chapter 10

[1]Uhnak, *The Ledger,* ch. x.
[2]Uhnak, *The Ledger,* ch. ii.
[3]O'Donnell, *Dial 577 R-A-P-E,* ch. xii.
[4]Creasey, *Theft of Magna Carta,* ch. viii.
[5]O'Donnell, *Dial 577 R-A-P-E,* ch. xvi.
[6]Procter, *Moonlight Flitting,* ch. xix.
[7]Burns, *Angle of Attack,* ch. xiv.
[8]O'Donnell, *Don't Wear Your Wedding Ring,* ch. vii.
[9]O'Donnell, *No Business Being a Cop,* ch. iv.
[10]Uhnak, *The Ledger,* ch. ii.
[11]O'Donnell, *No Business Being a Copy,* ch. xiv.

Chapter 11

[1]Ball, *Johnny Get Your Gun,* ch. vii.
[2]Ball, *The Eyes of Buddha,* ch. xi.
[3]McBain, *Fuzz,* ch. vi.
[4]Shannon, *Spring of Violence,* ch. v.
[5]Ball, *Johnny Get Your Gun,* ch. vii.
[6]McClure, *The Sunday Hangman,* chs. xiii-xiv.
[7]Shannon, *Spring of Violence,* ch. iv.
[8]McClure, *The Caterpiller Cop,* ch. xii.
[9]McClure, *The Gooseberry Fool,* ch. viii.

Chapter 12

[1]This episode seems to grow more sensational in Meyer's memory with the passage of time. In *Lady Killer* (ch. ii) we are told that the Gentile kids tied him to a stake but did not actually light a fire. In *Hail to the Chief* (ch. ii) Meyer remembers how the fire was doused by a providential rainstorm.
[2]McBain, *Calypso,*ch. vi.
[3]McBain, *The Empty Hours,* pp. 149-50
[4]McBain, *Ten Plus One,* ch. iv.
[5]McBain, *Hail, Hail, the Gang's All Here!,* pp. 65-70.
[6]Wilcox, *Long Way Down,* ch. xv; *Aftershock,* ch. x.

[7]Uhnak, *The Witness*, ch. xix.
[8]Egan, *Wine of Violence*, ch. ix.
[9]Wilcox, *Hiding Place*, ch. xx.
[10]McBain, *Bread*, ch. iv.
[11]Wilcox, *Aftershock*, ch. ii.
[12]McBain, *Ghosts*, ch. vi.
[13]McBain, *Sadie When She Died*, ch. iv.
[14]Uhnak, *The Bait*, ch. viii.

Chapter 13

[1]Burns, *Speak for the Dead*, ch. xiii.
[2]Gilbert, "Patrick Petrella," in *The Great Detectives*, pp. 167-9.
[3]Gilbert, *Petrella at Q*, p. 158.
[4]Gilbert, *Blood and Judgment*, ch. ii.
[5]O'Donnell, *No Business Being a Cop*, ch. ii.
[6]O'Donnell, *No Business Being a Cop*, ch. iii.
[7]Gilbert, *Blood and Judgment*, ch. xv.
[8]Shannon, *Case Pending*, ch. xv.

Chapter 14

[1]*World Authors, 1950-1970* (New York: H.W. Wilson, 1975), pp. 338-9.
[2]*Current Biography Yearbook, 1963,* (New York: H.W. Wilson, 1964), p. 93.
[3]Creasey, *A Splinter of Glass*, chs. viii, xv.
[4]Cresey, *Inspector West Cries Wolf*, chs. ii, xxi.
[5]Creasey, *A Part for a Policeman*, ch. v.
[6]Marric, *Gideon's Week*, ch. iii.
[7]Marric, *Gideon's Power*, ch. xvii.
[8]Marric, *Gideon's Night*, ch. xvi.
[9]Marric, *Gideon's River*, ch. xiv.
[10]Marric, *Gideon's Drive*, ch. xvii; *Gideon's Power*, ch. vii.
[11]Marric, *Gideon's Drive*, ch. xxi.
[12]Creasey, *Alibi*, ch. viii.
[13]Marric, *Gideon's Drive*, ch. vii.
[14]Creasey, *A Splinter of Glass*, ch. xiv.

Chapter 15

[1]*The Chief Inspector's Statement*, I,ix.
[2]*Hell is a City*, I,ii.
[3]*Killer at Large*, ch. iii.
[4]*A Body to Spare*, ch. xxii.
[5]In the entry on McBain in *Twentieth Century Crime and Mystery Writers* (New York: St. Martin's Press, 1980), I incorrectly identified McBain's Deaf Man as the first series villain in a procedural series (p. 1037). Dixie Costello was on the scene years before the Deaf Man.

[6]*Hideaway*, ch. xx.
[7]*The Pub Crawler*, ch. v; *Killer at Large*, ch. ix; *Moonlight Flitting*, ch. xviii.
[8]*Hideaway*, ch. xviii.

Chapter 16

[1]Afterword to the Mystery Library edition of *Last Seen Wearing*— (Del Mar: Univ. of California-San Diego, 1978), pp. 253-5.
[2]"Plots and People," *The Writer*, 82, No. 12 (December 1969), 9-10.
[3]"The Mystery Versus the Novel," in *The Mystery Story*, pp. 71, 73.
[4]"Interview: Hillary Waugh," *Ellery Queen's Mystery Magazine*, Oct. 1977, p. 97.
[5]"Fred Fellows," in *The Great Detectives*, p. 107.
[6]*Sleep Long, My Love*, chs. i, xiv.
[7]*Pure Poison*, ch. xxii.
[8]*Sleep Long, My Love*, ch. vi.
[9]*Road Block*, ch. viii.
[10]*Pure Poison*, ch. ii.
[11]*The Con Game*, ch. xxiv.
[12]*The Late Mrs. D.*,ch. x.
[13]*Sleep Long, My Love,* ch. xv.
[14]*Pure Poison*, ch. v.
[15]*Prisoner's Plea*, ch. vii.
[16]*The Young Prey*, ch. xxvii.

Chapter 17

[1]Introduction to *The 87th Precinct*, p. vi.
[2]*Mortal Consequences*, p. 205.
[3]"The 87th Precinct," in *The Great Detectives*, p. 95.
[4]*The Mugger*, ch. i.
[5]*Let's Hear It for the Deaf Man*, ch. x.
[6]"The 87th Precinct," p. 91.
[7]"The 87th Precinct," p. 91.
[8]*The Heckler* (1960), *Fuzz* (1968), and *Let's Hear It for the Deaf Man* (1973).
[9]"An Interview with Evan Hunter-Ed McBain," *The Writer* , 82, No. 4 (April 1969), 11.
[10]*Fuzz*, ch. xi.
[11]*Killer's Payoff*, ch. vii.
[12]*The Empty Hours*, ch. xii.
[13]"Carella of the 87th," in *Murder Ink*, pp. 301-5.
[14]"The 87th Precinct," p. 97.
[15]*Give the Boys a Great Big Hand*, ch. vi.
[16]*See Them Die*, ch. xvi.
[17]*Fuzz*, ch. xiii; *See Them Die*, ch. xii; *Sadie When She Died*, ch. vii.

Chapter 18

[1]*Rally to Kill*, ch. iv.

[2]*To Kill a Witch*, ch. viii.
[3]*Draw Batons!*, ch. viii.
[4]*Children of the Mist*, ch. i.
[5]*Pilot Error*, ch. ii.
[6]*Live Bait*, ch. i.
[7]*Children of the Mist*, ch. iv.
[8]*Draw Batons!* ch. iii; *The Tallyman*, ch. viii; *Pilot Error*, ch. i.
[9]*Pilot Error*, ch. vii.

Chapter 19

[1]"Inspector van der Valk," in *The Great Detectives*, pp. 252-3.
[2]*World Authors, 1950-1970*, p. 496.
[3]"One Man's Mote," *Times* (London) *Literary Supplement*, 20 Jan. 1966, p. 37.
[4]Timothy Foote, "Crime as Punishment," *Time*, 29 July 1974, p. 65.
[5]"Inspector van der Valk," p. 255.
[6]*The King of the Rainy Country*, pp. 5-6; *A Long Silence*, p. 87.
[7]*A Long Silence*, p. 59.
[8]*Criminal Conversation*, I,ii.
[9]*Criminal Conversation*, II,xix.
[10]*Tsing-Boum*, ch. vii.
[11]*Strike Out Where Not Applicable*, pp. 211-15.
[12]*Double-Barrel* IV,v.
[13]*Gun Before Butter*, p. 33.
[14]*Gun Before Butter*, pp. 10, 29.
[15]*Strike Out Where Not Applicable*, p. 19.

Chapter 20

[1]"Polis! Polis!" p. 334.
[2]"The Police in Society: The Novels of Maj Swojall and Per Wahlo," *The Armchair Detective*, 12 (Spring 1979), 175-6.
[3]*Encyclopedia of Mystery and Detection*, p. 408.
[4]Nancy Ellen Talburt and Lyna Lee Montgomery, "The Swedish Policeman: A Study of Sjowall and Wahloo," paper presented before the Popular Culture Association, Chicago, April 1976. Copy provided by the authors.
[5]*The Locked Room*, ch. xxvi.
[6]*The Terrorists*, ch. xvi.
[7]*The Fire Engine That Disappeared*, ch. ii.
[8]*The Abominable Man*, ch. xxx.
[9]*The Abominable Man*, ch. xvii; *The Terrorists*, ch. xx.
[10]Martha Duffy, "Martin Beck Passes," p. 58.

Chapter 21

[1]*Long Way Down*,ch. xx.
[2]*Doctor, Lawyer...*, ch. xvi.

[3]*Long Way Down*, ch. vii.
[4]*The Lonely Hunter*, ch. xvi.
[5]*Long Way Down*, ch. xiv.
[6]*Long Way Down*, ch. ii.
[7]*Hiding Place*, ch. ii.
[8]See, for example, *The Disappearance*, ch. xix; *Dead Aim*, ch. v.
[9]"Writing and Selling the Police Procedural Novel," *The Writer*, 89, No. 1 (January 1976), pp. 20-2.

Chapter 22

[1]Trekkersburg is a fictitious city, usually identified with Pietermaritzburg.
[2]"Apartheid in the Novels of James McClure," *The Armchair Detective*, 10 (October 1977), 348.
[3]*The Steam Pig*, ch. xi.
[4]*The Caterpillar Cop*, ch. xiv.
[5]*The Sunday Hangman*, ch. vi; *The Caterpillar Cop*, ch. xiv.
[6]*The Steam Pig*, ch. iii.
[7]*The Caterpillar Cop*, ch. ix.
[8]*The Gooseberry Fool*, ch. xiii.
[9]*The Caterpillar Cop*, ch. v.
[10]"Apartheid in the Novels of James McClure," p. 348.
[11]*The Steam Pig*, ch. v; *The Caterpillar Cop*, ch. xii.
[12]*The Steam Pig*, ch. xi.
[13]*The Steam Pig*, ch. xiv.
[14]*The Caterpillar Cop*, ch. iv.
[15]*The Steam Pig*, chs. iv, x; *The Sunday Hangman*, ch. iii.
[16]*The Steam Pig*, ch. iv.
[17]*The Sunday Hangman*, ch. vi.

Chapter 23

[1]*Adventure, Mystery, and Romance*, p. 164.
[2]"Interview: Lawrence Treat," p. 116.
[3]"The Police Procedural," in *The Mystery Story*, pp. 163-87.
[4]"Routines and Rules for the Police Procedural," pp. 17-19; 46.
[5]In *The Art of the Mystery Story*, pp. 189-96.
[6]*Murder for Pleasure*, p. 12.
[7]In *Detective Fiction: Crime and Compromise*, pp. 420-1.
[8]"Briefly Noted," *The New Yorker*, 22 Oct. 1973, p. 174; "Getting the Ax," *Newsweek*, 8 Oct. 1973, p. 112.
[9]"Expiatory Symbolism in Lawrence Sanders' *The First Deadly Sin*," paper presented before the Popular Culture Association, Detroit, April 1980. Copy provided by the author. A revision of this paper appears in *Clues* 1, No. 2 (Fall/Winter 1980), 71-6.
[10]*The Japanese Corpse*, ch. iv.
[11]*Tumbleweed*, ch. xviii.
[12]*The Corpse on the Dike*, ch. xiii.
[13]*Death of a Hawker*, ch. xi.
[14]*Tumbleweed*, chs. x, xiii.
[15]*Death of a Hawker*, ch. vii.

Index